IMAGES of America
THE NORCONIAN RESORT

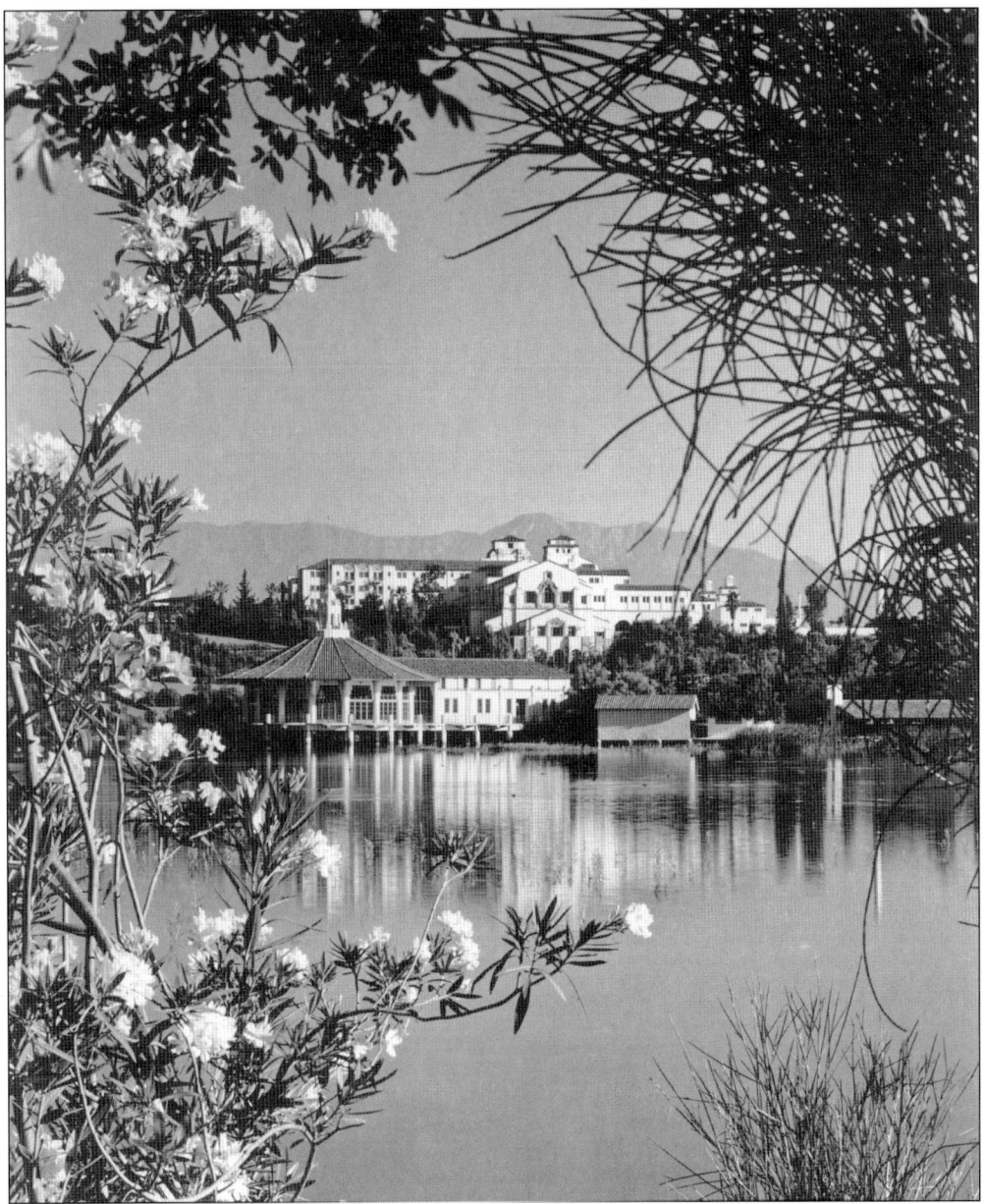

THE NORCONIAN RESORT SUPREME, C. 1938. Opened in 1929 by Rex B. Clark in the tiny, rural town of Norco, California, the Norconian Resort Supreme dazzled. A majestic, white palace, visible for miles and built as a monument to recreation, attracted the rich and famous before being crushed by the Great Depression. Today the Norconian is a one-of-a-kind national treasure that still has the ability to astound.

ON THE COVER: Shown in February 1929 in an image by renowned Riverside, California, photographer A. E. Field, the Norconian simply shimmers and sparkles. With the magnificent San Gabriel Mountain range as a background, the Resort Supreme, overlooking and surrounding beautiful Lake Norconian, was very likely the finest and most complete recreational resort ever built on the West Coast. (Norco Historical Society.)

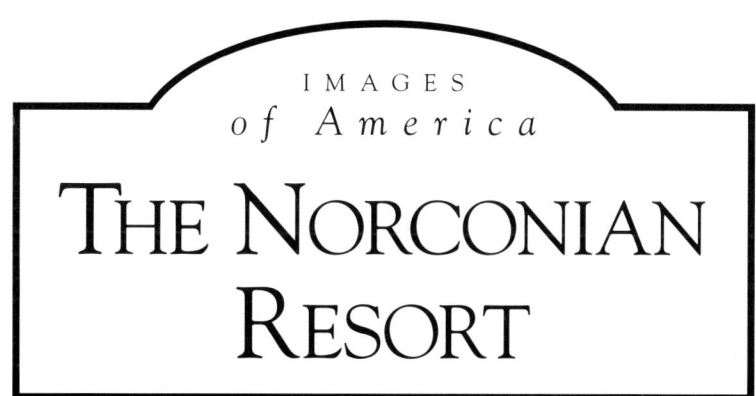

IMAGES of America
THE NORCONIAN RESORT

Kevin Bash and Brigitte Jouxtel

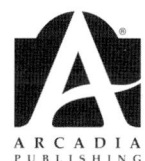

Copyright © 2007 by Kevin Bash and Brigitte Jouxtel
ISBN 978-0-7385-5559-1

Published by Arcadia Publishing
Charleston SC, Chicago IL, Portsmouth NH, San Francisco CA

Printed in the United States of America

Library of Congress Catalog Card Number: 2007928544

For all general information contact Arcadia Publishing at:
Telephone 843-853-2070
Fax 843-853-0044
E-mail sales@arcadiapublishing.com
For customer service and orders:
Toll-Free 1-888-313-2665

Visit us on the Internet at www.arcadiapublishing.com

*To Angelique, who inspires us daily with her
passion, common sense, and intelligence.*

CONTENTS

Acknowledgments		6
Introduction		7
1.	Rex B. Clark and Norco	9
2.	Building the Dream	19
3.	A Golfer's Paradise	37
4.	Olympic Gold in Norco	43
5.	The Norconian Resort Supreme	51
6.	Hollywood in Norco	99
7.	Patients, Prisoners, and Ph.D.s	115

ACKNOWLEDGMENTS

Thank you to the Norco Historical Society, who, unless otherwise noted, provided the majority of the photographs in this book. Other contributors were Peter Clark, Corona Public Library, University of California Los Angeles, University of Southern California, Ed Lotterman, Los Angeles Public Library, University of Pittsburgh, Brigitte Jouxtel, U.S. Navy Archives, Tom Sito, Louis Zehfuss, Bison Archives, Scripps College, and the Motion Picture Academy of Arts and Sciences.

Thank you to the Corona Public Library Board of Trustees, who provided access to archival copies of two local newspapers. Most important was the *Corona Daily Independent*, and unless otherwise noted, all quotes are from that newspaper. We are also grateful for access to the *Norco Beacon* and the book *The Navy in Corona* (Fleet Analysis Center, 1979). Also used was the invaluable *Los Angeles Times*.

Thank you to Ellen Revelle, who graciously supplied hours of information regarding her father, Rex Clark.

Thank you to those who made on-site research possible: California Department of Corrections, especially Warden Guillermina Hall, Lt. Michael Brownell, Terry Thornton, and Chief Dennis Ellison; Department of the Navy, including Capt. Robert Shafer, Lt. Stephanie Murdock, Comm. Harrison Hueblein, Lt. Comm. William Lauper, Jeanne Easum, Gloria Deets-Breyer, Chief Douglas Clark, and Orrin Anderson; Norco City Council, particularly Kathy Azevedo and Hal Clark, Debbie McNay, Chief Jack Fry, City Manager Jeff Allred, and Ron Snow. Thank you to the Corona Public Library staff, particularly Sandra Brautigam-Strader, Christopher Dixon, Brent Fite, Vera Garcia, Theresa Hodges, Karli Mahoney, Shanika Norman, Jennifer Marlatt, Diana Miranda, Amy Ragland, Marvin Sinson, Chris Smith, and Deborah Jennifer Villegas.

From esteemed libraries, we thank Mark Wanamaker, Miles Kreuger, Simon Elliot, Dace Taub, Carolyn Cole, Dr. Mellissa Conway, Darian Davies, and Judy Harvey Sahak. Special thanks to Velma Hickey, Laurie Urie, Helene Demeestere, Betty Bash, and Mary Winn.

And thank you to the storytellers: Ray Harris, Robert Peister, Gene Peister, Bob Allen, Karlene Allen, Phil Newhouse, Lyle Draves, Vickie Draves, Regina Dotson, Dwight Tyler, Jo Ann Gordon, Sammy Lee, Gwene Barbao, Dennis Kent, Rudy Ramos, Benjamin Cricket, Mike Nugent, Edna Johnson, Rueben Lemus, Lolita Lemus, Augie Ramirez, Larry Key, Pat Barker, John Barr, B. J. Hill, Don Stowe, George Milner, Shirley Gilbraith, Harold Davis, Don Stowe, Jack Gordon, and Howard Hansclik.

INTRODUCTION

The most intriguing aspect of the Norconian Resort Supreme may not be its fabulous history, magnificent ceiling paintings, or the wonderful art deco, mission revival, and Mediterranean–style architecture; perhaps the most remarkable aspect of the former "playground to the stars" is that it still stands and no one seems to know it.

Unlike so many wonderful and long-gone resorts, theaters, and other structures built during this golden age of architecture, we can still look up and see the red-tiled towers, walk across the marble floors, touch the exquisite tile work by the light of original chandeliers and fixtures, gaze at beautiful murals and paintings, and find our image in mirrors that still bear the initials of the Lake Norconian Club. Almost the entire resort complex still exists despite two decades as a naval hospital, 60 years' service as a top-secret naval warfare testing center, and 40 years as a prison. Unfortunately, after surviving for 80 years and despite its prominent position on the National Register of Historic Places, the days of the Norconian Resort Supreme may be numbered because of officially sanctioned neglect and destruction, politics, and an uninformed, perhaps uncaring, public.

The Norconian was built by Rex B. Clark in the town he founded: Norco, California. In the early 1920s, Clark, a brilliant businessman buoyed by a wife with millions, purchased 15 square miles in the middle of nowhere with the idea of founding a community where people could live off the land they owned by developing chicken and rabbit farms and all manner of agriculture. While a well was being drilled in 1924, a "hot mineral spring" was discovered. Clark, who believed in doing things "big," announced he was going to construct the greatest recreational resort ever built on the West Coast, perhaps in the whole United States, and then did it.

On February 2, 1929, the Norconian Resort was given to the world with a star-studded grand opening. Complete with boating, airfield, horseback riding, mineral baths, tennis, golf, and swimming, the resort simply astounded. The Olympic pools attracted some of the greatest Olympic swimmers and divers of all time. Several films were shot at and around the Norconian, and celebrities flocked to the resort. Greta Garbo and Clark Gable were frequent guests, and Will Rogers and Wallace Beery regularly flew into the Norconian Air Field. On the championship golf course could be found Buster Keaton, Bing Crosby, and even Babe Ruth. Major motion picture studios, Lions Club, Kiwanis, Rotary, Shriners, American Legion, and dozens of other organizations held gigantic picnics as well as national, state, and county conventions on the lush grounds.

Unfortunately, the Norconian never made a nickel. As it opened just months before "Black Tuesday," the Depression hit the resort hard. Another mark against the "millionaire's playground" was its location. Norco, California, of the 1920s was known for lettuce and chickens: meaning once you stepped off the resort's manicured lawns, there wasn't a whole lot to do in the small town. Worse, the Depression was equally devastating to the promising community, with many farms and ranches going belly-up, and perhaps driving through such poverty to enjoy a weekend in luxury may not have been appealing to those still fortunate to have money.

By 1941, the Norconian was up for sale, and the asking price was $2 million, less than half of its cost to build. The United States was quietly preparing for war, and the navy came calling; the resort's plentiful water supply, top-of-the-line power plant, and room to expand provided a perfect location for a hospital. On December 8, 1941, the day after the Japanese attack on Pearl Harbor, the Norconian Resort became the U.S. Naval Hospital.

This book primarily chronicles the Norconian era (1927–1941), but equally fascinating are the years following the resort's closure. Perhaps World War II was the old playground to the stars' finest hour. The naval hospital was an exemplary facility making extraordinary advances in the treatment of tuberculosis, malaria, and polio. Wheelchair basketball may well have been born at the facility or at the very least was given a huge boost on the wheels of the fabulous "Rolling Devils." Wounded men from Pearl Harbor, Peleliu, Iwo Jima, and other distant Pacific battlefields recovered in luxury at the naval hospital. And Hollywood again called—movie star Kay Francis was in charge of morale and troop entertainment, and many of the stars who once were guests at the resort now spent their weekends visiting patients. After the war, the patient load dropped, and the hospital closed in 1949 only to reopen again in 1951 to receive wounded from Korea. In 1957, despite heavy public outcry and a moderately heavy patient load, the hospital closed for good.

In 1951, the National Bureau of Standards moved into the empty isolation wards on the eastern portion of the old Norconian golf course. The best minds in the country were brought together in the interest of national defense to work primarily on guiding and fusing missile systems. Since then, many name and mission changes have occurred on this base described by Congressman Ken Calvert as "crucial to our nation's security." The experimentation and evaluation of all manner of weaponry carried out in that 400-acre, heavily guarded facility has saved countless U.S. soldiers' lives.

In 1963, ninety-four acres of the old resort became the Californian Rehabilitation Center (CRC). Using the former hotel building, the navy-built hospital wing, gymnasium, chapel, and patient barracks, the State of California, in an unprecedented effort, attempted to circumvent heroin addiction.

Today CRC is a Level II correctional facility; a medium-security prison housing at times as many as 5,000 inmates guilty of a wide variety of crimes. Inside, some truly extraordinary prison officials and officers, despite horrific overcrowding, lack of funding, public disinterest, and even scorn, keep the public safe and continue to man programs that offer even the most wretched a way out of drug addiction.

In 2002, the State of California deemed the old hotel building seismically unfit and—despite the building's history, architecture, landmark status, and multiple recommendations to the contrary—deemed a retrofit too expensive and ordered the old hotel abandoned. Despite the mandated protections in place to preserve national treasures, a 20-foot-high fence was put up around the building, the water and power turned off, and the building was officially designated a "black building," a structure sealed up and left to die from the inside out. In the dark, rainwater seeps over breathtaking paintings, chandeliers, and stunning tile. Raccoons and feral cats roam the empty hallways and defecate on the marble floors. Just as planned, the "shining white monument to health" is dying.

On the navy-controlled side of the old resort, thanks to the efforts of countless navy and civilian officials, the lake still remains, as do the pavilion, old chauffeurs' quarters, and garage. Unfortunately, navy budget cuts have severely limited the resources needed to maintain these treasures also on the National Register, and their fate is in limbo.

It would appear at this time that only an informed and interested public, on a local, statewide, and national level willing to lobby our elected officials, can save this complex of some of the finest and most extraordinary structures ever built.

One
REX B. CLARK
AND NORCO

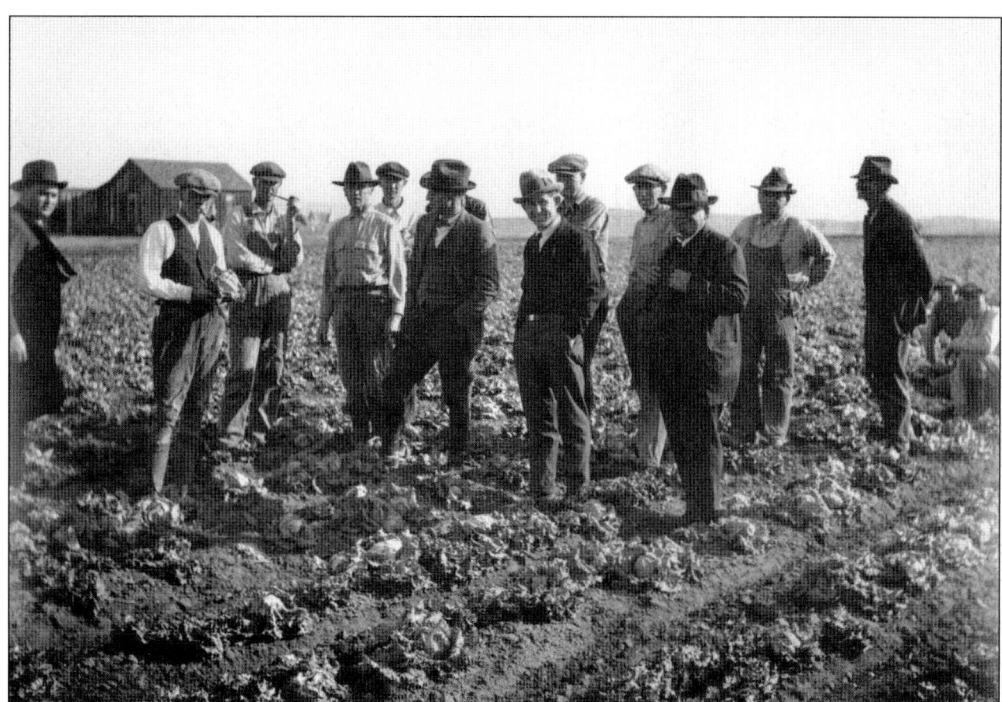

REX CLARK, C. 1922. In profile at center, the founder of Norco stands with a group of unidentified men in a field of lettuce, reveling no doubt that Norco, then known as Orchard Heights, was California's lettuce king. In 1920, Clark personally purchased 600 acres of Orchard Heights and controlled another 4,400 as principal shareholder of the North Corona Land Company, the company that built early Norco. (Peter Clark.)

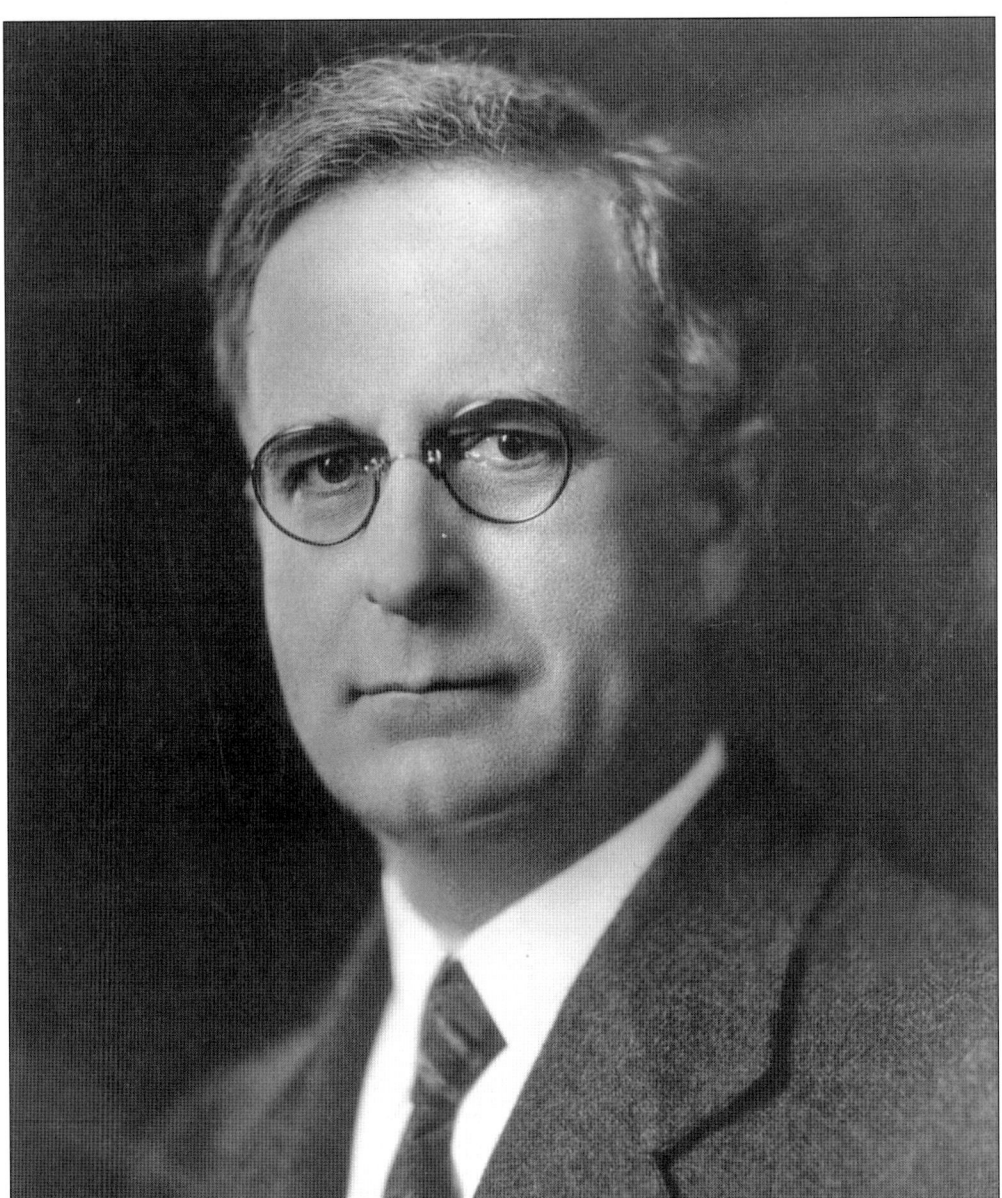

REX BRAINERD CLARK, 1927. Born 1876 in Detroit, Clark was the son of an actuary, sang in the church choir, and was ambitious. He married Grace Scripps but did not get along with his new father-in-law, the powerful newspaper founder James Scripps. Barred from the Scripps family business, Rex Clark started a large stationery store but after some noted success went bankrupt and suffered a nervous breakdown. To help her husband recover and perhaps escape the glare of her father, Grace Clark took her husband west to La Jolla, California, to stay with her uncle, famed publisher E. W. Scripps. The Clarks loved California and decided to stay. Upon his recovery, Rex demonstrated a talent for land speculation and development. Eventually Rex and Grace, with their three children, Rex, William, and Ellen, settled in Julian, California, to raise cattle and apples and start a freight company. It was in Julian where Clark began his longtime affair with Emma "Jimmie" Snyder, and her move to Los Angeles prompted yet another Clark family relocation to Pasadena and the acquisition of Norco.

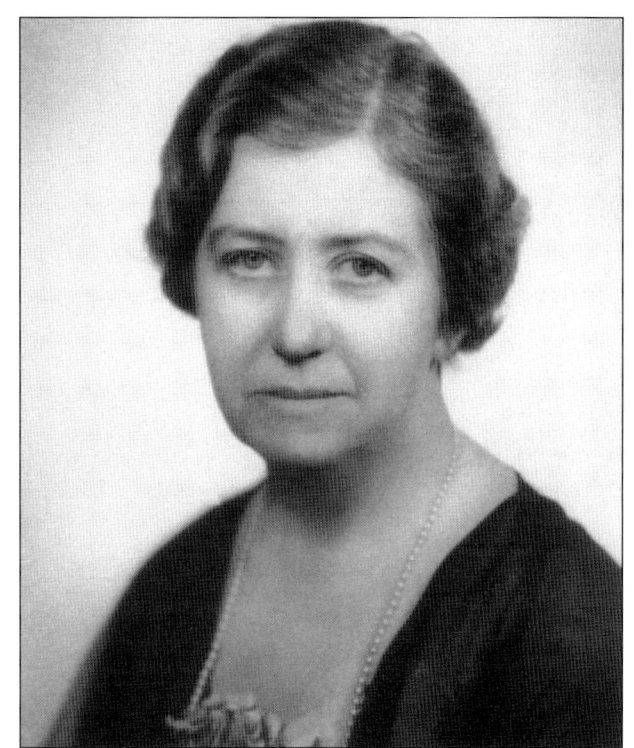

GRACE MESSINGER CLARK, C. 1932. It was likely Grace Clark's Scripps family inheritance and trust fund that in part or perhaps entirely financed the building of Norco and the Norconian Resort. An adventurous individual, she was the first woman to drive an automobile in Detroit, and Sierra Street in Norco was so named for her founding membership in the Sierra Club. (Scripps College.)

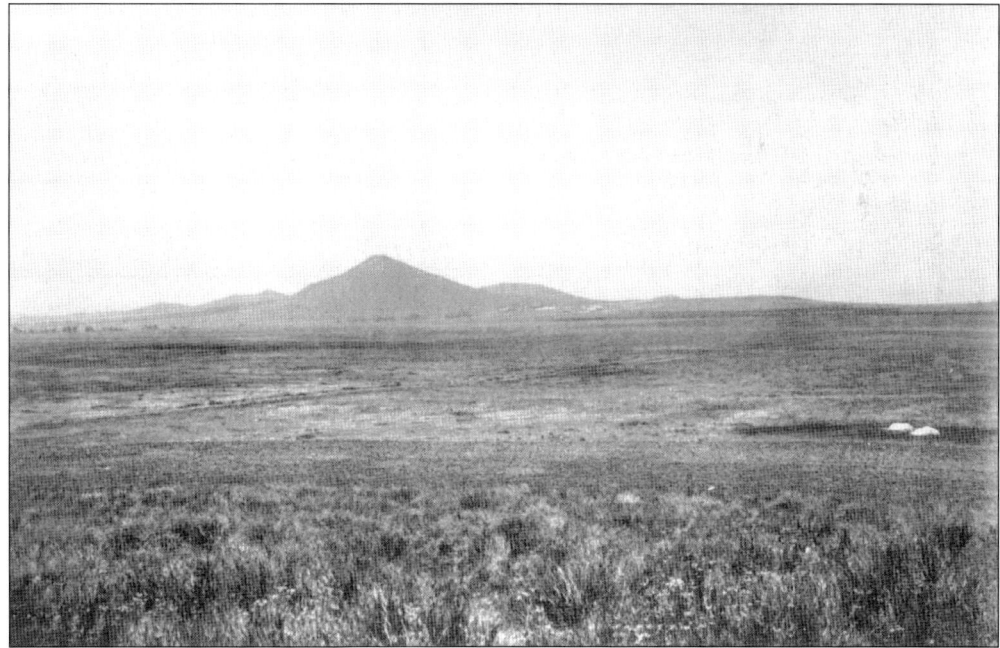

ORCHARD HEIGHTS, C. 1922. Once named Citrus Belt, this agricultural area of 5,000 acres was renamed Orchard Heights during a 1920 Corona Chamber of Commerce promotional campaign to encourage the development of a new northern suburb. In the distance is Beacon Hill and very little else. Apricots, peaches, potatoes, and other crops were grown successfully; however, water was expensive with too few wells and pipelines that frequently malfunctioned. (Peter Clark.)

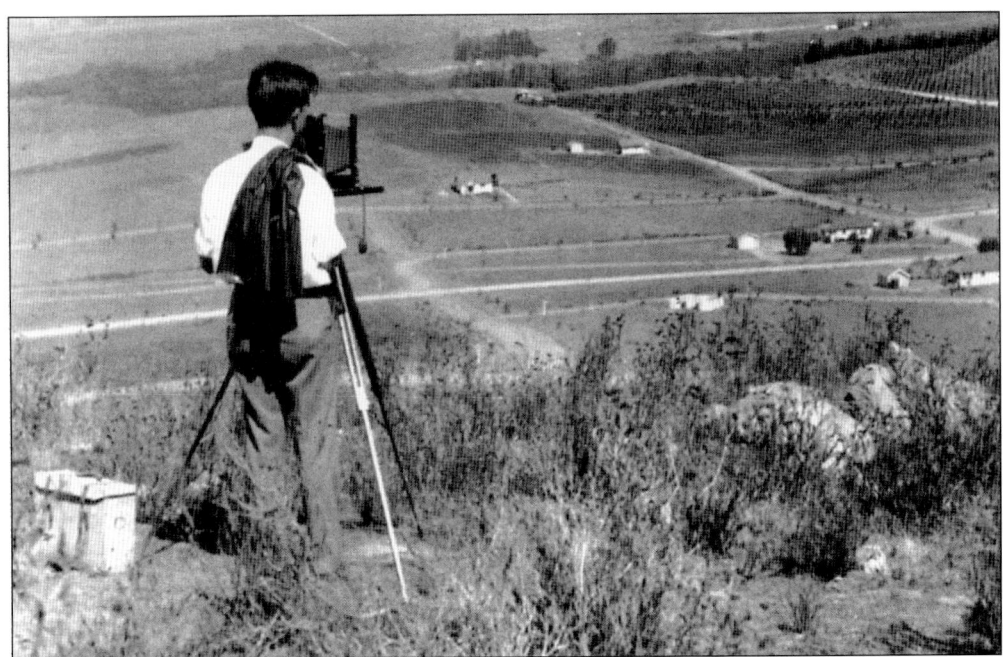

REX SCRIPPS CLARK, C. 1923. The oldest son of Rex Clark suggested the name of "Norco" for his father's new town. Known as "Scripps," he managed the North Corona Land Company, was Norco's first postmaster, and coached the company baseball team. A photographer who captured thousands of images of both Norco and the building of the Norconian, Scripps parted with his father and never saw the completed resort. (Peter Clark.)

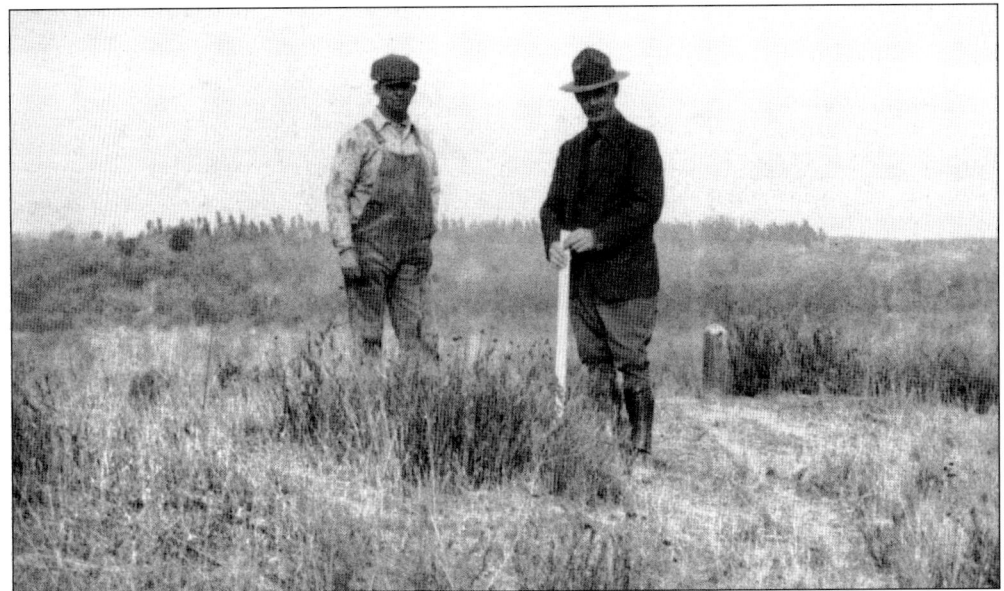

CAPT. CUTHBERT GULLY, C. 1922. "Bert" (right), as he was known to his closest friends, served in the Engineers Corps during World War I; afterward, he was forever known as Captain Gully. Serving as Norco's chief engineer on and off for over 40 years, he was responsible for laying out the streets of the fledgling community and between 1921 and 1923 completely upgraded the area water system, installing new pumps, lines, and reservoirs. (Peter Clark.)

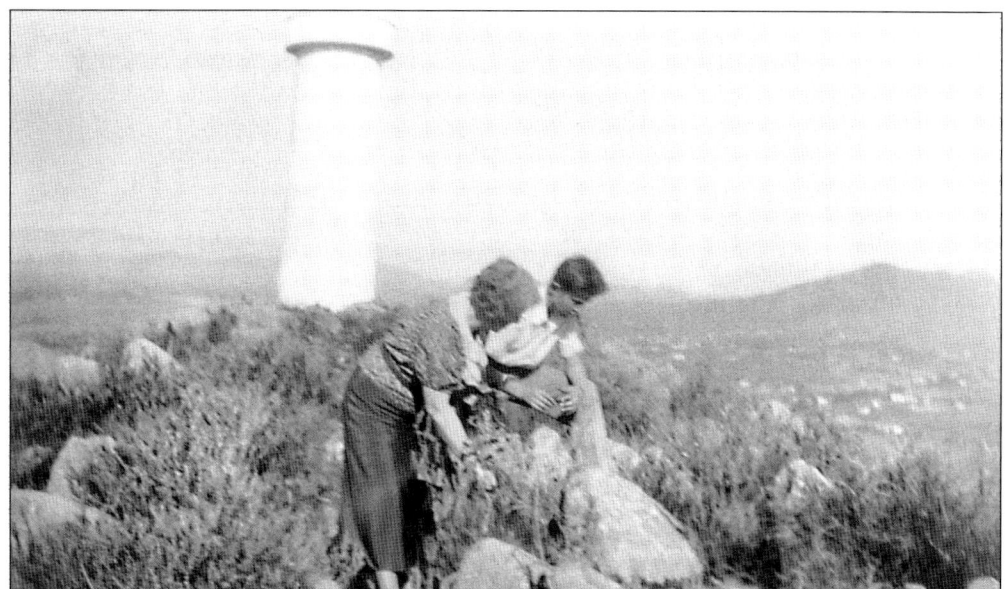

THE BEACON, C. 1935. As a promotional device to sell the first homes in Norco, a lighthouse was mounted atop Beacon Hill. Advertisements encouraged homebuyers to "follow the Beacon" to Norco. This partial image is the only known close-up photograph of that wonderful structure. The beacon was torn down by 1957; however, the footings remain to this day. In the foreground stand Sophie Zehfuss and her son Louis. (Louis Zehfuss.)

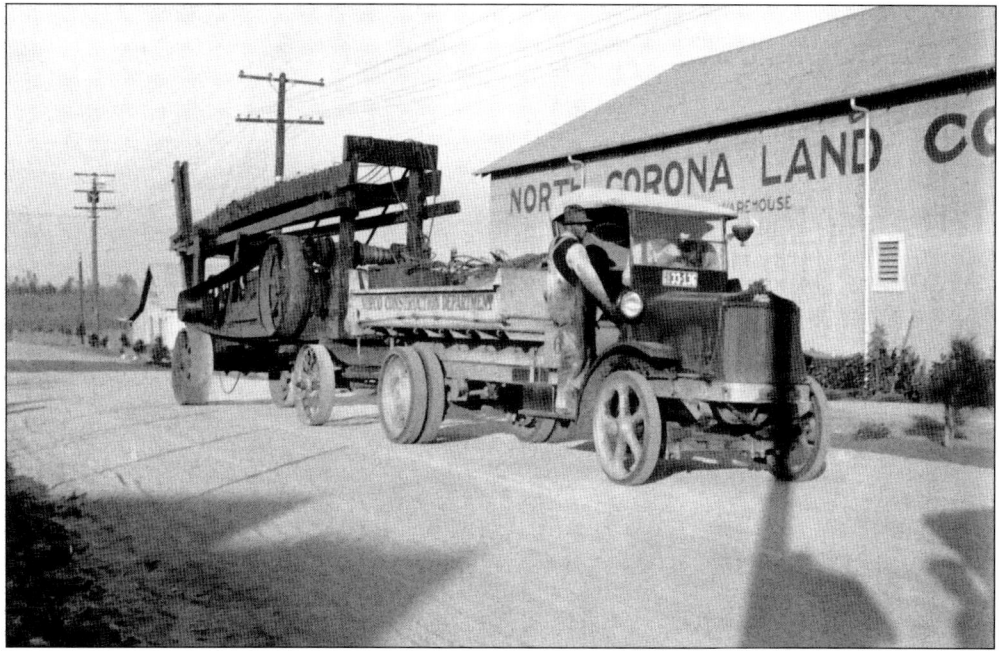

NORCO CONSTRUCTION DEPARTMENT, C. 1923. Rex Clark established a manufacturing center off Norco's Detroit Street (named in honor of his hometown and a symbol of industry), complete with tile and brick works, machine shop, gravel works, pipe company, drilling operation, blacksmith shop, tractor repair shop, plumbing shop, lumber yard, and so forth. The early Norco homes were constructed of materials and labor from this center, as was the Norconian Resort. (Peter Clark.)

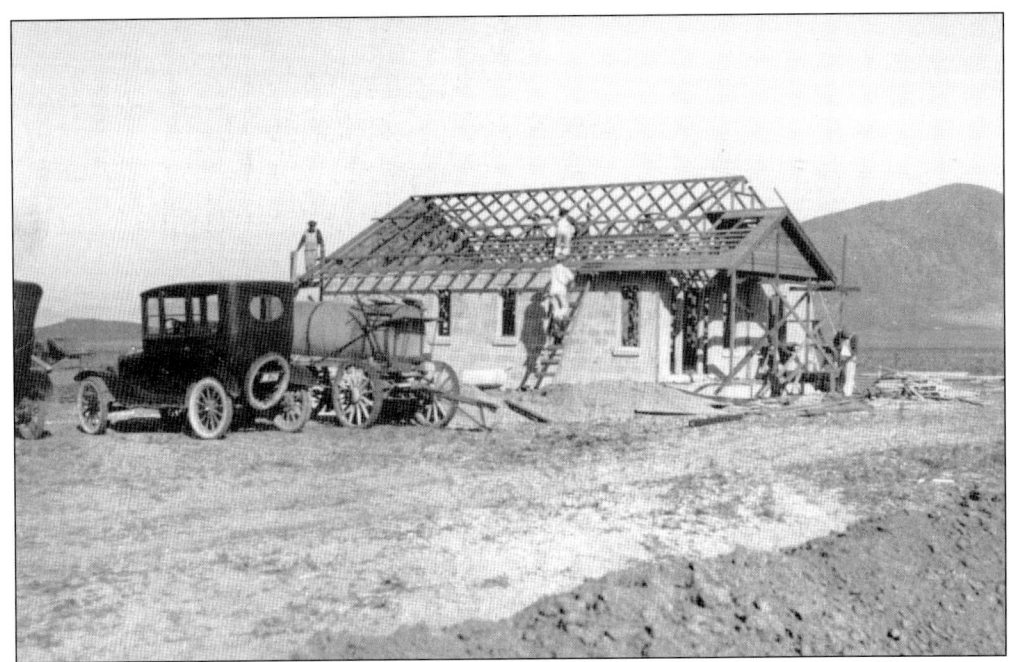

BUILDING A HOME, 1923. The initial houses were small, generally wood-sided or block structures. Electricity did not arrive until the late 1920s, and outhouses were the norm. Cheap water was the key to community success, and a home purchase brought with it shares of the Orange Heights Water District, a community-owned water company whose monthly rates rose and fell like the stock market. (Peter Clark.)

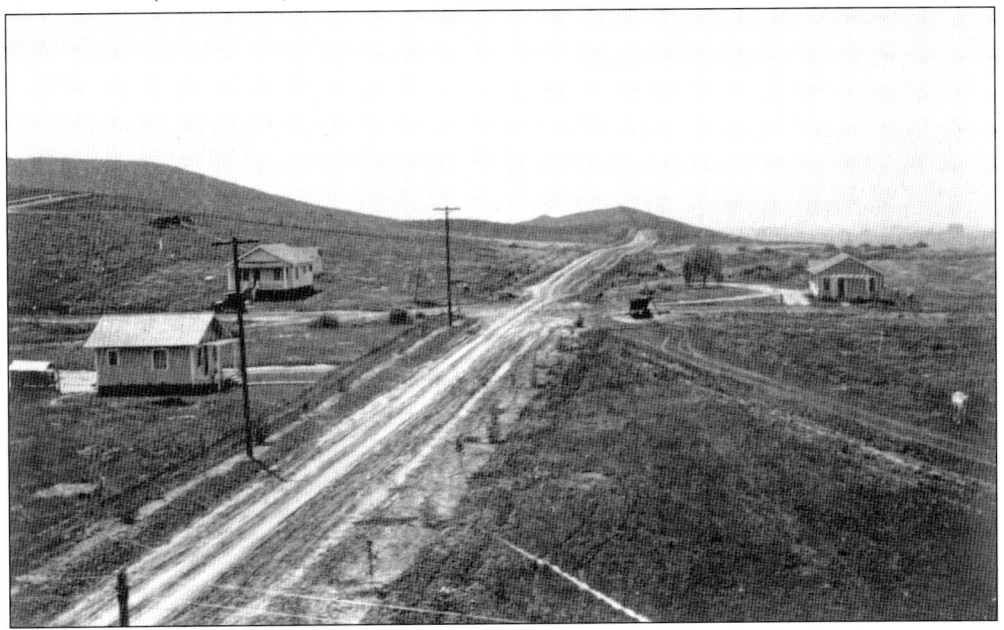

NORCO, 1922. Rex Clark, in the spirit of the "Cow, Sow and Plow" self-reliance movement, advertised homes on lots of 5 and 10 acres where "a go-getter" who worked hard could grow what he needed to live and raise his family. Ironically, Clark at the time lived in Pasadena on a gigantic estate in complete luxury and likely never pushed a plow in his life. (Peter Clark.)

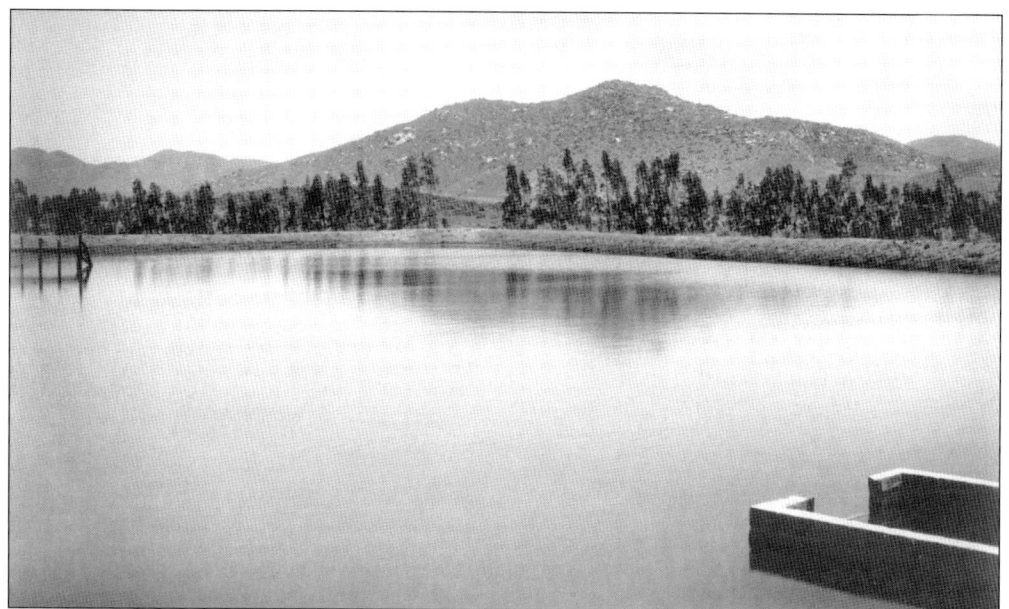

WATER RESERVOIR, 1923. Water was supplied via open reservoirs. Gene and Robert Peister, old-time Norco residents, remembered well swimming and fishing in these forbidden ponds. Gravity was used as a means to pressurize water into Norco homes and fields; the water tasted terrible, and frequently guppies, frogs, and small fish would work their way out of a kitchen faucet. (Peter Clark.)

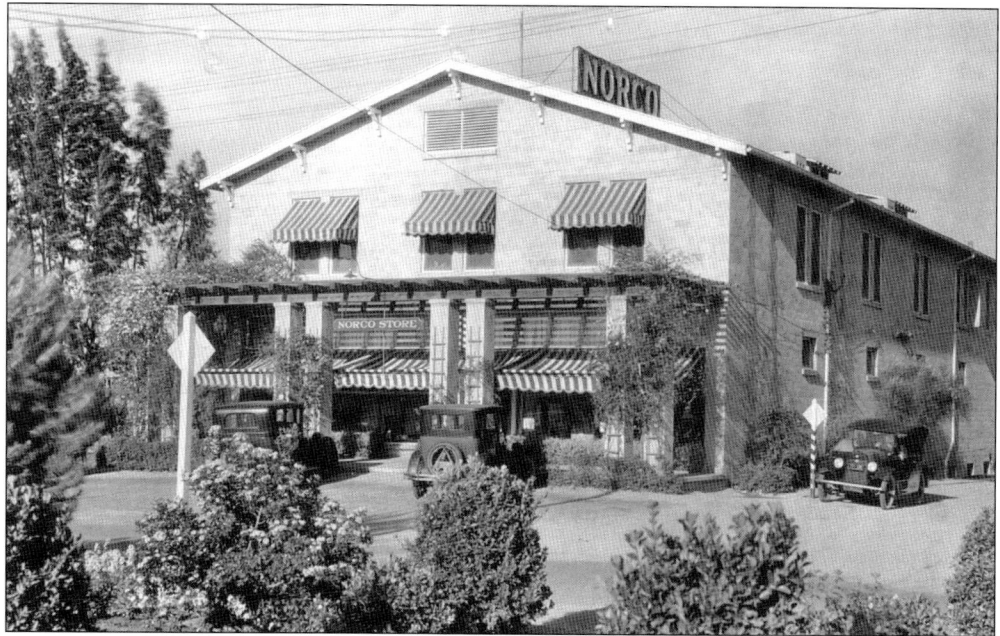

NORCO STORE, 1923. The single most important structure in early Norco, this building housed the Norco Grill, meeting hall, butcher shop, and community library, sold all manner of hardware and feed supplies, and even contained several apartments for company employees. It was the scene of countless major meetings, both locally and regionally, and it is said the food served by the Norco Grill was superb, specifically the chicken dinners. (Peter Clark.)

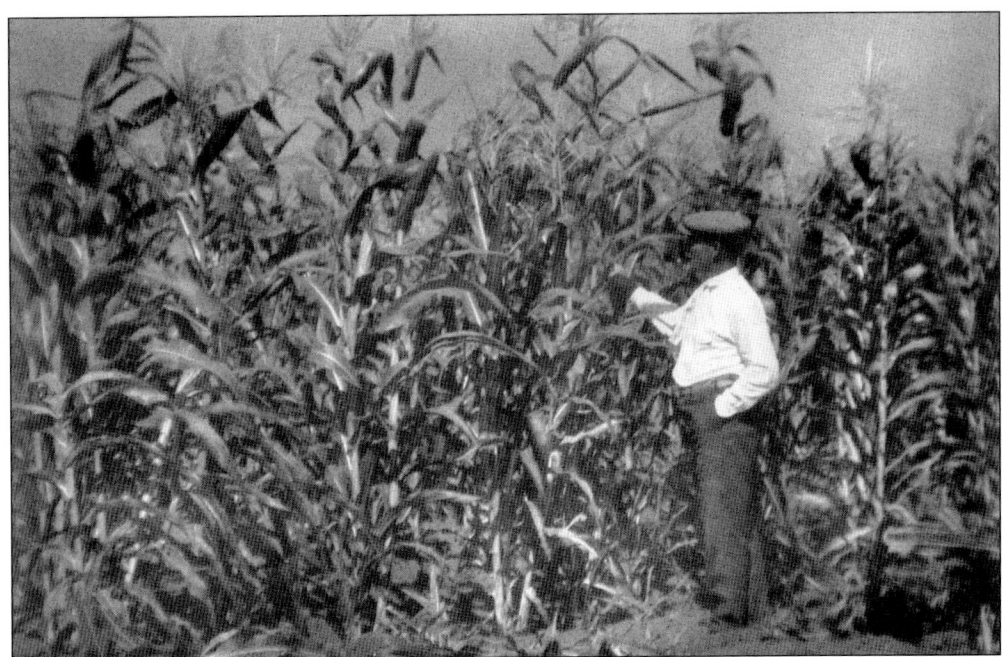

CORN, 1923. By 1923, Norco was an agricultural center to be reckoned with. The community exported eggs, pelts and furs, frying hens, corn, apricots, tomatoes, potatoes, onions, berries, and dozens of other kinds of produce bearing the "Norco Brand." Norco in the early 1920s was a lettuce, poultry, and rabbit capital of California. Rex Clark in later correspondence claimed there was nothing like a Norco watermelon. (Peter Clark.)

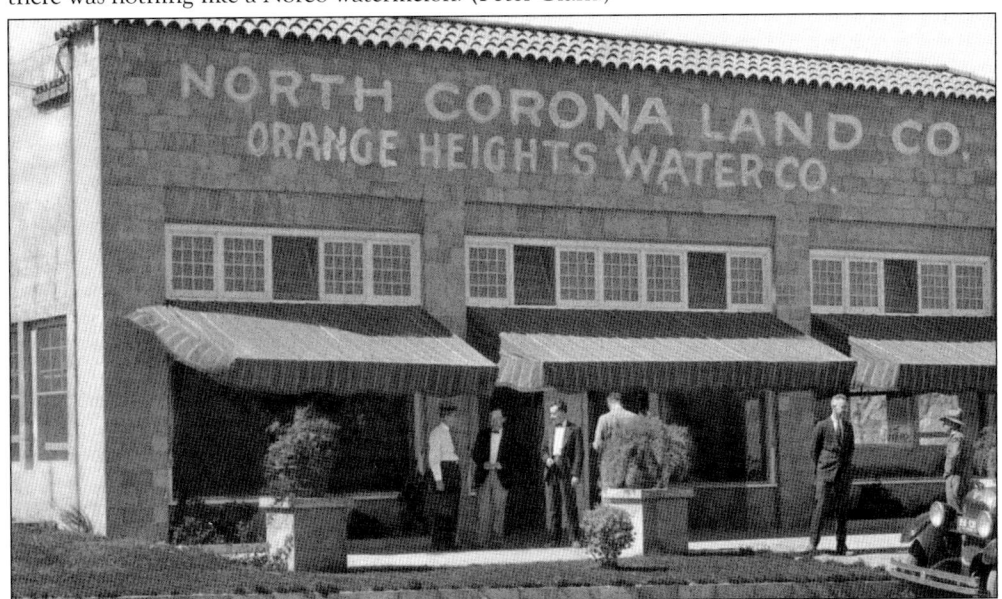

NORTH CORONA LAND COMPANY, 1924. NCLC, claiming $600,000 in operating capital, was formed to oversee the development of Norco and would later serve the same function for the Norconian Resort. Rex Clark, as president, claimed 51 percent ownership, and Emma Jimmie Snyder, Clark's mistress, was vice-president and crucial to the early development of Norco. Until the 1930s, the main headquarters was located in Los Angeles. (Corona Public Library.)

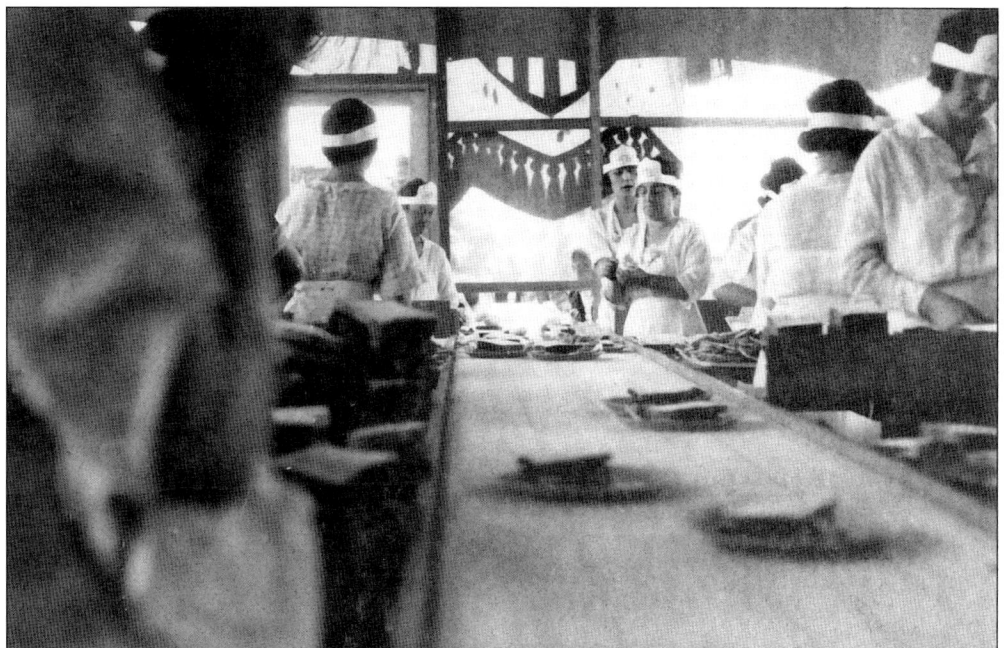

NORCO DEDICATION DAY, MAY 13, 1923. To feed the thousands expected to show for Norco's grand opening, an assembly line and conveyer belt delivery system was developed. The initial homes for sale sold out by the end of the day. Rex Clark himself oversaw the pie-eating contest and gave speeches. Other events were a greased-pig chase, tug-of-war, and a brass band concert. (Peter Clark.)

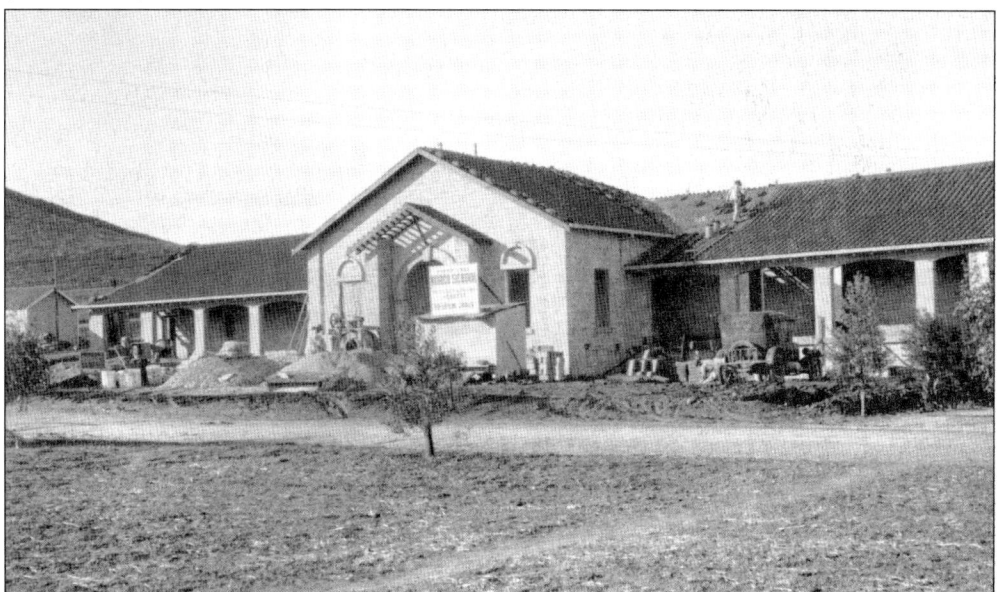

NORCO SCHOOL, 1924. Rex Clark felt his community, tired of having their students bused to Corona, should have their own school. Designed by famed architect G. Stanley Wilson, the school opened in early 1925 and quickly began service as yet another meeting place for the community. L. M. Crary, in 1925, was the first Norconian elected to the Corona School Board; unfortunately, he died before finishing his term. (Peter Clark.)

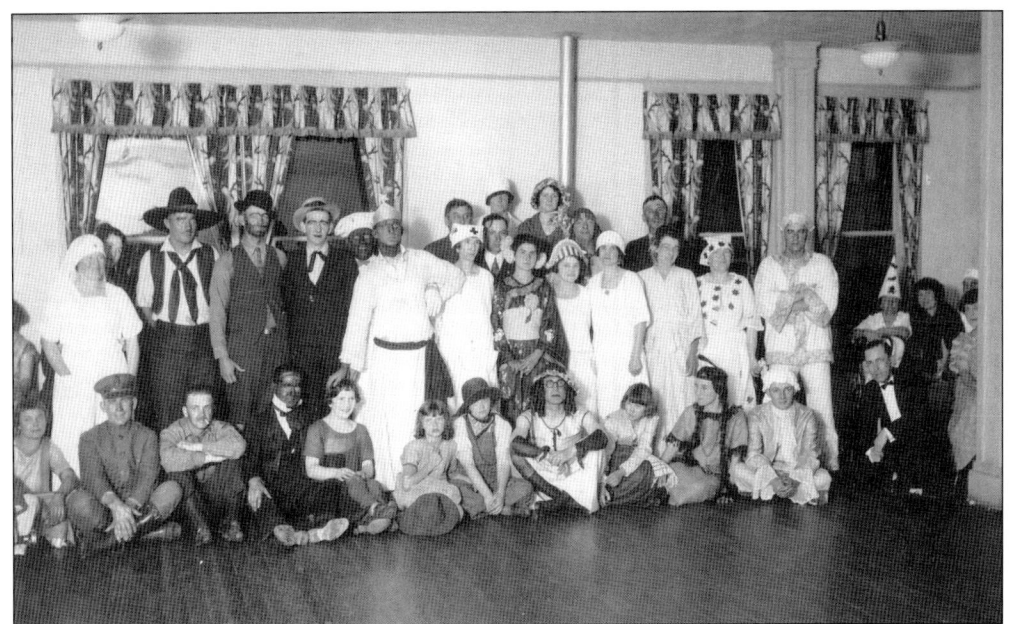

COSTUME PARTY, 1924. Norco, though under county jurisdiction and not a city, boasted a "mayor," a volunteer fire department, and several civic organizations. The town motto was "Acres of Neighbors." Here in the Norco Grill is one of many events chronicled in local papers. The participants are unidentified; however, there could well be a poultry farmer, concert violinist, and railroad magnate side by side in this photograph. (Peter Clark.)

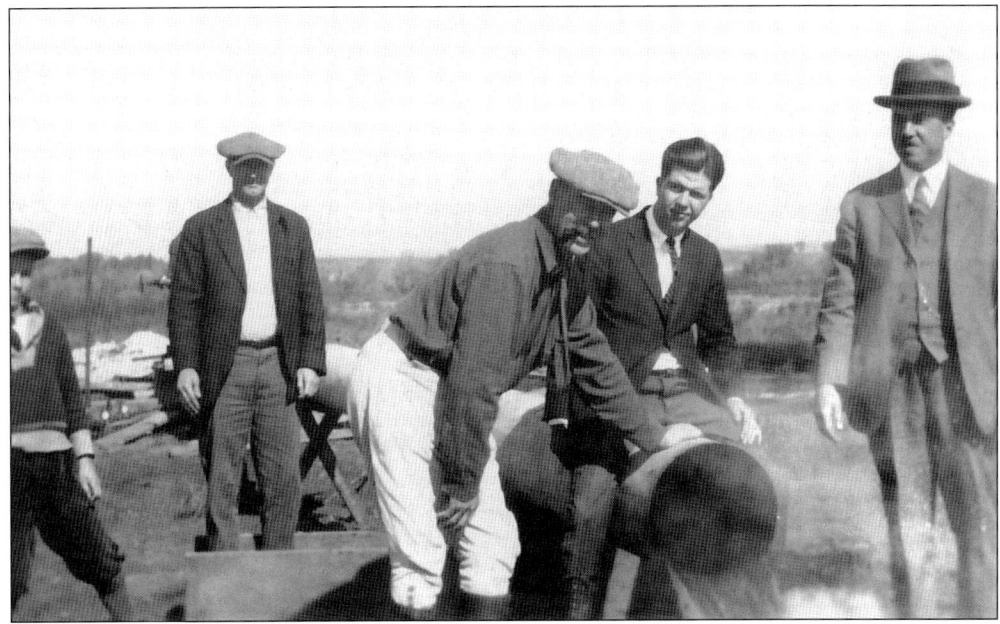

HOT WATER, 1924. The Norconian began with the discovery of naturally occurring water, heated to 126 degrees and chock-full of minerals. Rex Clark's daughter, Ellen Revelle, stated the find was an accident and remembered her father's excitement bringing home a jar of water and his irritation when she confessed, "It tasted awful." The "magical elixir of health" still tastes awful today. (Peter Clark.)

Two

Building the Dream

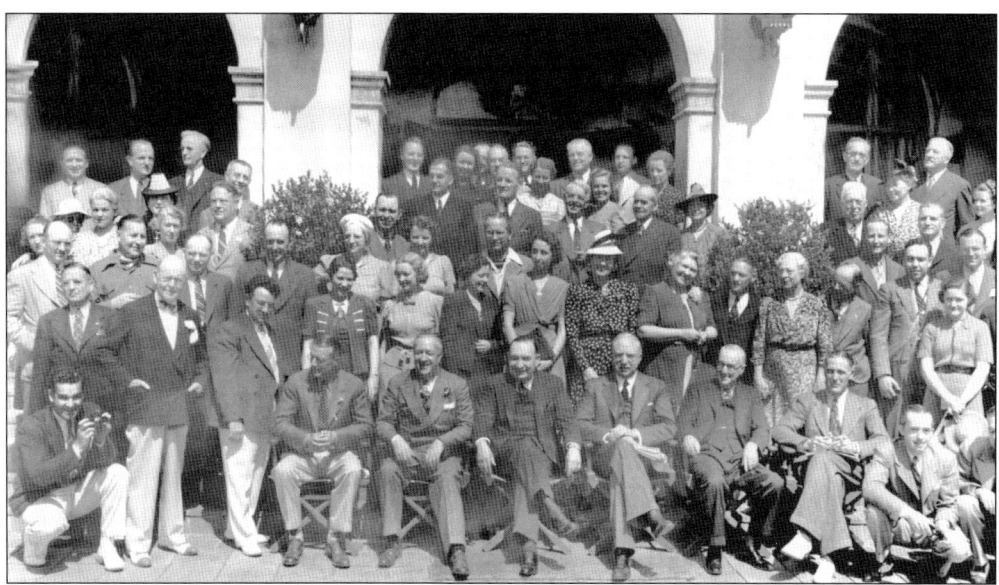

NORCONIAN FRONT STEPS, 1939. Rex Clark, top row, third from left, is seen here hosting the California Hotelmen's Convention. Clark has been described as a "dictator" and "wonderful man who would do anything for you." Clark once said that he always dreamed of building a "resort supreme dedicated to recreation," and yet his daughter stated her father took no pleasure in the family nature walks and, in fact, avoided exertion.

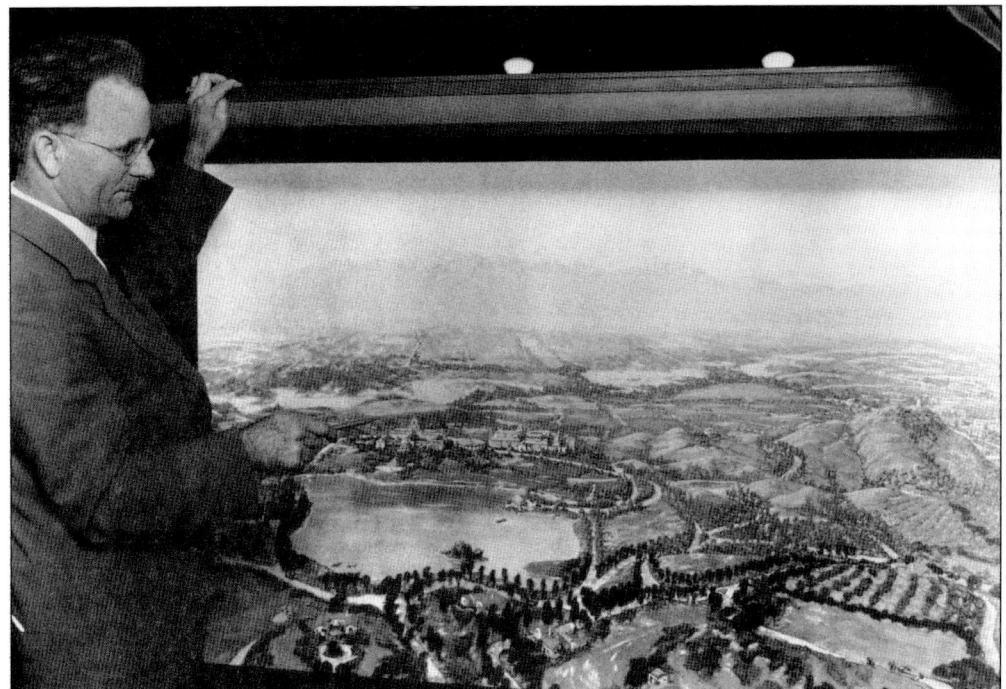

NOT JUST CHICKEN FEED, 1926. During the closing hours of the first-annual Norco Rabbit Show, Rex Clark announced, "An imposing hotel and landscape garden is to crown one of the Norco hills." The budget for the project was $1.5 million and included an inn, 60-acre lake, private pools, baths, lounges, gymnasiums, two large outdoor pools, and "everything to be desired by those seeking health and recreation." Stated Clark, "Norco's future would be assured."

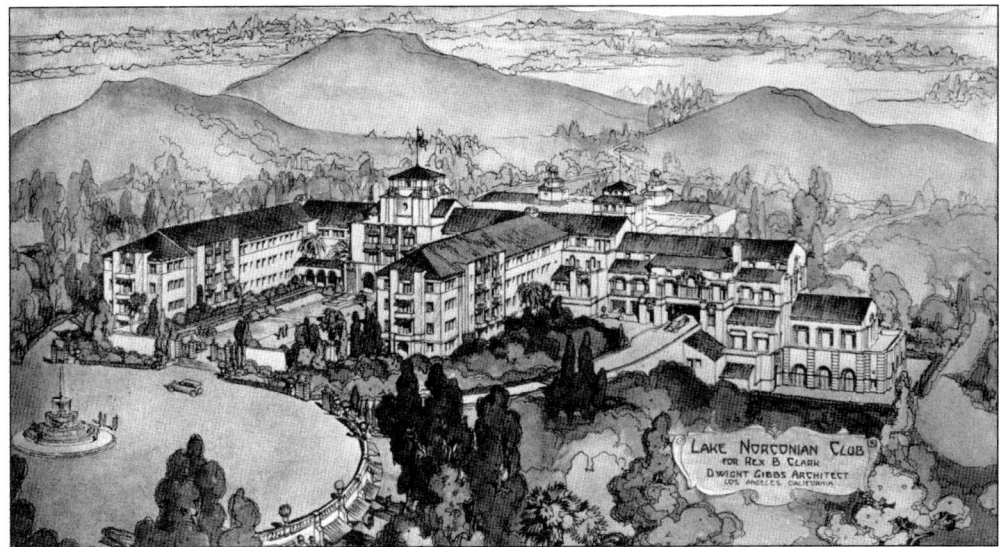

NORCONIAN CLUB ARCHITECTURAL RENDERING, 1927. Dwight Gibbs was the architect in charge of designing the combination inn, bathhouse, and pools. Previously he had designed the magnificent Carthay Circle Theatre in Los Angeles, the Mesa Theatre in Costa Mesa, and the interior of the Pasadena Playhouse in Pasadena. An advocate of California mission style, Gibbs was quite proud of his ability to blend "old Spanish touches" with a "modernistic treatment."

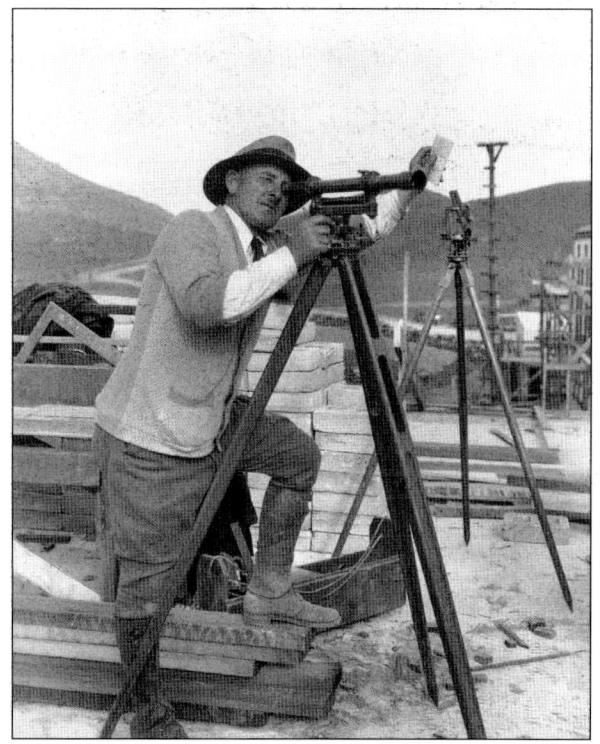

CAPTAIN GULLY, C. 1928. On July 25, 1927, Bert Gully, chief engineer for the North Corona Land Company, began to survey the area destined to become the jewel of the Resort Supreme: the hotel and spa. Old-timers remember Gully exactly as seen in this photograph—hat, riding breeches, and knee-high boots; also remembered was the huge, convertible Maxwell roadster he drove for decades. (Corona Public Library.)

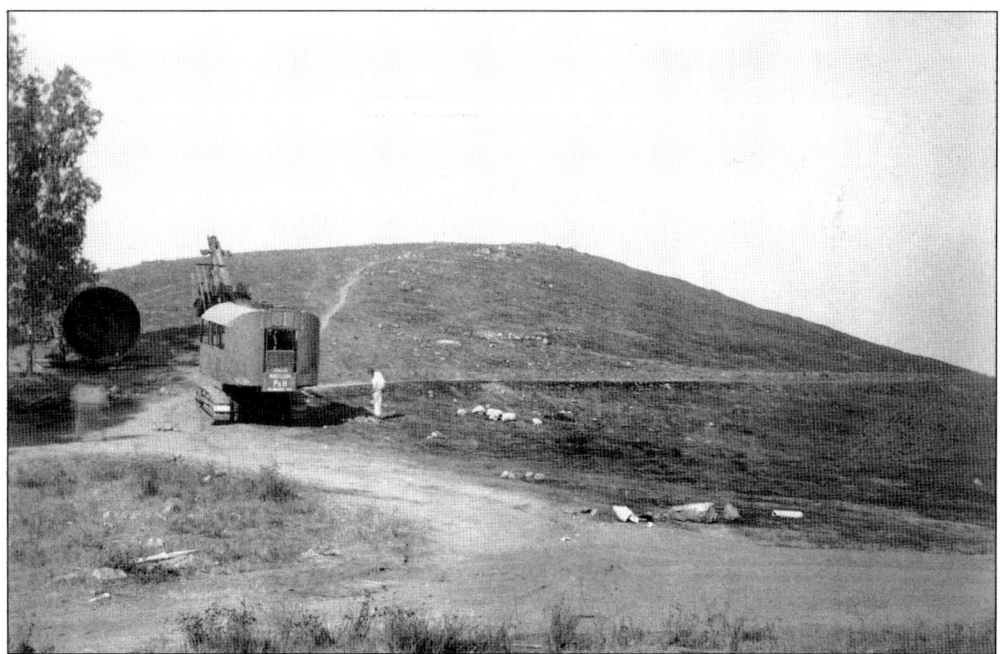

GROUND-BREAKING, AUGUST 15, 1927. This photograph was taken only moments before ground was broken for the "resort supreme." The *Daily Independent* stated, "Rex Clark gave one of his inspirational speeches, then told the mighty earth movers to do the work of man." In a few months, the paper would further write, "Even his associates could not fathom the plan to transform those bare, ugly hills into a creation of beauty."

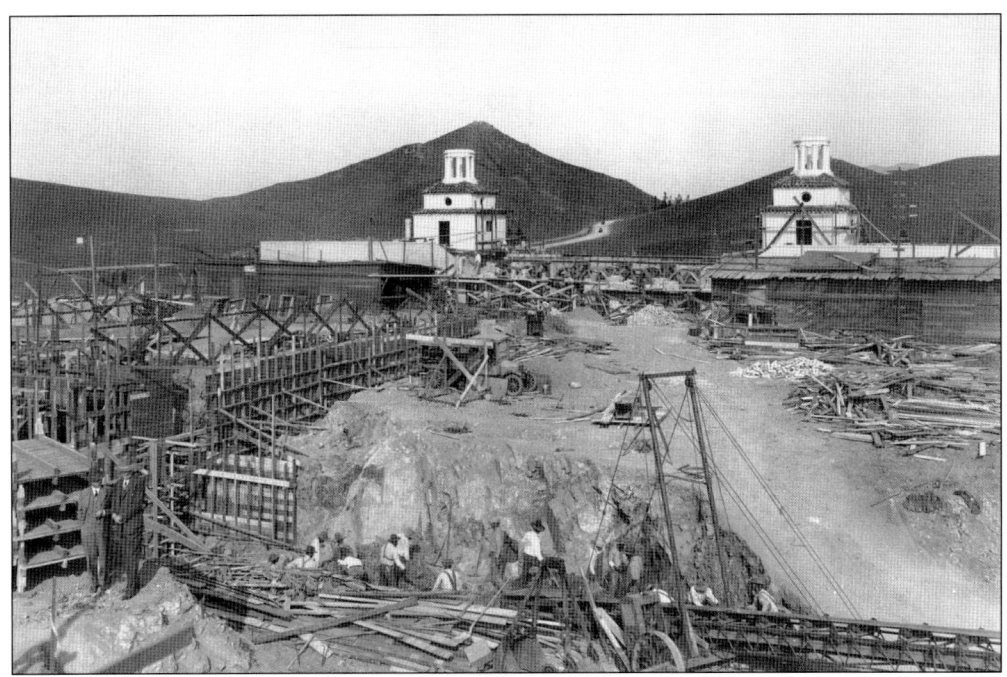

EAST VIEW FROM HOTEL SITE, DECEMBER 12, 1927. Five months later, the twin towers soon to overlook the outdoor pools are in place. In the foreground are the underground service tunnels being cut into the granite. The work is grueling, as the rock at times must be chipped away with chisel, pick, and shovel. In the mid-ground, masons lay block to complete one of many observation decks.

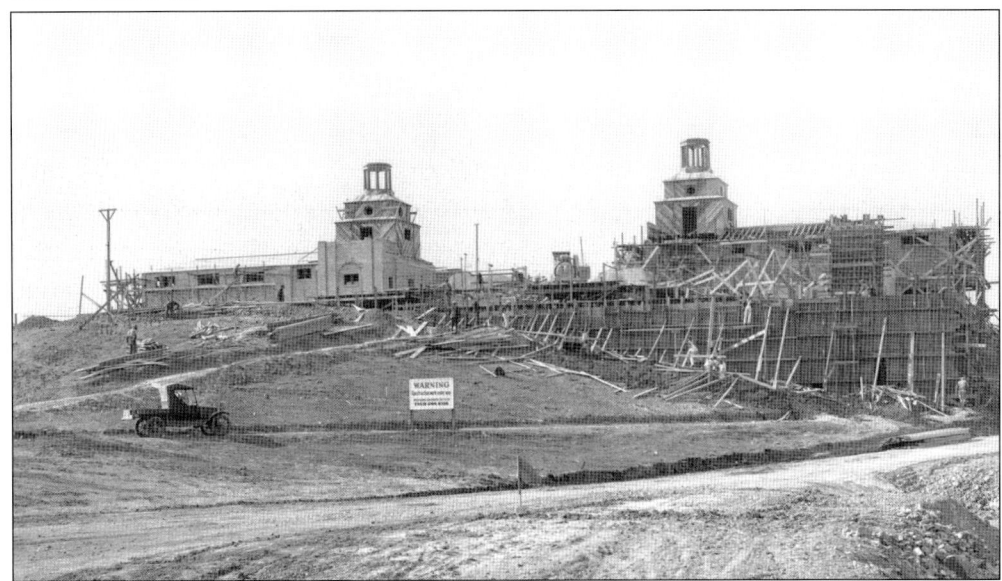

WEST VIEW, DECEMBER 15, 1927. The majestic towers would dramatically greet visitors as they descended into the valley, exactly why Rex Clark built them first. He wanted "momentous" publicity to "let the world know he was up to something unique out in Norco." It worked, as Clark, his project, and the Norconian were daily topics in newspapers and magazines on a local and national scale.

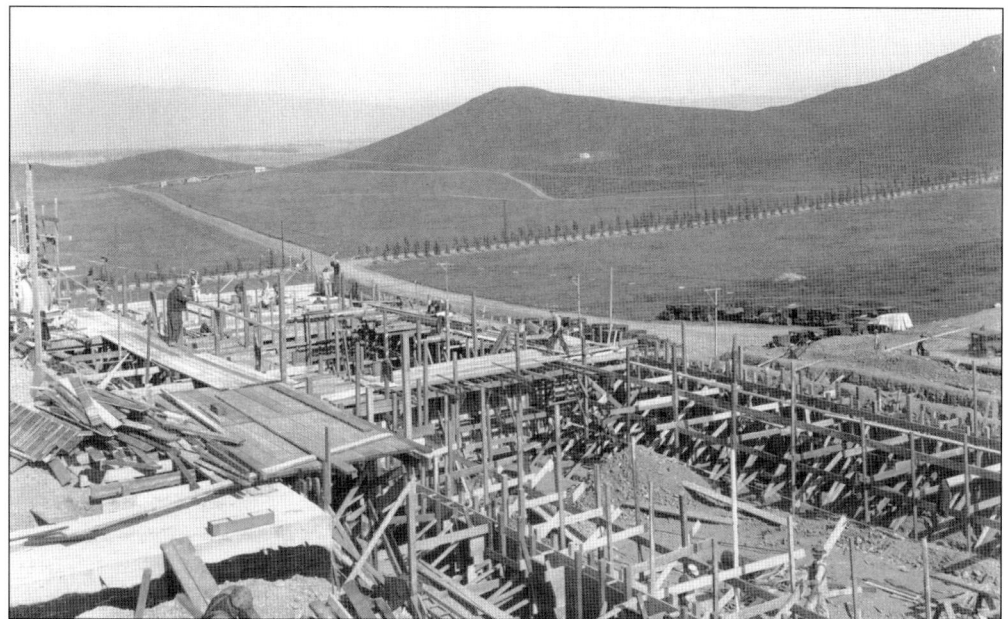

POOLS CONSTRUCTION, DECEMBER 15, 1927. In this photograph, forms are readied for what will soon be two outdoor competition pools. According to the *Daily Independent*, on January 2, 1927, a "force of 210 men, without a single stop . . . poured concrete continuously for 29 hours. 2,400 sacks of cement and 400 cubic yards of sand and rock were used to complete the walls of the swimming pool and the filter room."

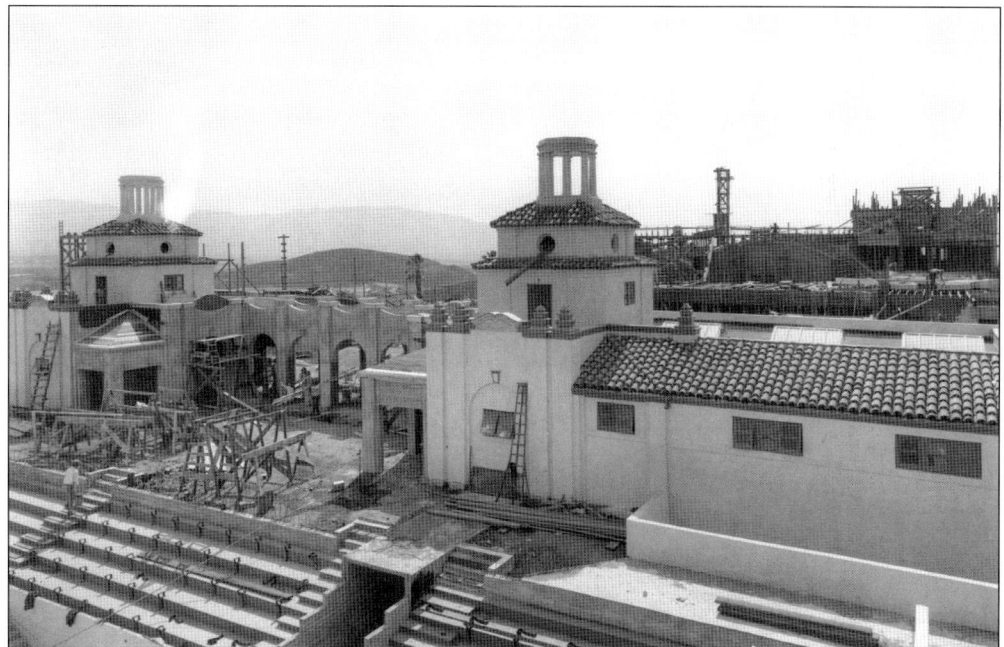

THE POOL GRANDSTANDS, 1928. The tunnel at the bottom of the photograph will lead to the changing rooms. In the middle to the right will be a sunporch and snack bar, and under the left tower will be a café. To the rear of the photograph can be seen the main hotel being erected. The pool would host swimming guests and competitions months before the opening of the hotel.

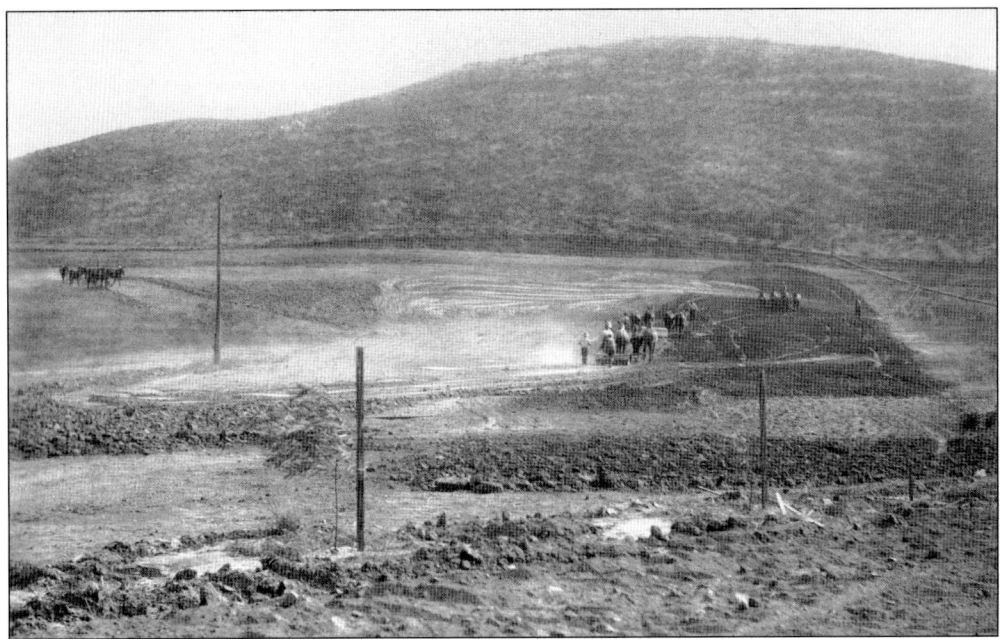

NORTH VIEW LAKE EXCAVATION, SEPTEMBER 3, 1927. To the rear is the hill upon which the hotel and bathhouse will sit, and in the foreground is what will soon become Lake Norconian. The planned lake will cover approximately 60 acres with two dams constructed with granite construction debris to hold back the water. The lake at its deepest will be 8 feet and take one month to fill.

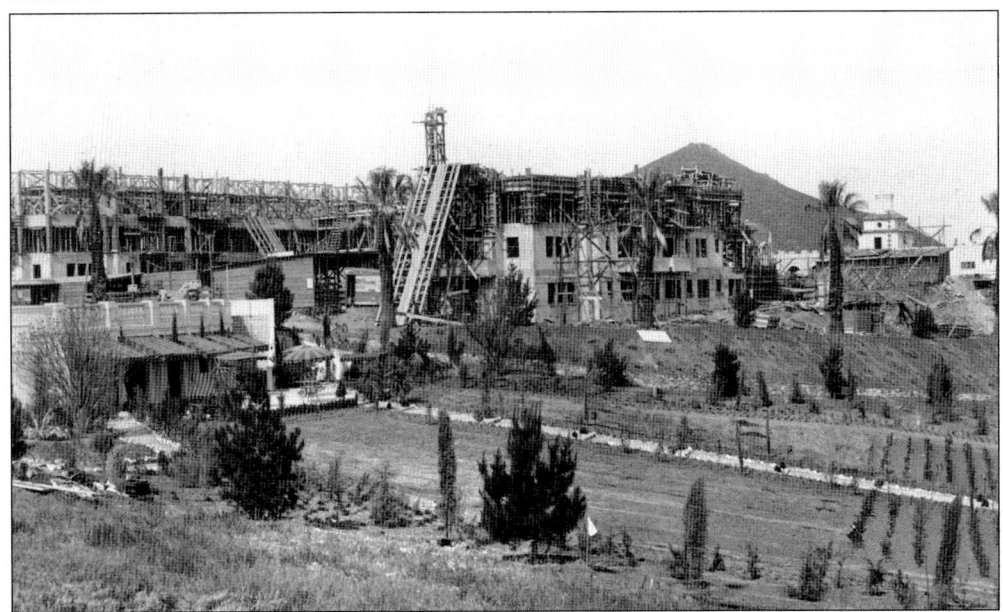

TEA ROOM, APRIL 12, 1928. The snow-white, Mediterranean-style building (lower left) was finished almost a year before the Norconian grand opening and was booked solid for months in advance. Rex Clark was delighted to share every aspect of his "master project," and the patio of the tea room overlooking the lake was the perfect vantage point. Directly behind, the hotel has been framed and blocks are being set.

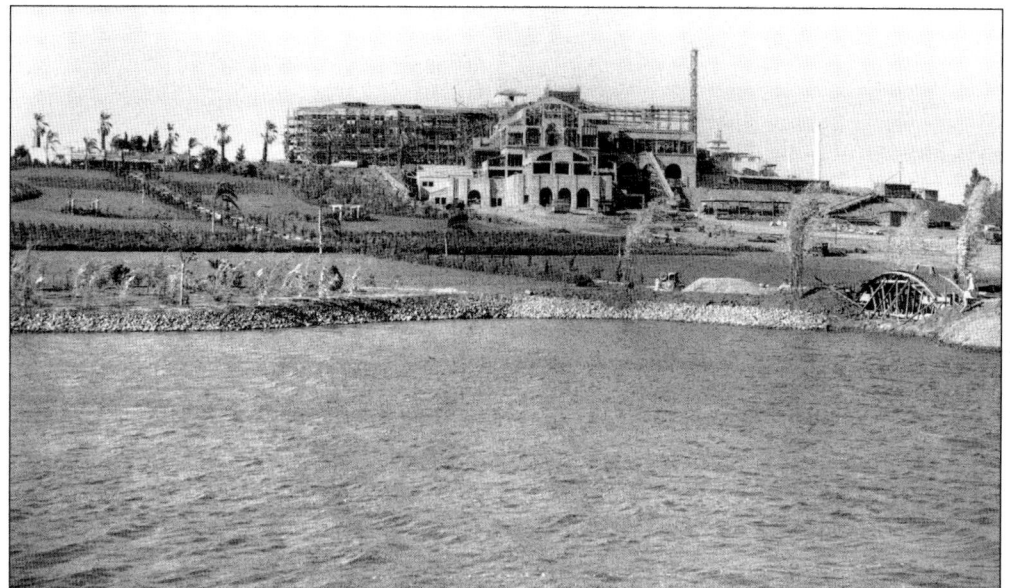

NORTH VIEW, OCTOBER 15, 1928. The lake is now filled, landscaping is in place, and the inn and bathhouse jut skyward. This amazing spectacle had the desired effect and attracted hundreds of visitors, inspired multiple editorial comments, and made news across the nation. The *Daily Independent* wrote, "That man Rex Clark is going to put Norco on the map with the grandest project you have ever seen."

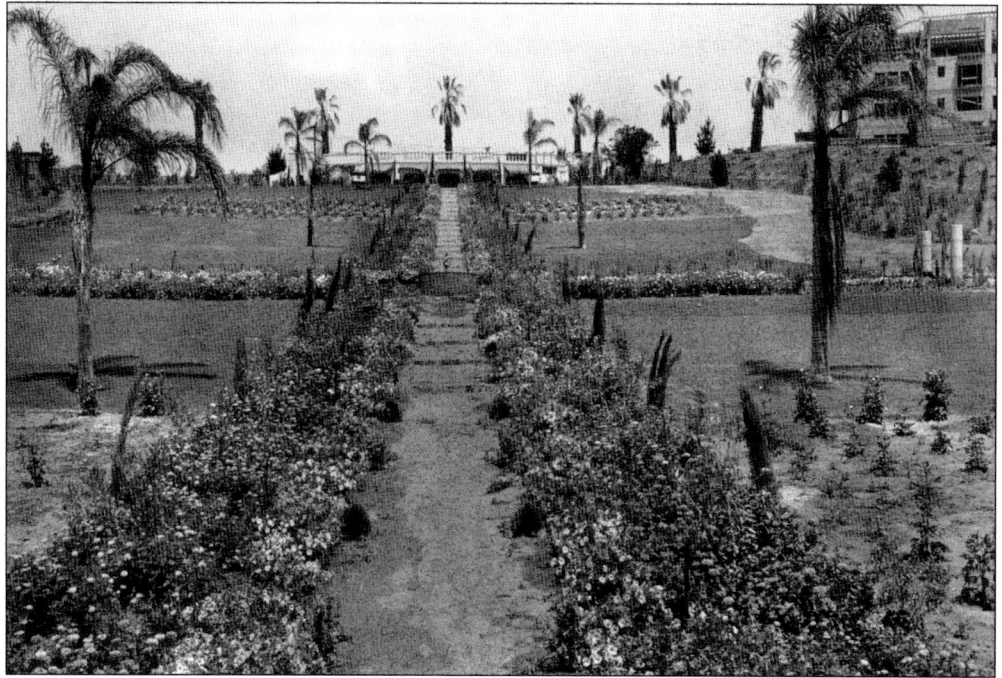

TEA ROOM NORTH VIEW, 1928. A 900-foot terraced walkway leads from the lake to this cozy cafe. The path is of gray, finely processed gravel, lined with granite rocks paralleled by rows of hibiscus, oleanders, and cypress. Other walkways lead away through rose gardens, bowers of jasmine, and viewing pavilions. A fountain of red tile and granite provides a rest stop as one hikes the hill.

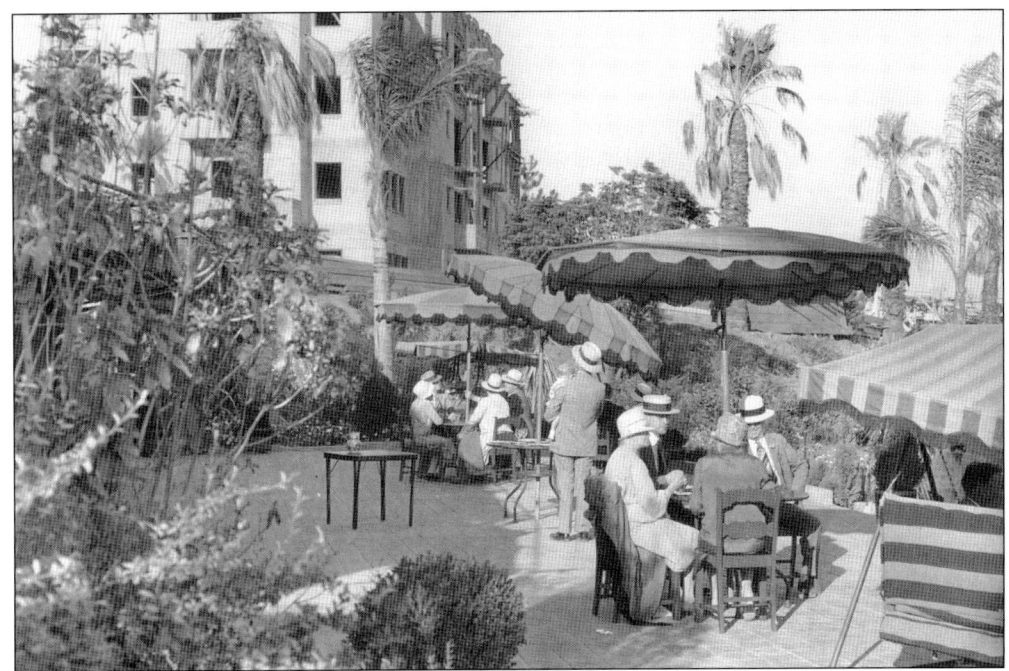

Tea Room Terrace, 1928. Larger than the interior, the red-tiled patio is adorned with round tables and, according to the *Daily Independent*, sheltered by "colorful orange and green umbrellas, palms, ferns and other exotic shrubbery." Tea was served using silver tea sets manufactured by Gorham specifically for the Norconian that bore the resort's crest. Looming above is the windowless, unfinished inn.

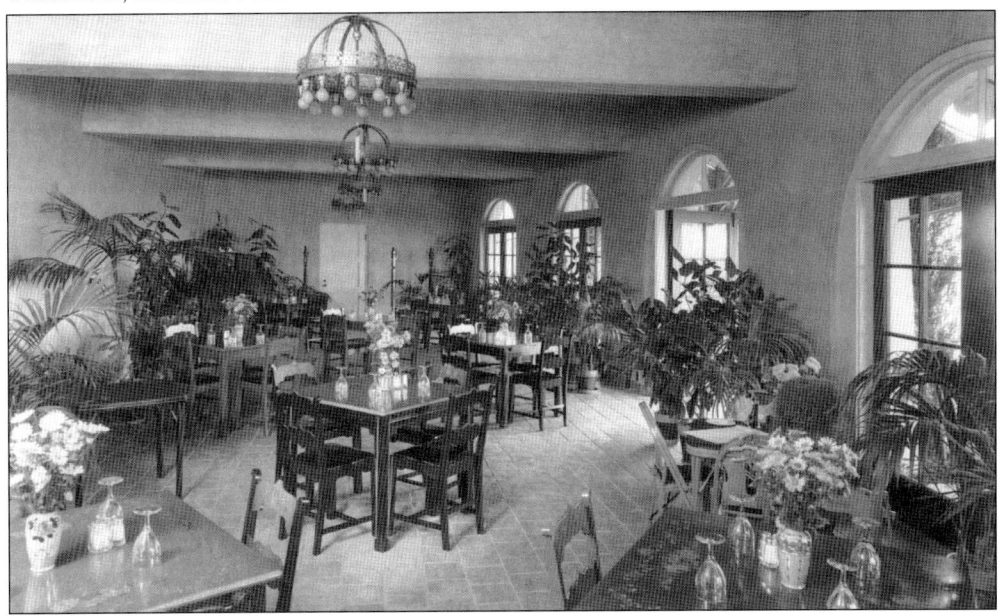

Interior Tea Room, 1928. The walls were painted apple green, with copper chandeliers and decorated with palms of different varieties. A great deal of publicity was made over the use of the electrical appliances. New to Norco, the Edison Company itself installed the kitchen equipment complete with range, hot plates, toasters, waffle irons, refrigerator, and soda fountain.

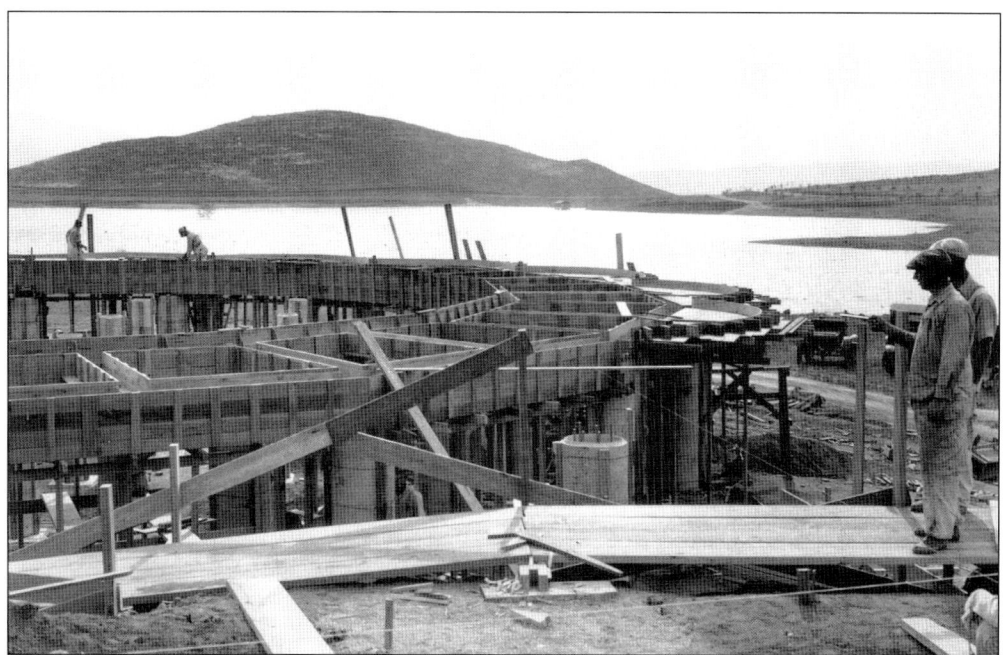

PAVILION CONSTRUCTION, 1928. News accounts tell of the rush to complete the structure called both the Pavilion and Casino for the May 22, 1928, opening hosting the Riverside County Chamber of Commerce. The conference successfully took place but in a slightly unfinished building. The Norco Grill catered, serving one of their "chicken dinners for which Norco is famous."

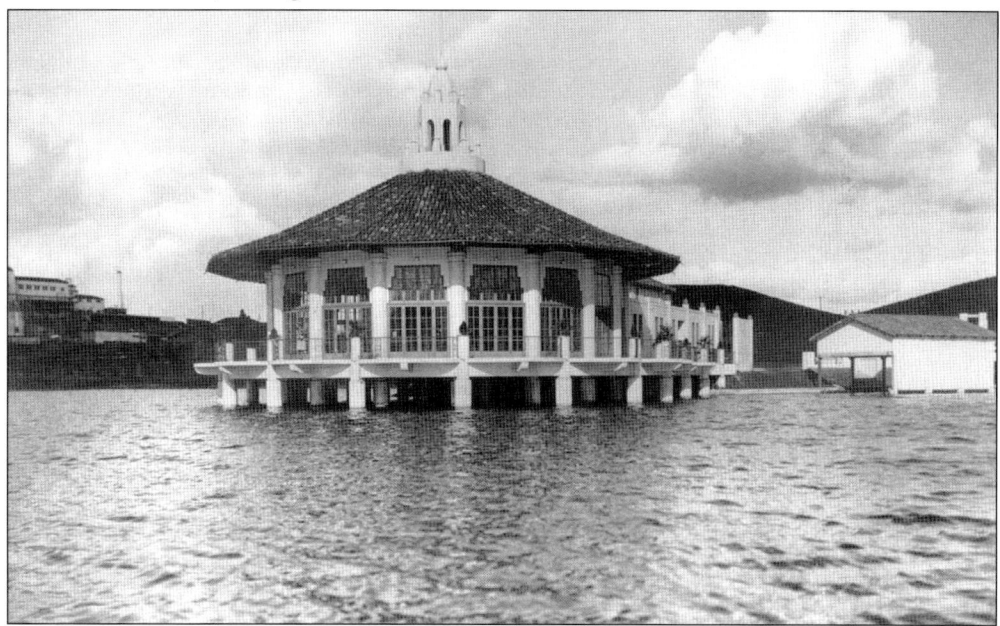

PAVILION EAST VIEW, 1929. Jutting 100 feet into the lake, 60 feet across, and circular in shape, the Pavilion was proclaimed "magnificent." Large glass windows completely encircled the dance floor and could be opened to "take advantage of the lake breezes." Complete with a cafe and soda fountain, the pavilion was a central location where guests could relax after golf, tennis, or horseback riding. Atop the dome sits a revolving beacon.

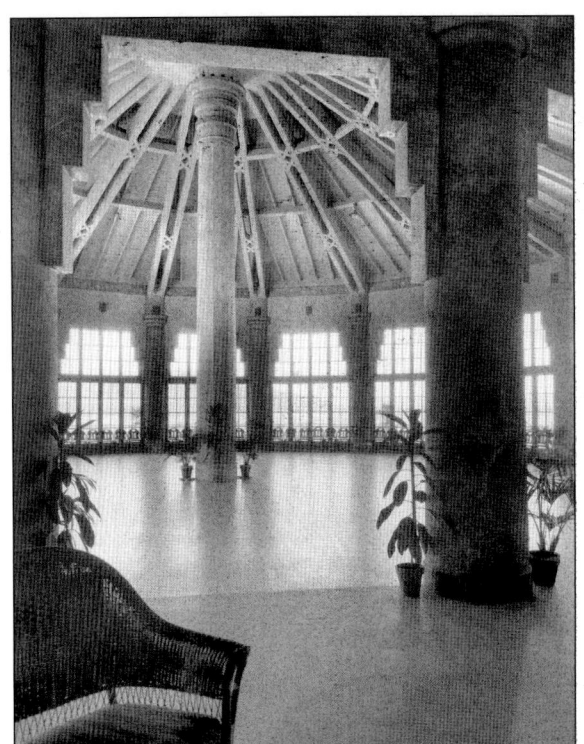

PAVILION INTERIOR, 1929. The maple dance floor hosted many a senior prom. The wicker chairs were handmade, and the 45-foot-high ceiling to this day is stunning. In the film *Top Speed*, a dance sequence appeared to take place in this very room. However, in the movie, there is no center support beam; clearly an almost exact duplicate had been created on a Hollywood soundstage.

PAVILION VIEW FROM TEA ROOM, 1929. The pathway to the boathouse and the Pavilion are finished. As for its use as a casino, George Milner, a longtime employee of both Clark and later the navy, insists he personally witnessed slot machines being tossed from the Pavilion veranda into the lake in 1949. Subsequent dives into the shallow lake to find gambling paraphernalia came up empty.

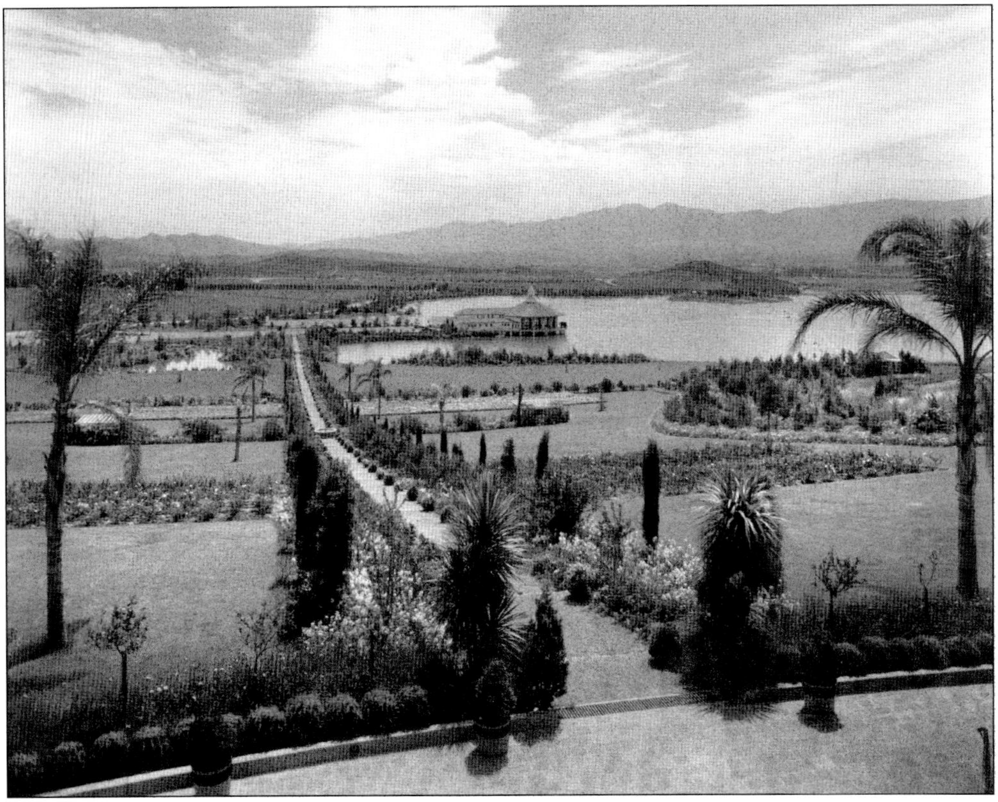

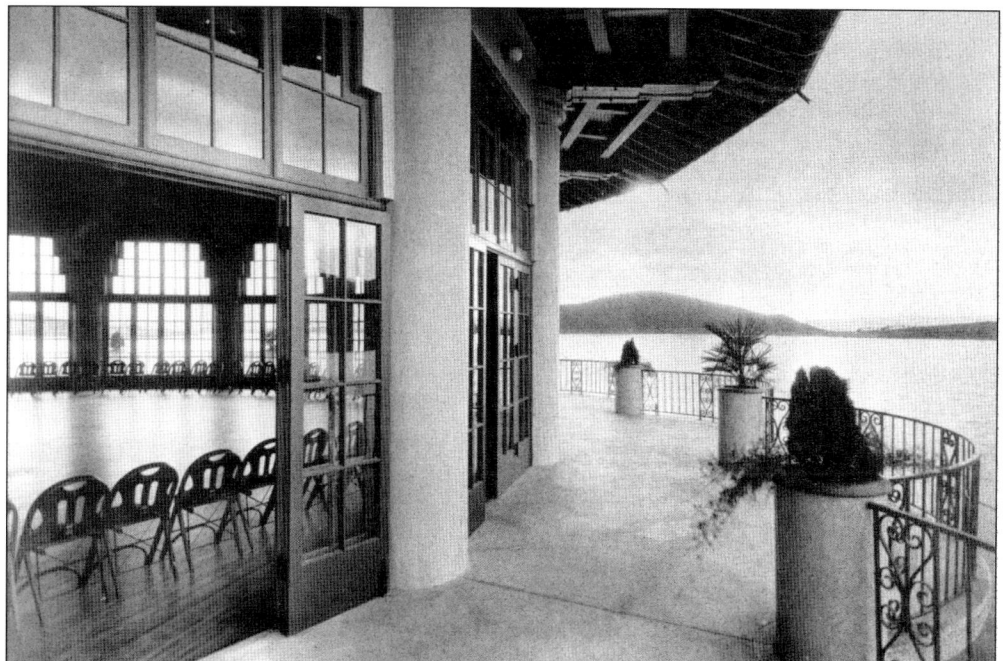

PAVILION PROMENADE DECK, 1929. Two old-timers insist that bootleg liquor was only allowed at the Pavilion during Prohibition so evidence could be tossed the into the lake should the sheriff "pull a raid." However, Ellen Revelle (Rex Clark's daughter) and Mike Nugent, a former caddy at the resort, adamantly insist no alcohol was allowed prior to the lifting of the federal ban in 1933.

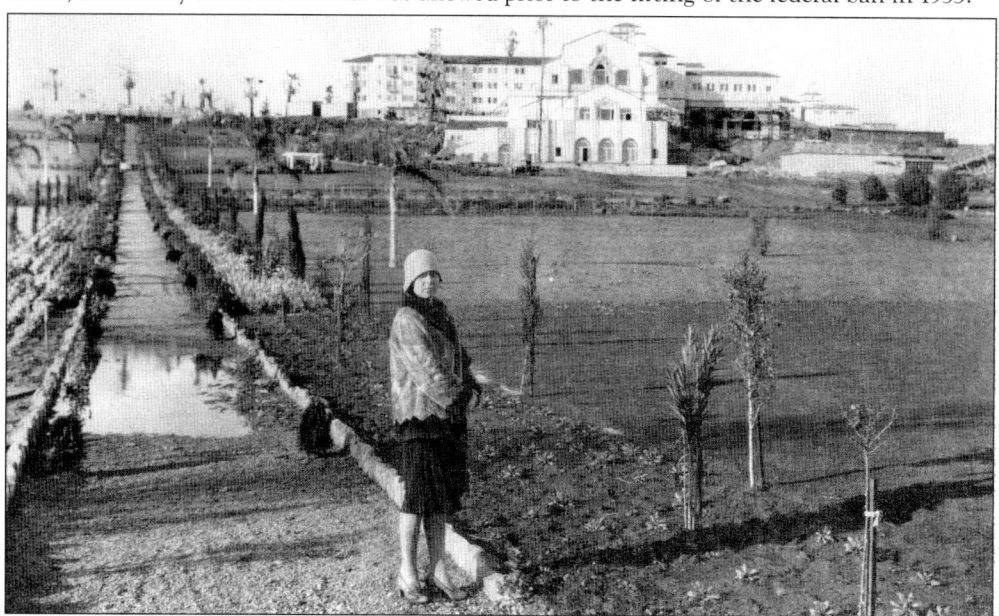

CHAMBER OF COMMERCE COUNTY MEETING, 1928. The Pavilion opened May 22, hosting what was proclaimed the best Riverside County Chamber meeting ever. Rex Clark was the guest speaker and waxed poetic about Norco, stating the community's slogan "Norco does it!" was well earned and that the residents were "hand-picked." Clark went on to say his hotel would be open to "only the most desirable people" with proper recommendations.

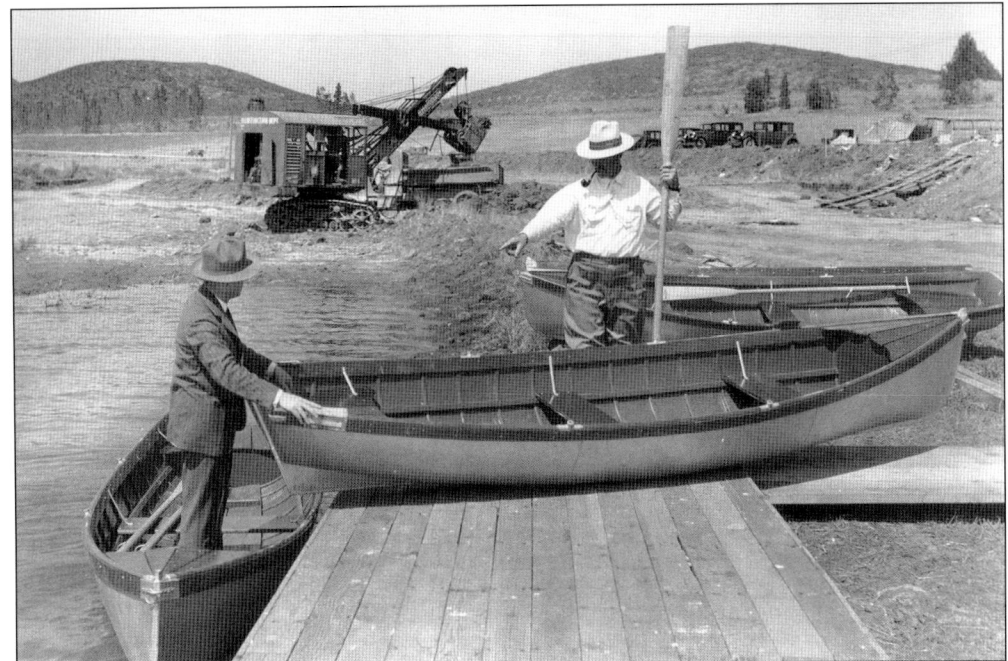

BOATHOUSE DOCK VIEW WEST, 1928. As the pad for the future Pavilion is being leveled in the background, just enough water has been let into the lake to test 25 brand-new rowboats. The future boathouse is to be 150 feet in length and will have two launch moorings and two docks large enough to accommodate 30 canoes and 30 rowboats.

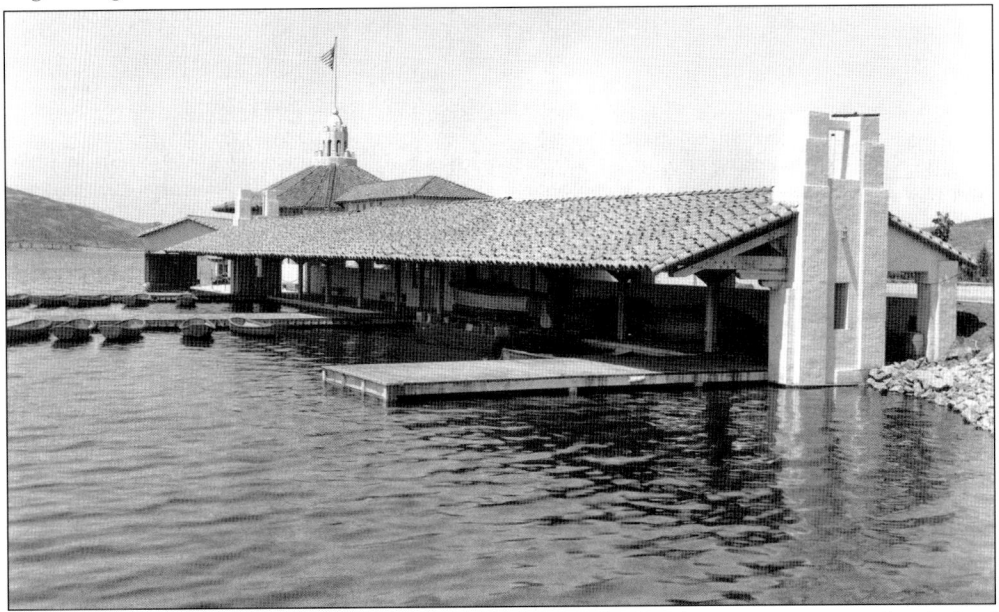

BOATHOUSE VIEW WEST, 1929. Opened in July 1928, the boathouse was yet another hub of activity at the resort. Canoes, rowboats, and motorboats all gave the average guest yet another avenue of recreation. For others, the launch ramps and docks would service speedboat races, endurance swim competitions, a movie location, and the starting point for Duke Kahanamoku to give surfing demonstrations on the lake.

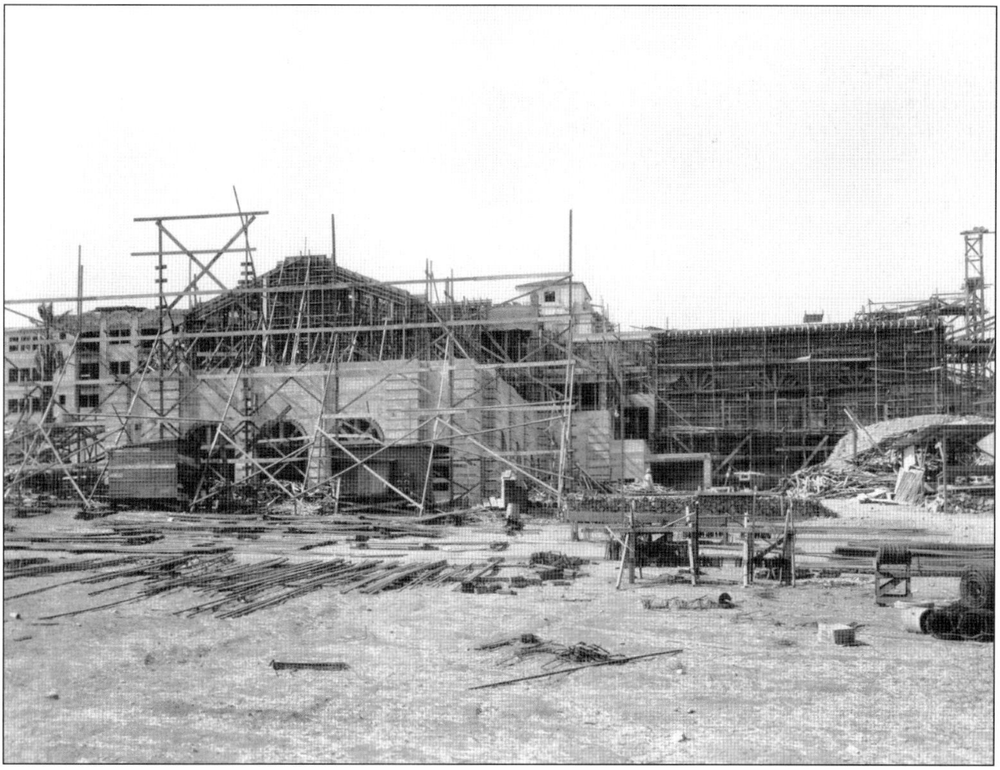

NORTH VIEW NORCONIAN, 1928. The *Daily Independent* reported that this "skeleton" sits on solid rock-and-concrete foundations with piers running throughout the structure, tied together with reinforced concrete beams on which the "massive tiled roof will rest." This is "for general safety and extra precautions against earthquake damage." The floors will be "of solid concrete pan construction," and the resort will be "magnificent and last forever."

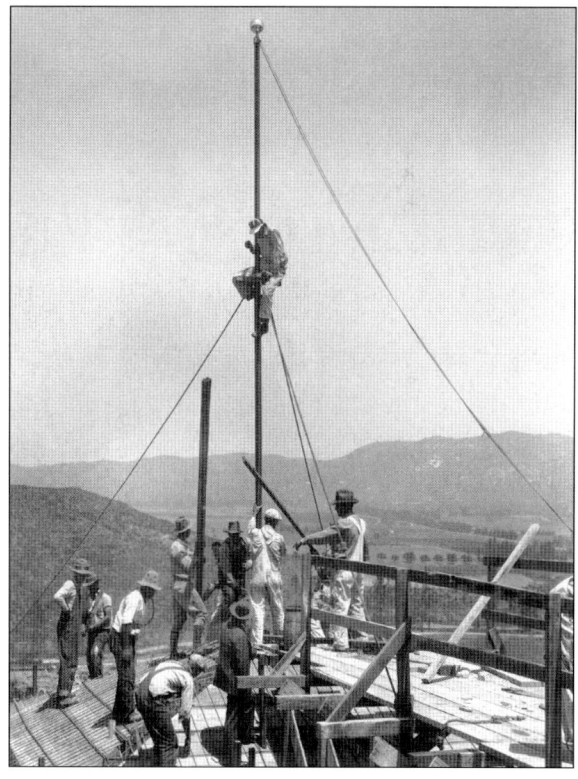

FLAGPOLE, 1928. The *Daily Independent* carried the news that Rex Clark considered the first raising of "the flag of the United States over the Norconian a great day." Norco, using the yardstick of county building permits, was declared the fastest growing community in the "entire Southland." In 1928, Norco building costs totaled $1,239,700, second only to the city of Riverside.

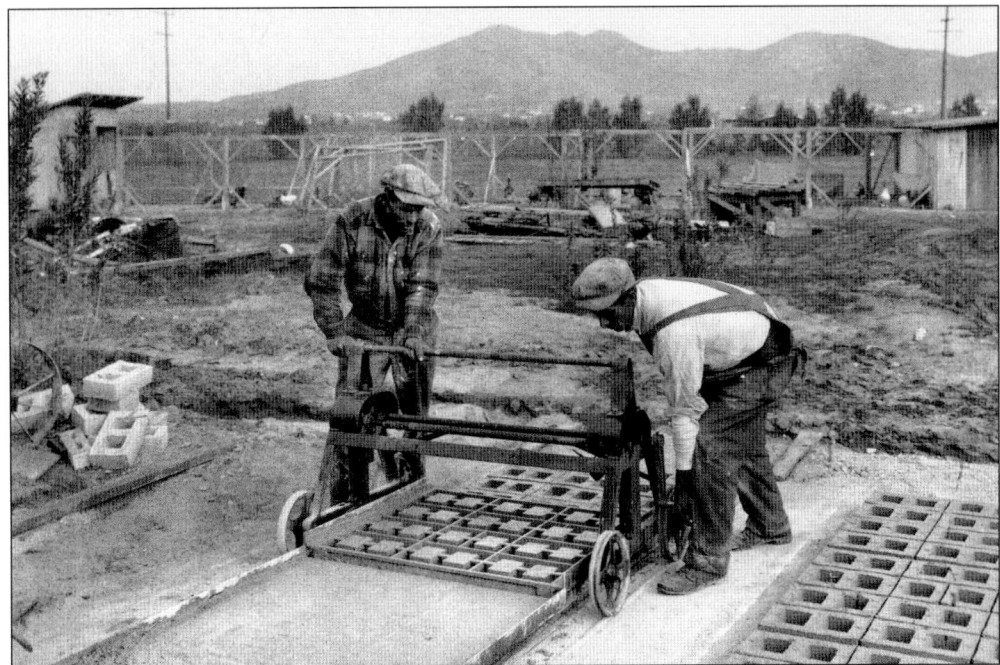

BLOCK MANUFACTURING, 1927. Rex Clark utilized two forms of masonry material, the standard concrete block and a "stone tile." Both were manufactured in Norco and both were used extensively in the construction of the Norconian and Norco in general. The stone tile was not the common block but was said to be stronger, easier to lay, and far more flexible to suit a wider variety of construction needs.

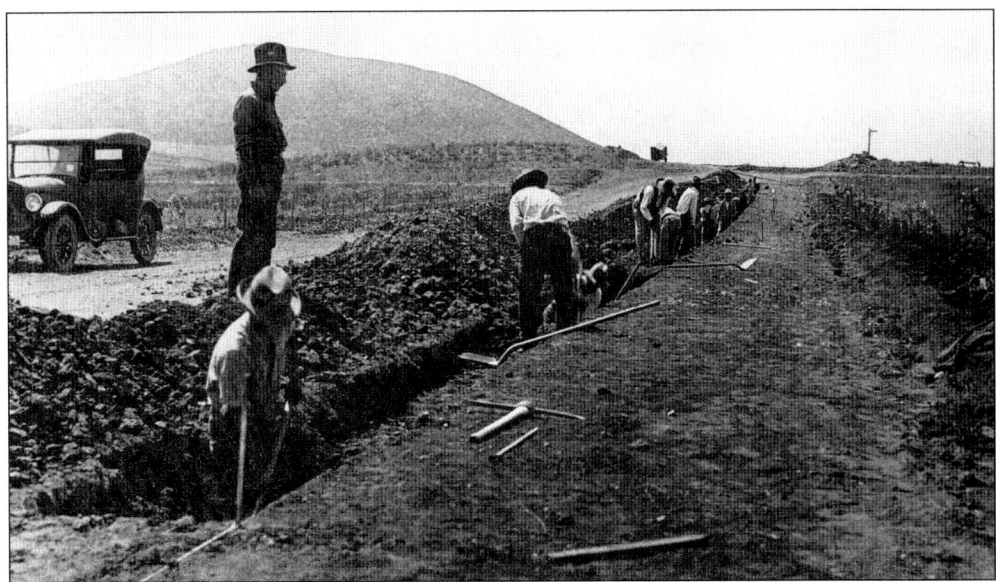

DIGGING HOT WATER PIPELINE, 1927. The pipeline supplying the precious hot mineral water to the bathhouse was 1.5 miles long. The pipe itself was 12 inches in diameter and, because of the "corrosive nature of the water," required the conduit to be of wood construction. After several disasters, specialists in the difficult art of laying watertight wood pipe were brought in to complete the job. (Peter Clark.)

PAYDAY, 1928. Rex Clark paid his employees personally and in cash. Accompanied by armed guards, Clark would pick up bags of money from a local bank and dramatically motor his way to the Norco Store. During the construction of the Norconian, payroll on many occasions exceeded $25,000 per week: approximately $52 a man. In Riverside County, only the City of Riverside exceeded the Clark payday. (Corona Public Library.)

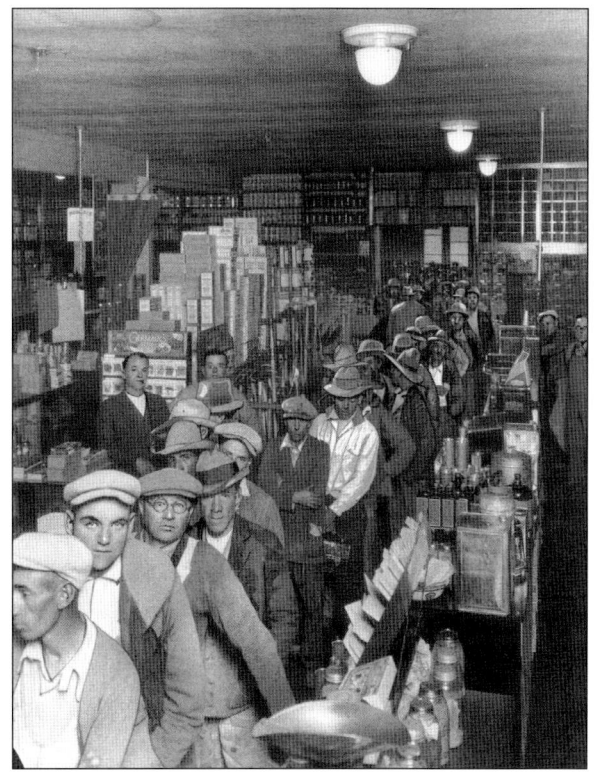

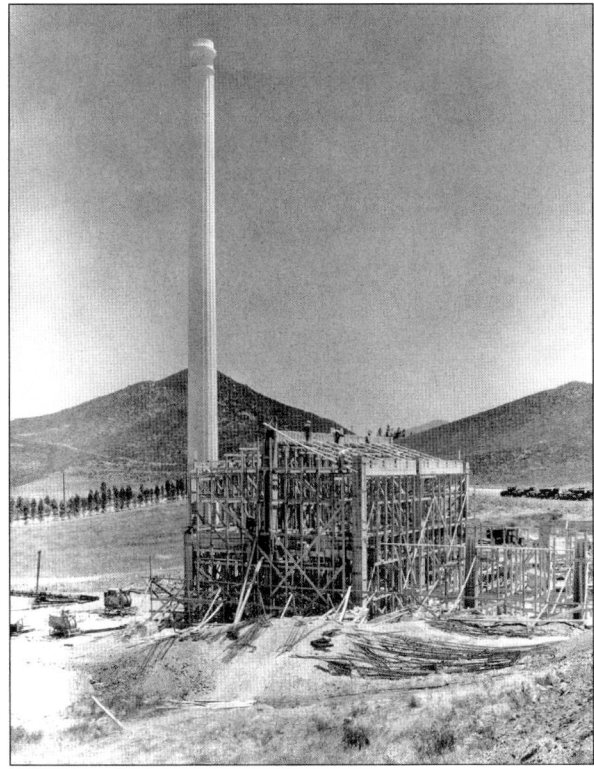

POWER PLANT CONSTRUCTION, 1928. Approximately $155,000 was spent to make this the most cutting-edge power facility on the West Coast. It was designed to supply light, water, and power to the entire resort. Inside, the floors were done in red tile and, as reported by the *Daily Independent*, "fittings such as flywheels, handrails and the like will be chromium plated for a finish more durable and attractive than nickel."

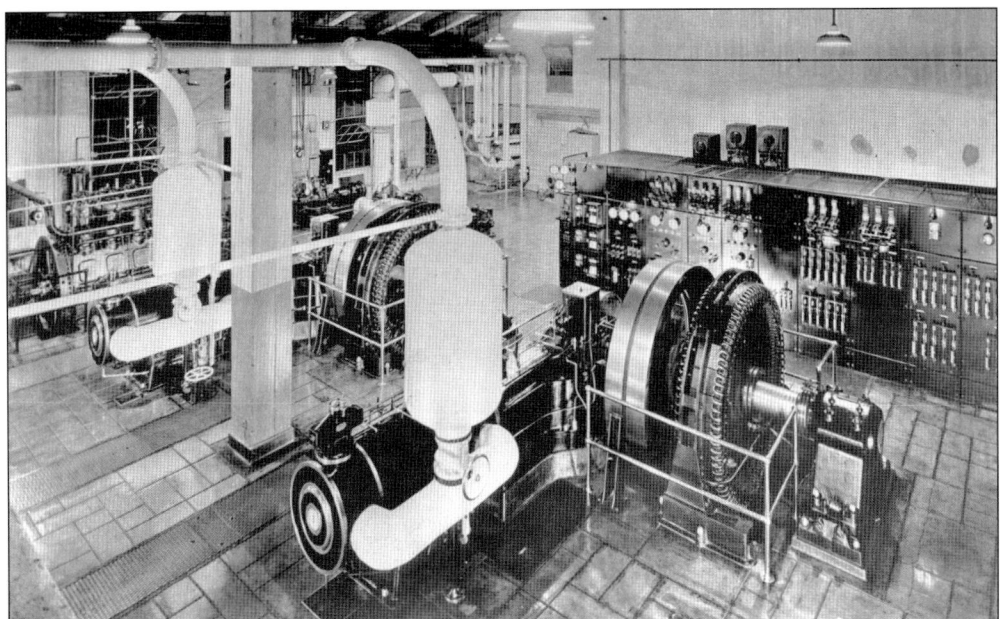

POWER PLANT INTERIOR, 1928. Designed specifically for the Norconian Resort by Benedict Electrical Company, the switchboard, recording devices, gauges, electrical components, and other electronics were state of the art and very likely comprised one of the finest and most modern electrical systems in the United States. Later a primary reason for the navy's interest in purchasing the resort was the excellent power system and the huge capacity it offered.

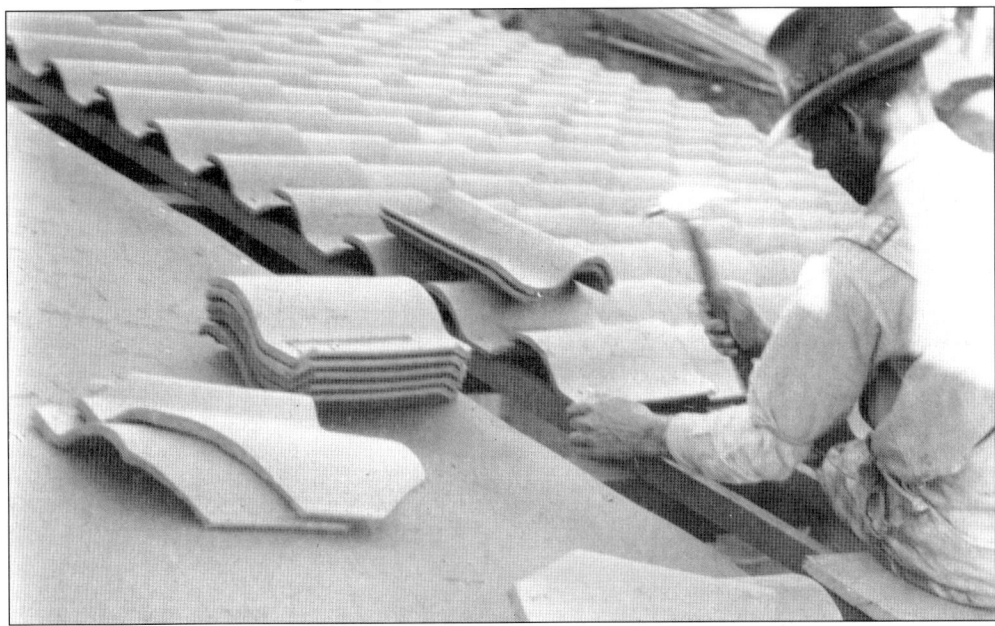

TILE ROOF, 1928. Corona, California's, True-Tile Corporation, managed by John Warfield and employing 15 men, produced 3,000 roof tiles per day with their biggest client being the Norconian Resort. Base clay from the Prado district and red clays from the Temescal Canyon were blended together in various combinations to produce different shades of roofing. The tiles were strong enough on the curved side to hold four men. (Peter Clark.)

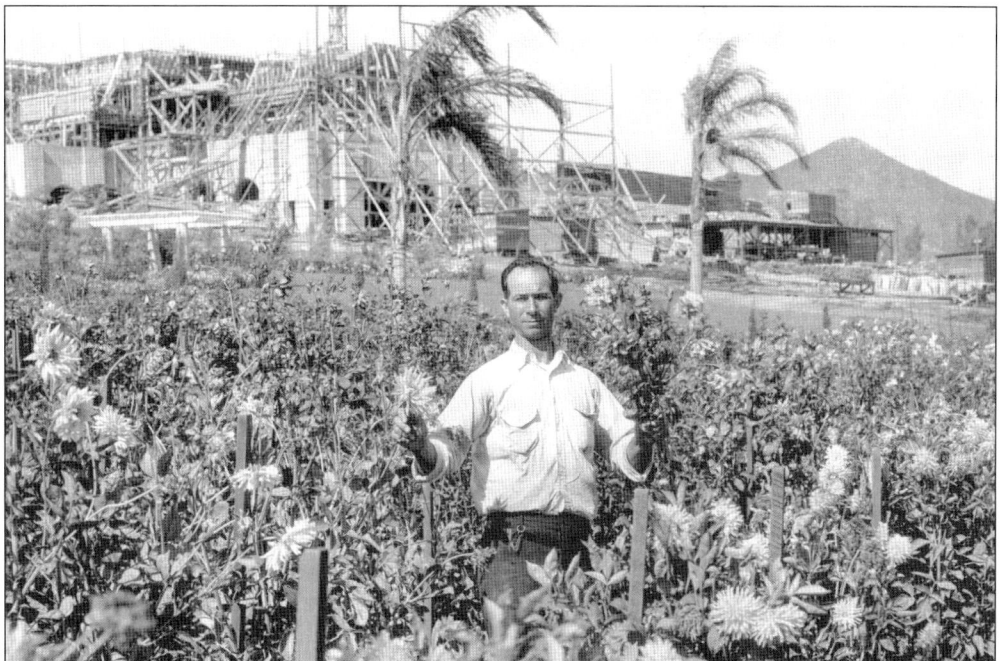

NORCO NURSERY, 1928. The Oak Knoll Nursery of Pasadena was purchased for $30,000 and moved in 26 sixteen-ton truckloads to Norco, instant new home to the largest nursery in Riverside County. Thousands of ornamental shrubs, trees, and plants were needed to landscape the gigantic resort. Pictured is John Strathus, the former owner, who not only sold his entire plant stock but his services as well for the next several years.

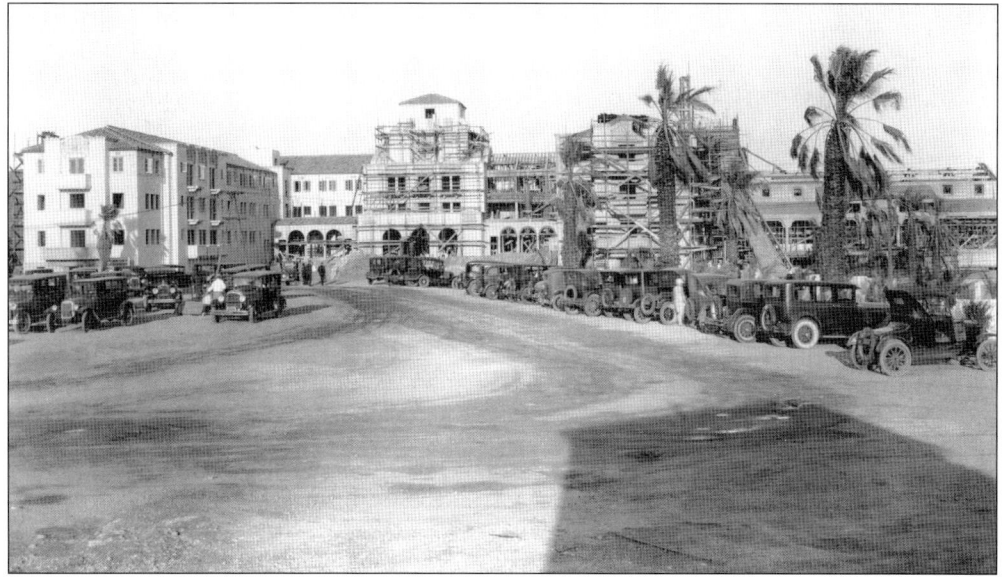

EAST VIEW NORCONIAN INN, 1928. News articles stating the number of guest rooms to be provided varied wildly over time from 97 to 250. What was not in doubt was Rex Clark's desire to create "a resort devoted to sports, health and rest," complete with tennis, medicinal baths, bass fishing, horseback riding, walking trails, championship golf, canoeing, and what would soon become the very famous outdoor pools.

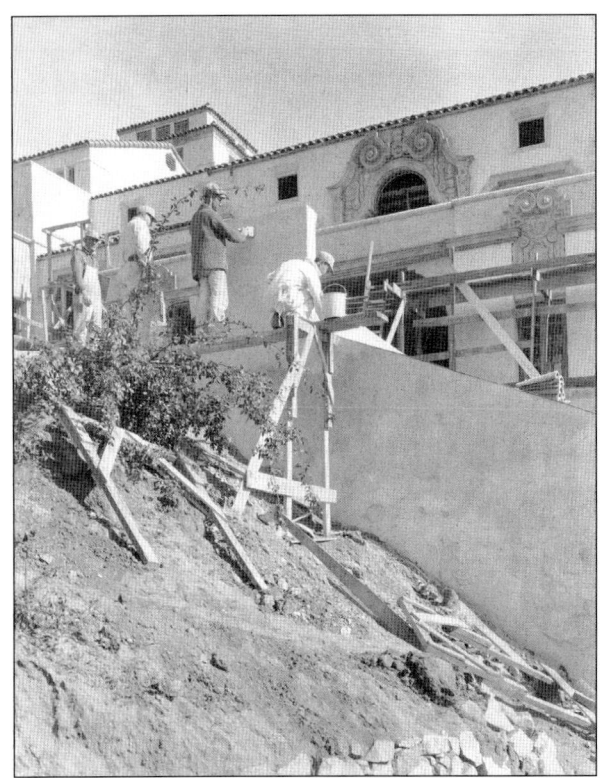

PAINTING, 1928. In this photograph, painters rush to apply a final coat in time for the grand opening. Clark's thoughts on his employees were: "We want a community of go-getters and in our construction work, we use all available Norco men and women. . . . But, I insist our workmen give us service. I despise a workman whom you have to watch, so once in a while our home people lose out."

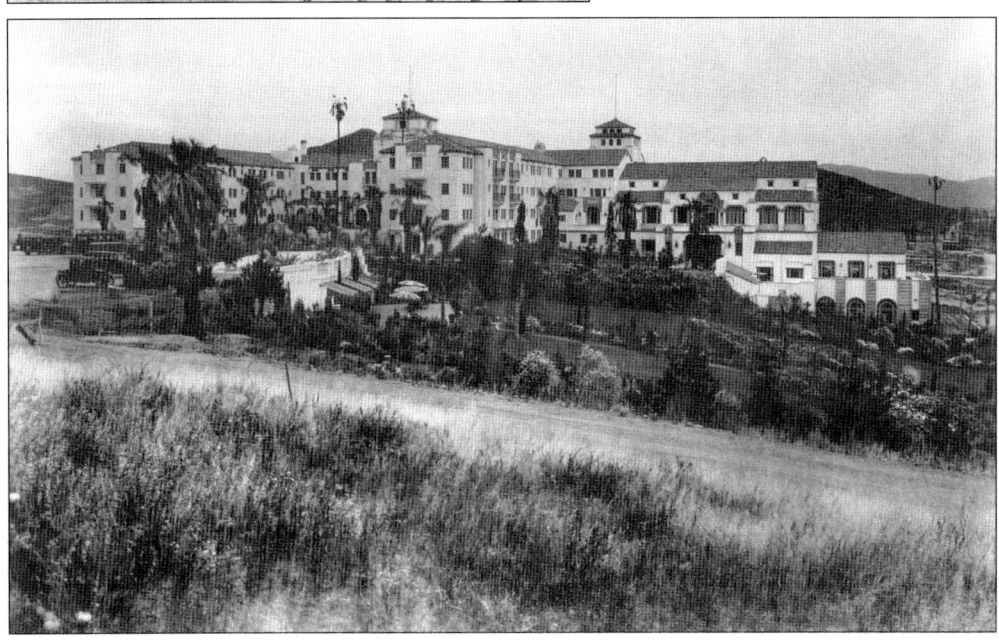

EAST VIEW NORCONIAN INN, C. 1929. The inn and bathhouse are finished, the landscaping is in place, the pools are filled, and the Norconian is ready for business. One can only imagine the impact this sight had on travelers as they approached from afar. The *Daily Independent* stated, "There never has been, nor will there ever be, a more breathtaking sight." (University of Southern California.)

Three
A GOLFER'S PARADISE

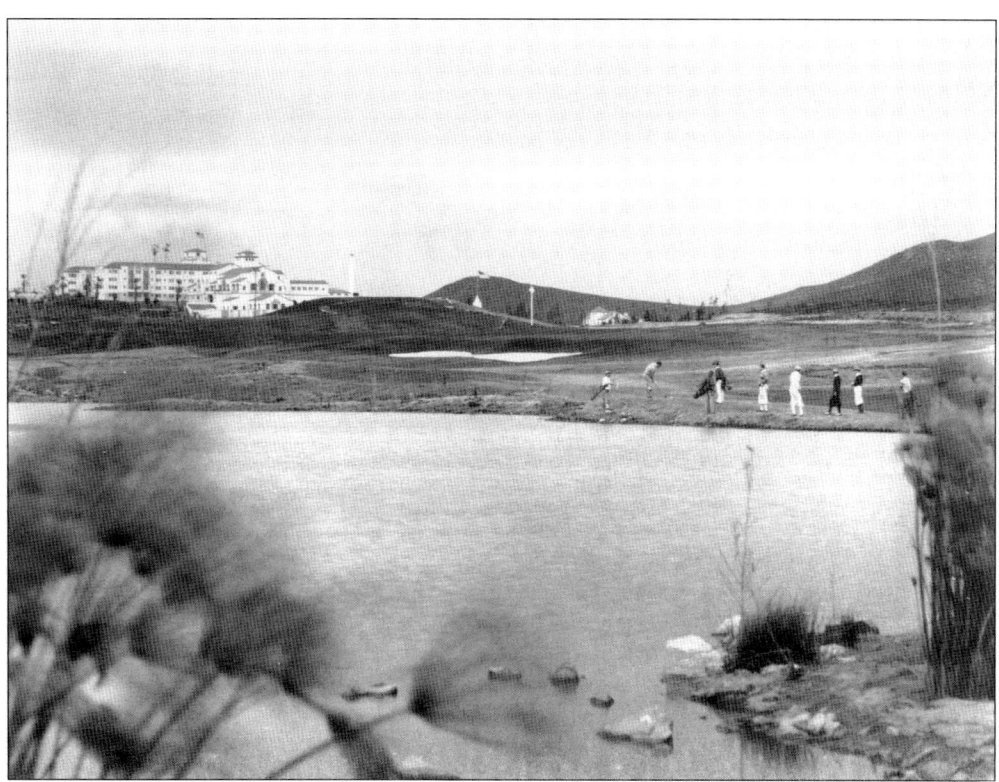

THE 18TH FAIRWAY, 1928. The golf course debuted just days before the grand opening of the resort. A Norconian sales brochure proclaimed that the 18-hole, all-grass golf course features wide fairways, "scientifically placed sand traps, . . . intricate water hazards, . . . an automobile driveway surrounding the course to enable spectators to follow the action, no parallel fairways and no shots into the setting sun. . . . The fastidious golfer will find the answer to his prayer."

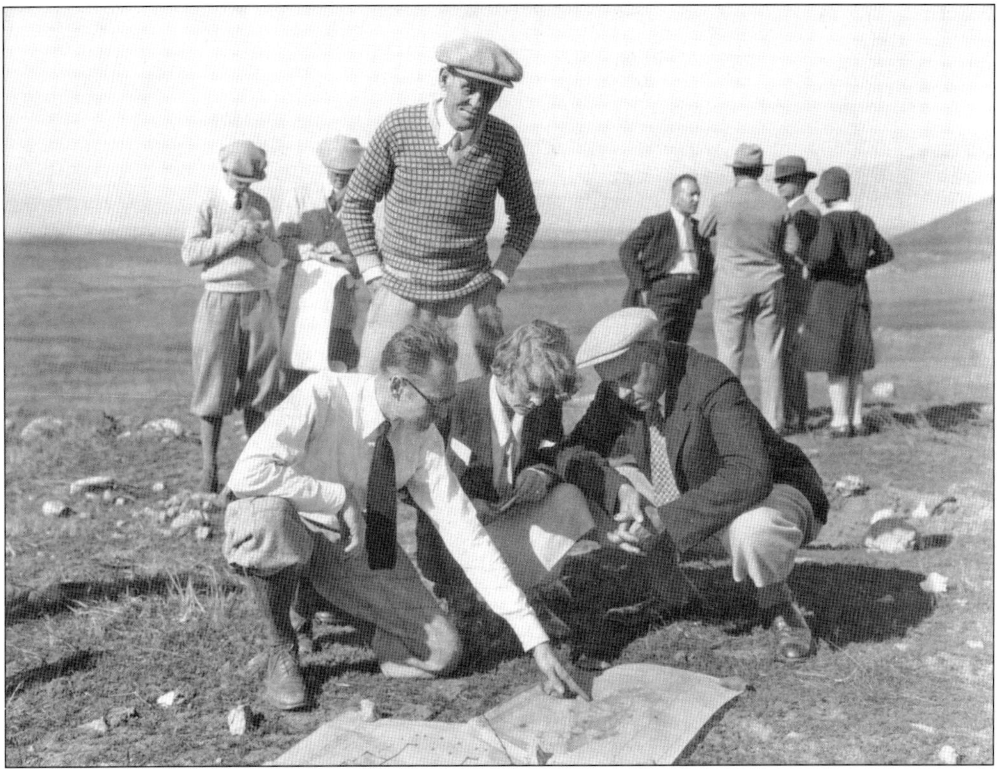

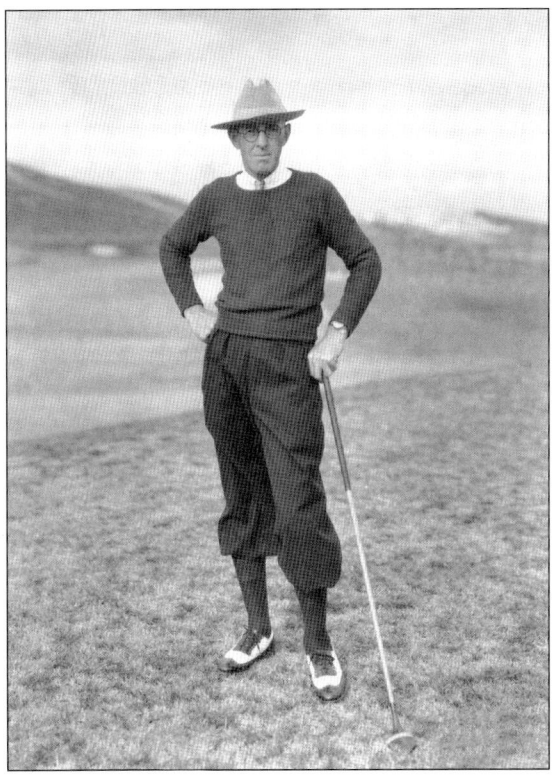

NORCONIAN GOLF COURSE, 1927. John Duncan Dunn (pointing) designed and built the Norconian links. Over his shoulder is golfer Thomas Paine; at lower right is Scott Chisholm, a golf personality who would later write that the Norconian course was the best on the West Coast. At upper right, semi-profiled with hat, is Rex Clark, and the woman to his right has been identified as Jimmie Snyder, his mistress. (Corona Public Library.)

JOHN DUNCAN DUNN, 1928. Descended from a distinguished line of Scottish golfers, Dunn was described as "America's foremost authority of golf courses." A leading teacher, writer, and designer of golf courses for over 50 years, Dunn laid out Catalina, Ekwanok, and Parkridge (now Cresta Verde) in Corona. Dunn's designs were considered exceptional, and his colorful lectures on all aspects of golf were in great demand.

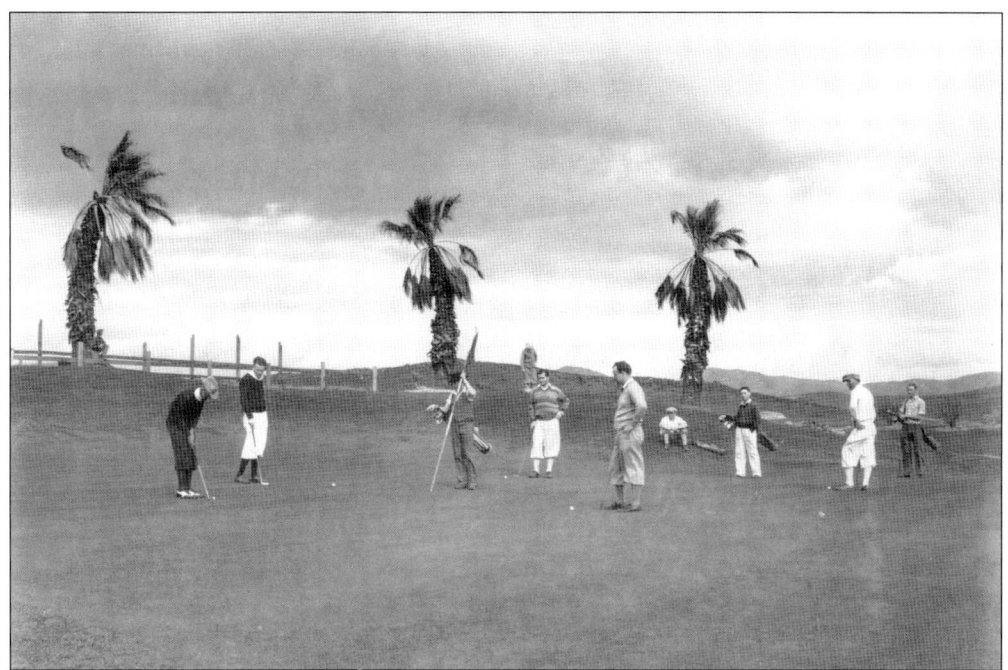

PUTTING ON THE 13TH GREEN, 1929. Charlie Paddock, "the world's fastest human," looks on as John Duncan Dunn sinks a put during what was likely the first round of golf at the Norconian. The gentleman at center has been identified as Jay Shoup, the Norconian's first resident pro. An advertisement declared the course to be a "golfer's paradise, a slice of heaven for the tired businessman."

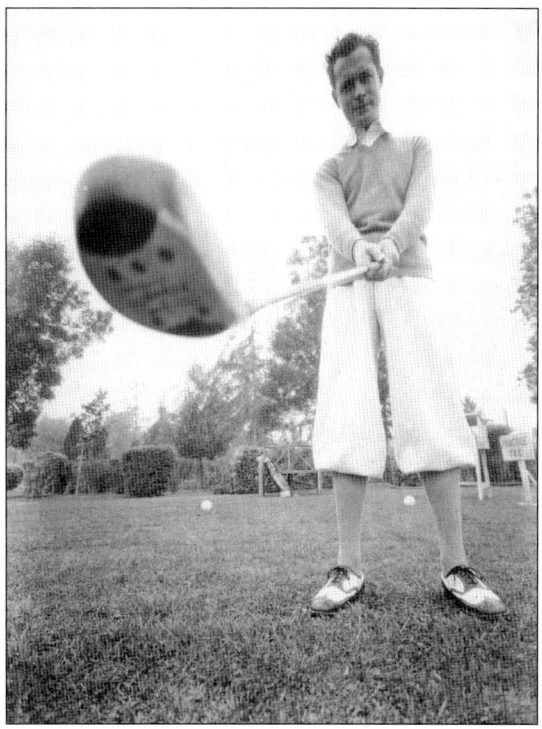

ON THE LINKS, C. 1930. Pictured is Robert Montgomery in a publicity photograph for a golf movie shot at the Norconian. This star actually played the Norconian links on several occasions, as did the best golfers and celebrities of the day. According to caddy Mike Nugent, "There was always somebody famous on that course." Buster Keaton and Bing Crosby were regulars, and on occasion one could even spot Babe Ruth.

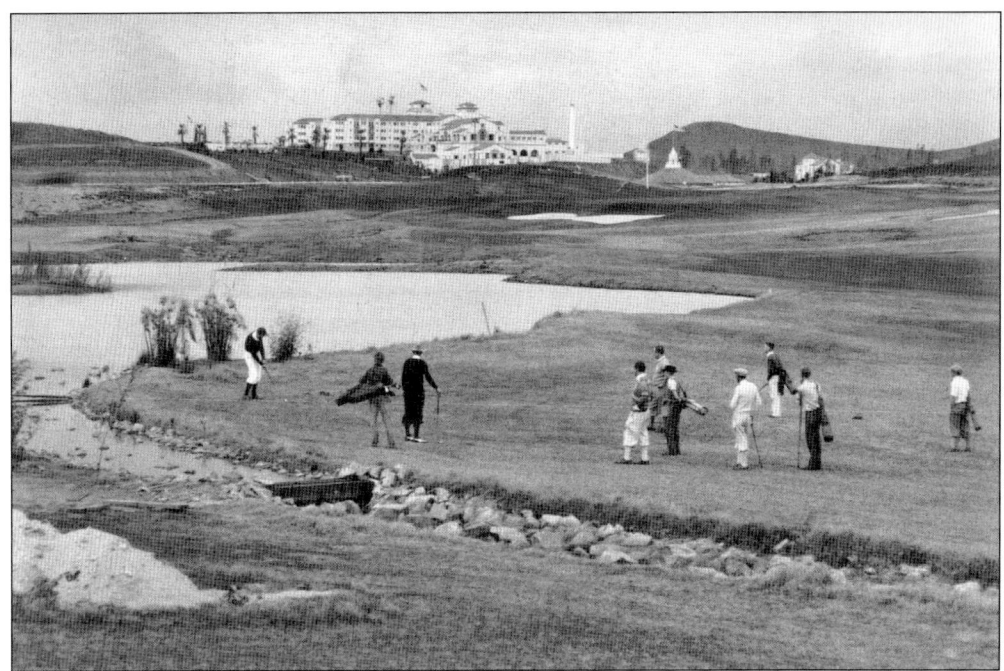

PADDOCK PUTTS ON THE 17TH GREEN, 1928. The *Daily Independent* claimed that Duncan Dunn was given unlimited funds, 15 miles of sprinkler line, numerous steam shovels, dump carts, graders, hundreds of tons of the finest top soil, the best grass seed, and as many as 80 workers to lay out the finest course in America—a sight to make a golfer's heart go "pitter-pat!" Note the hotel in the background.

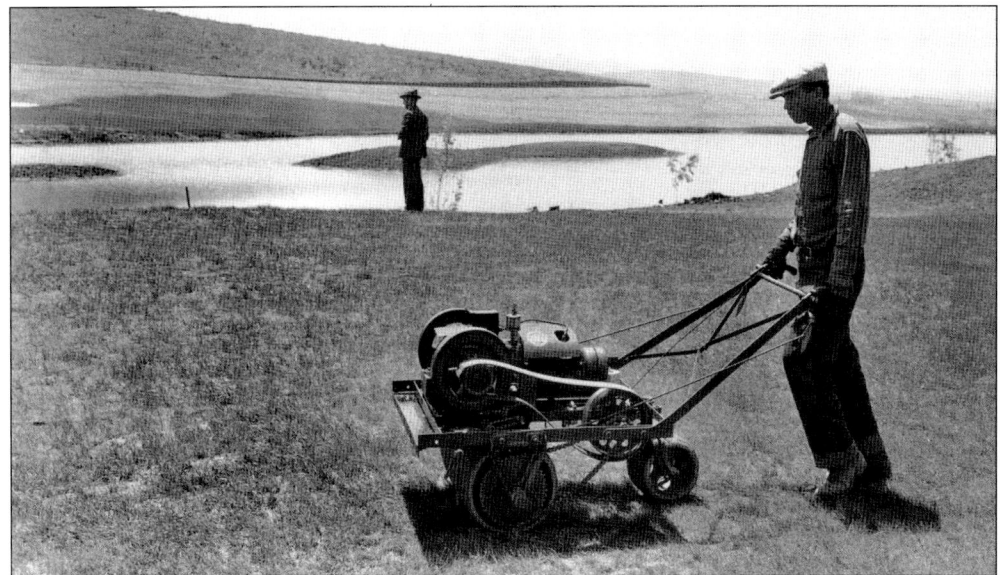

A LOT OF GRASS, 1928. Enormous numbers of men were required to cultivate and maintain the resort landscaping. The superintendent in charge was Epamuscemo Ramirez. Years later, his son Augustine ("Augie") Ramirez would become the superintendent of the Corona-Norco Unified School District, the first Hispanic American to reach such a post in Riverside County. In 2009, a school bearing Augie's name will actually be visible from the old resort.

SON OF A BARBER, C. 1935. Jess Hill may have been the finest athlete to come out of Corona, California. At the University of Southern California (USC), he held the national broad-jump record; as a running back, he led the Pacific Coast Conference in yards per carry and the Trojans into the Rose Bowl; and later he played baseball for the New York Yankees. He was also a regular on the Norconian links. (University of Southern California.)

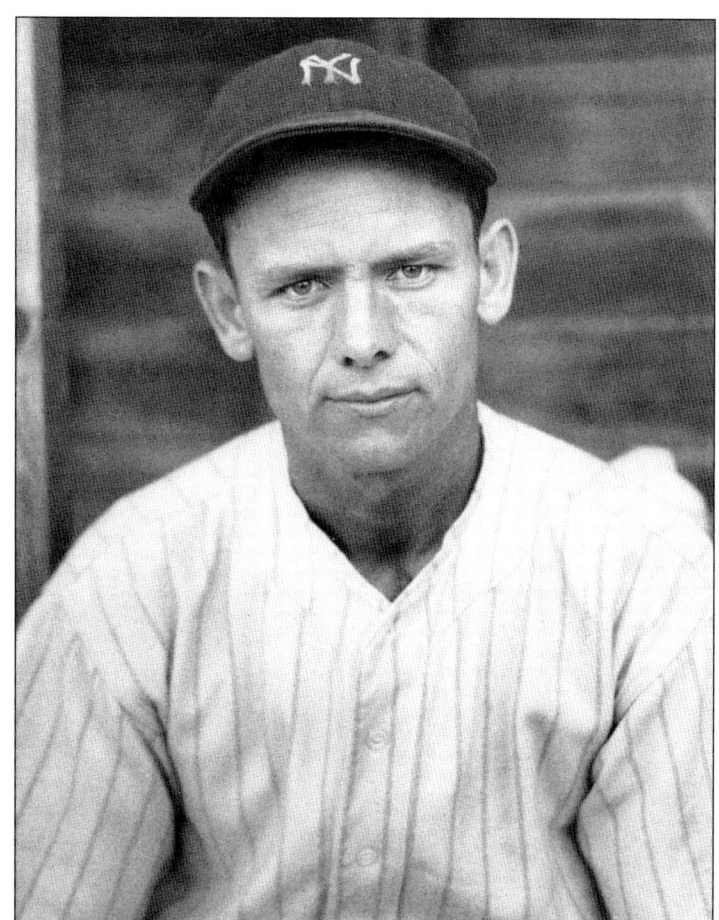

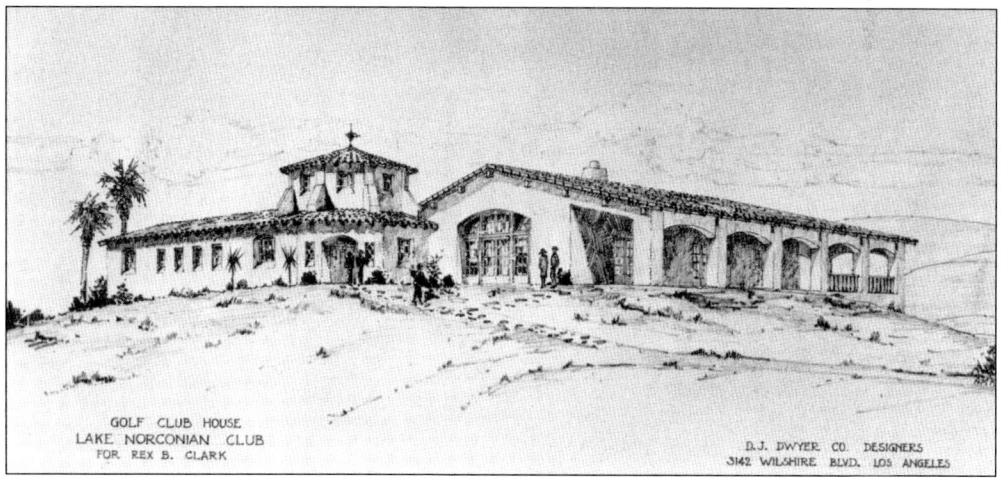

GOLF CLUBHOUSE RENDERING, 1928. Rex Clark envisioned a world-class clubhouse to go with his world-class golf course. The clubhouse would contain showers, dressing rooms, cafe, pro shop, and so on. Oddly, news accounts document at great length the building of this structure as well as small guest bungalows. However, while there is evidence that some cottages were built and a caddy shack, most assuredly the clubhouse was never even started.

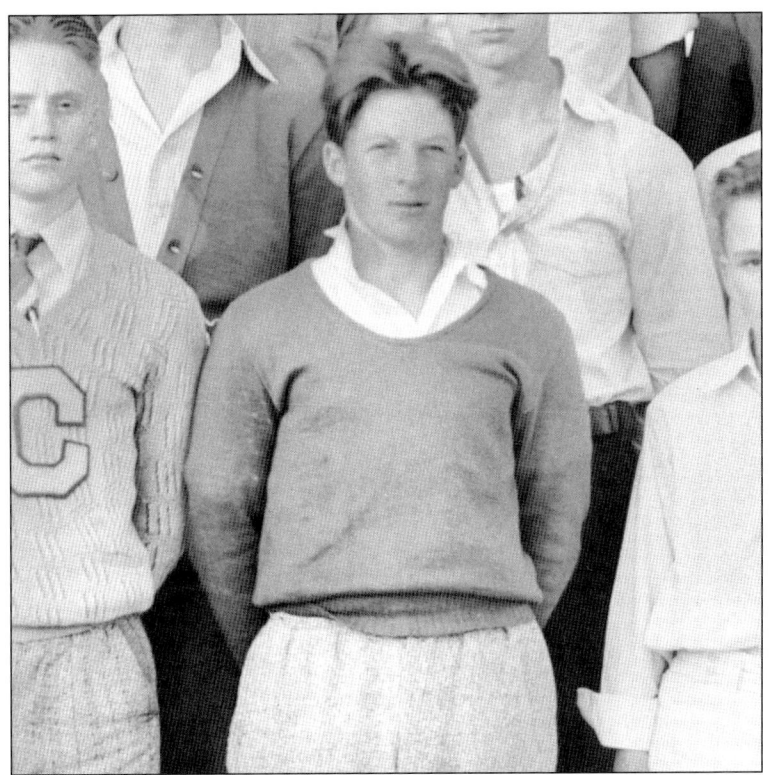

NORCONIAN HOLE-IN-ONE, C. 1928. High schooler Nevitt "Nevy" Rossiter (center) sank a 172-yard single drive into the seventh cup. Mike Nugent, fellow Norconian caddy, said, "If a hole-in-one was to be made, it would be the seventh given how that hole was laid out." Ira Landis, superintendent of Riverside Schools, made the other known ace in 1930. Nevy stands with his Corona High class of 1933. (Corona Public Library.)

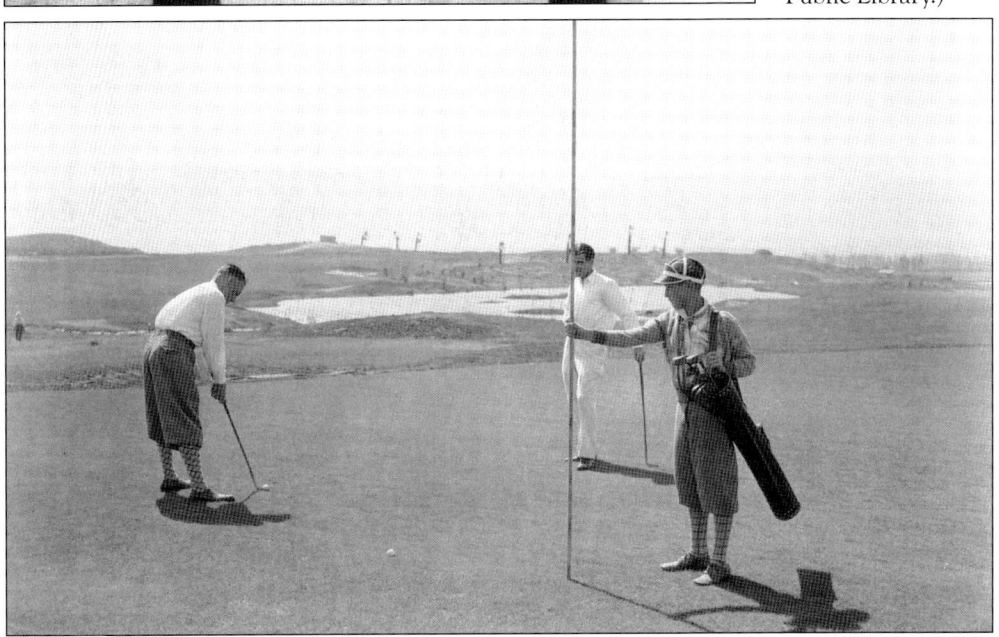

PUTTING, PROS, AND COURSE RECORD, C. 1929. The first club pro was Jay L. Shoup, who unfortunately passed away in 1929, followed by Harry Brooks, who according to Norconian caddy Mike Nugent was a wonderful golfer and teacher. Charlie Shung set the course record in 1929 with a score of 66. Olin Dutra held the putting record; 24 putts to 18 holes. (University of Southern California.)

Four

OLYMPIC GOLD IN NORCO

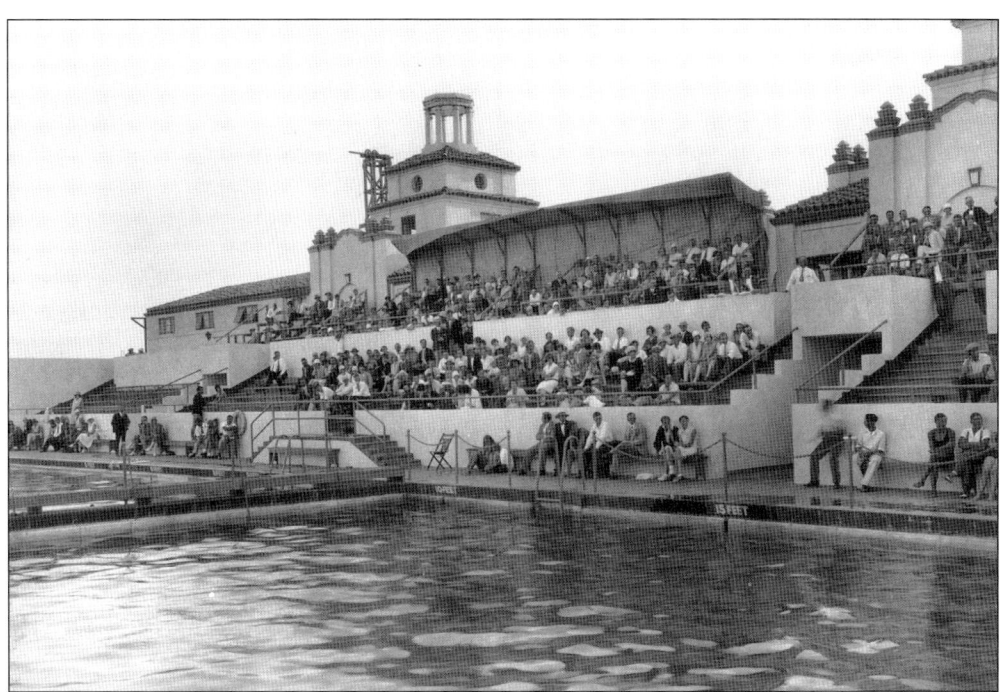

NORCONIAN POOL DEDICATION, MAY 20, 1928. Tiptoeing through construction debris, some 600–700 invited guests munched on a chicken buffet in the tea room, toured the almost completed golf course, listened to a "Los Angeles Orchestra," laughed as Rex Clark playfully pushed an unidentified inaugural swimmer into the pool, and witnessed something unusual in a poultry town like Norco: a world record.

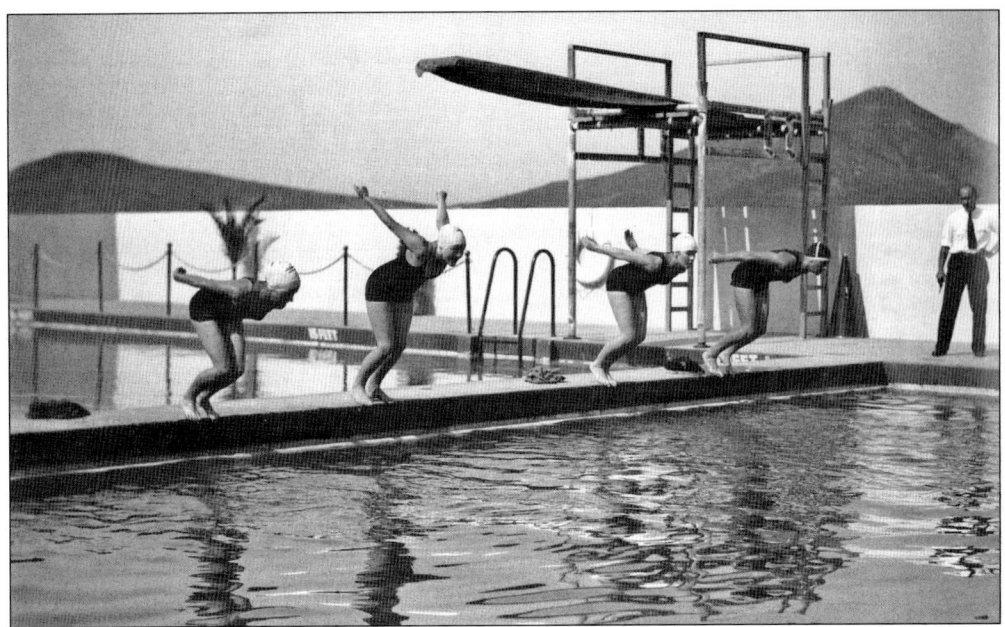

INAUGURAL RACE, 1928. The *Los Angeles Times* claimed this image of unidentified competitors at the beginning instant of their 100-meter freestyle race was one of the greatest sports photographs ever taken. Most certainly, this was the beginning of a long string of state, national, and world records to be set in the Norconian pools. The starter to the right is legendary coach Fred Cady. (University of Southern California.)

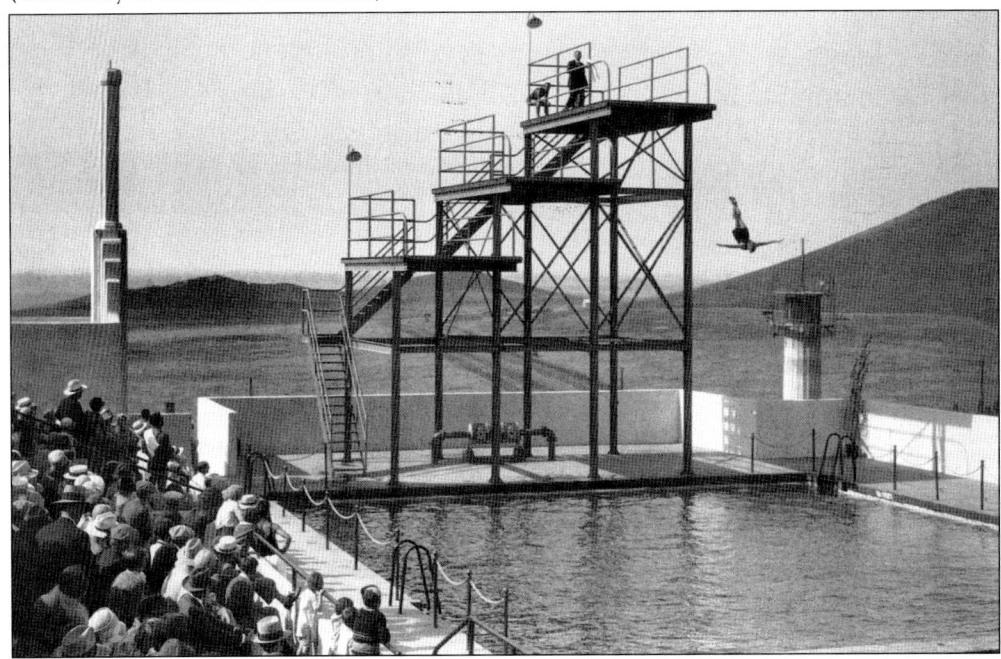

NORTH VIEW DIVING PLATFORMS, 1928. Old-time residents spoke repeatedly of the high dive platforms; many climbed the ladder, only to lose their nerve and climb right back down. The dive platforms were 5, 7.5, and 10 meters high, and the springboards to the right were 1 and 3 meters high. The competition swimming pool, small by today's standards, was 100 feet by 45 feet.

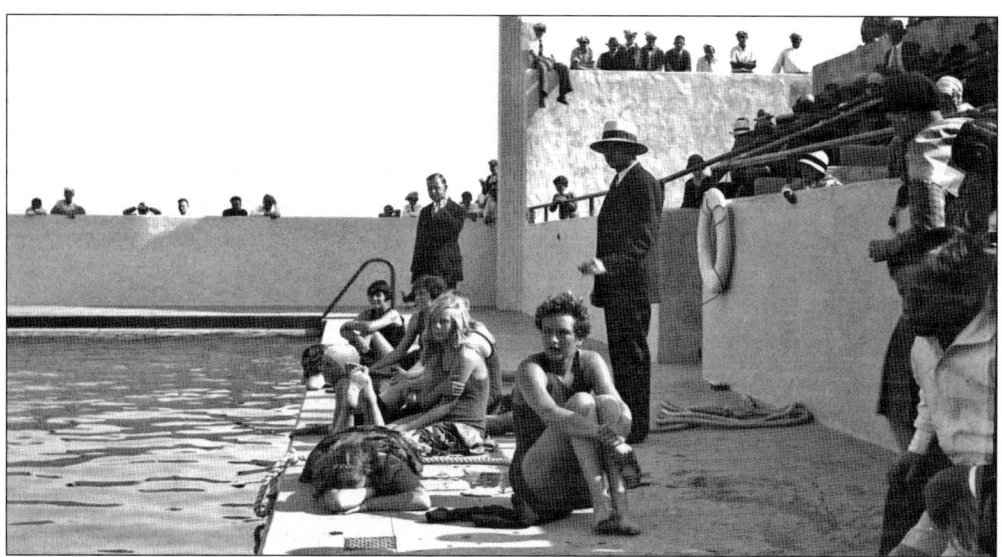

WORLD RECORD, 1928. Cecily Cuhna, center, is shown moments before a momentous swim. Paced by Olympian Austin Clapp, this 18-year-old heir to the fabulous Cuhna fortune in Hawaii will break the world record for the 400-meter swim in the brand-new Norconian pools. Considered a definite for the 1932 Olympics, she abruptly quit the sport to spend a lifetime traveling the globe, her world-class moment in Norco forgotten. (University of Southern California.)

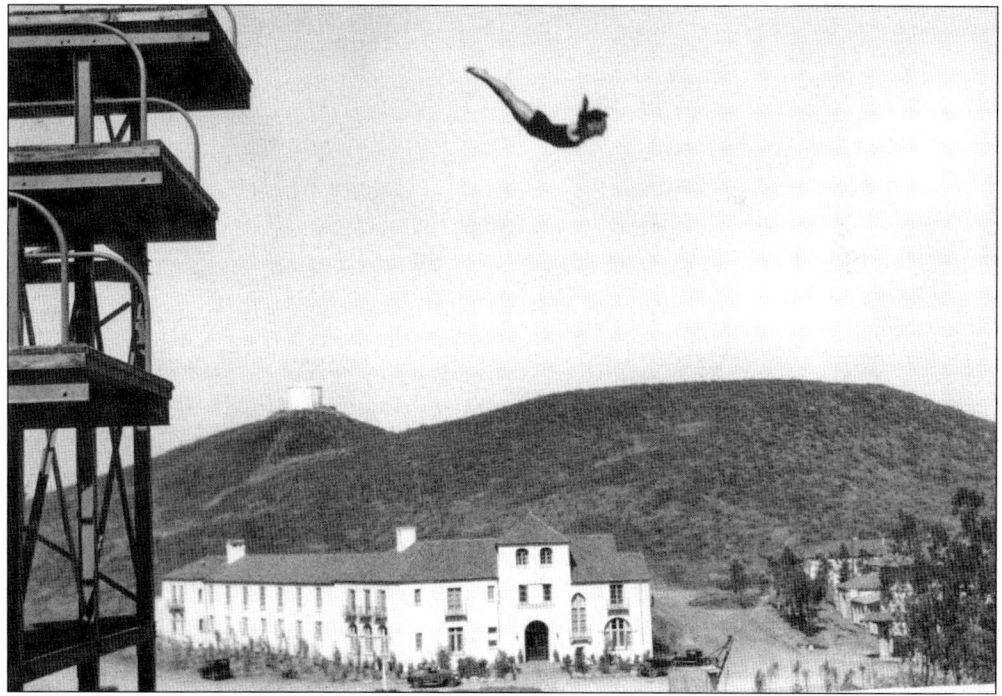

A LONG WAY DOWN, 1929. One of many Olympic divers to compete, train, and exhibit at the resort was Harold "Dutch" Smith. Wearing the heavy wool bathing suit of the time, Smith shows perfect diving form with the Norconian chauffeurs' quarters in the background. Smith, with fellow diver Farid Simaika, went on to invent "double diving," later known as synchronized diving and a popular Olympic event in 2000.

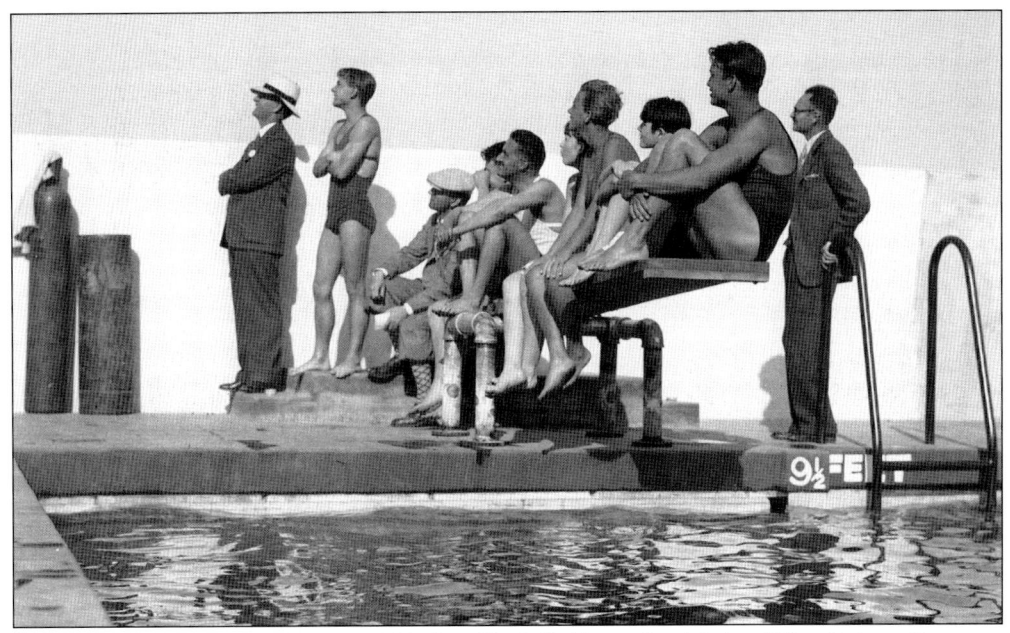

PACIFIC COAST CHAMPIONSHIPS, 1928. Rex Clark (left) watches Mickey Riley diving off-camera during the Southern California Diving and Swimming Championships, the first stateside appearance of the 1928 American Olympic Aquatic Team. Standing behind Clark is Dick Degener, the "Fred Astaire of Diving." Degener was undefeated at Michigan and was an Olympic bronze and gold medalist. At far right stands Walter "Doc" Beazley, the Norconian Club aquatics team coach. (University of Southern California.)

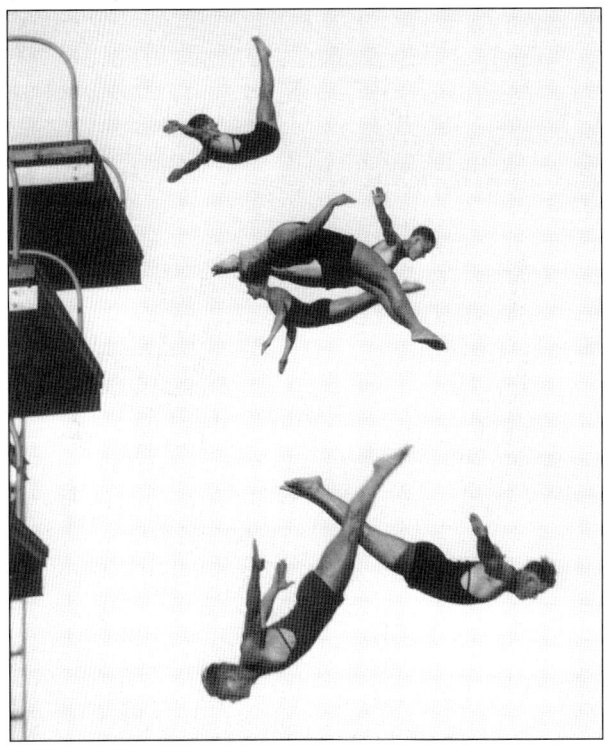

SYNCHRONIZED DIVING, 1928. Multiple divers leaping in tandem from the three platforms was extremely popular with Norconian guests. Norconian exhibition diver and Olympic coach Lyle Draves remembered, "Athletes, to maintain their amateur status could accept nothing for their efforts"; the coaches, however, "cleaned-up." In this fabulous photograph from left to right are (first, bottom row) Mickey Riley and Dutch Smith; (second, middle row) Frank Kurtz, Johnny Riley, and Peter Desjardins; (third, top row) Farid Simaika.

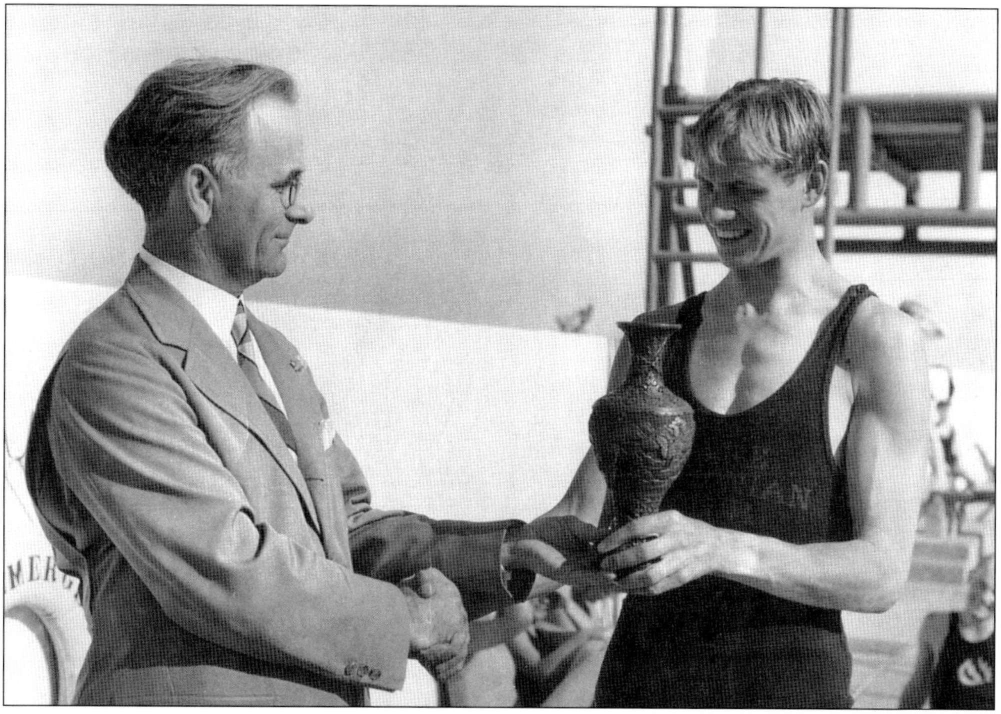

NORCONIAN CHAMPION, 1929. Rex Clark presents Olympian Arne Borg with a loving cup after the swimmer smashed the American 500-meter record. This was the era of the great athletic clubs, the best of which was the Los Angeles Athletic Club. However, on this day, Clark boasted Borg was swimming for the Norconian, hopefully a step toward building the strongest aquatics team in America. (University of Southern California.)

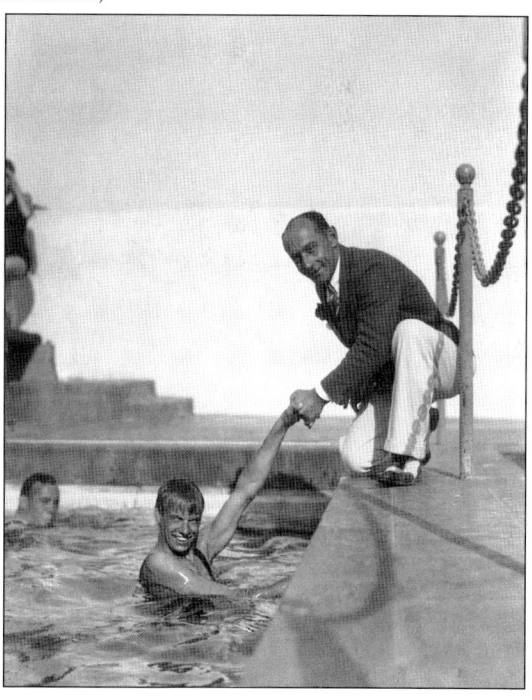

KING OF THE HILL, C. 1928. Fred Cady congratulates Arne Borg after his record-setting 500-meter swim. Cady, a former circus strongman, became one of the great diving coaches. His record was astounding: four Olympic diving teams, four Olympic gold medalists, head coach at USC for 33 years, and at one time, his divers held all U.S. and world diving championships. (University of Southern California.)

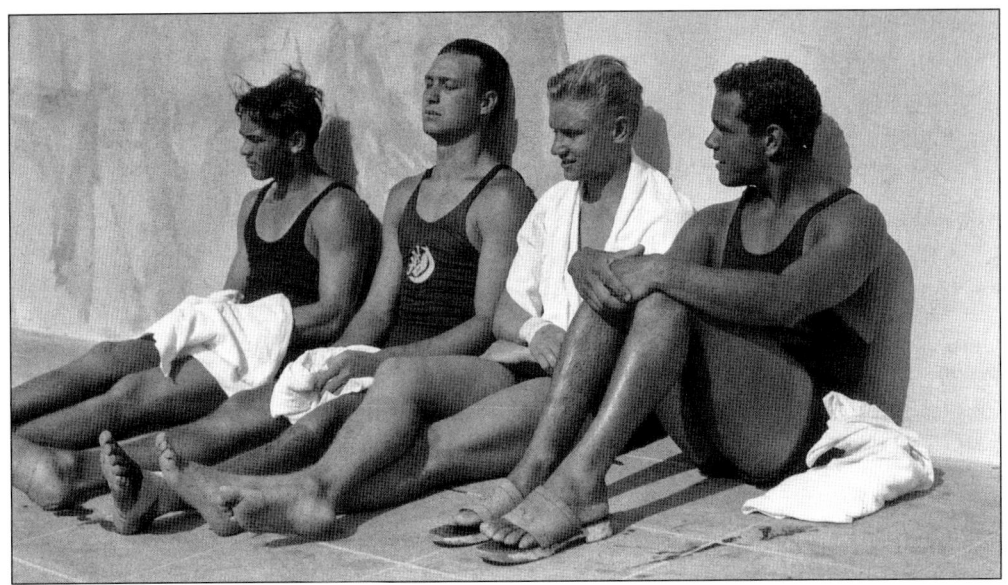

THE BEST OF THE BEST, 1928. Until the pools were built in Los Angeles for the 1932 Olympics, the Norconian boasted the only outdoor Amateur Atheletic Union (AAU) qualifying pools in Southern California: if an athlete competed in the 1928, 1932, or 1936 Olympics, they competed at the Norconian. Pictured from left to right are Farid Simaika (silver, bronze), Pete Desjardins (silver, two gold), Mickey Riley (bronze, two silver, gold), and Harold Dutch Smith (silver). (University of Southern California.)

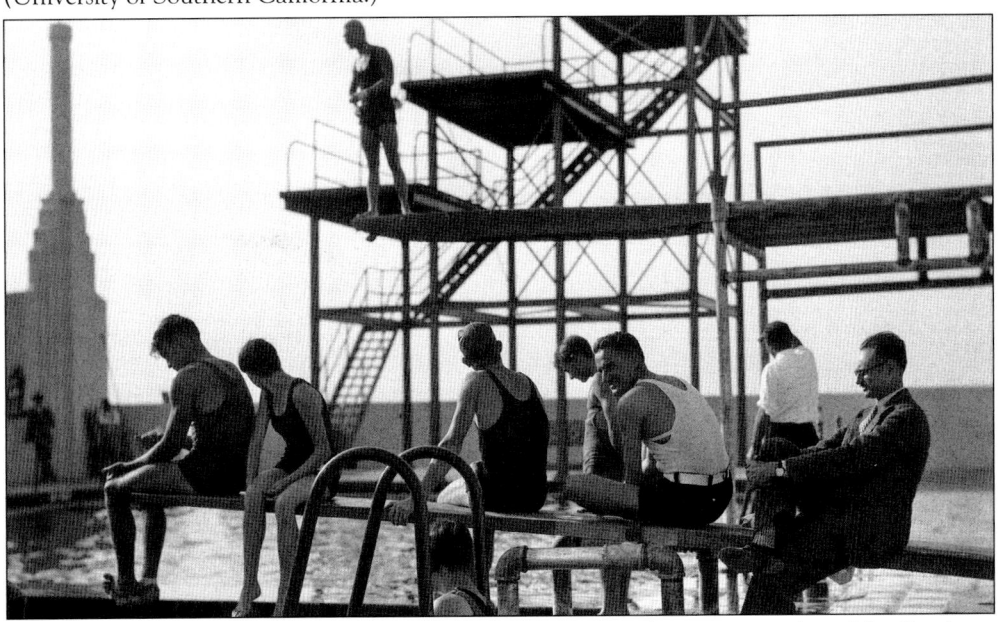

NORCONIAN BOARDS AND PLATFORMS, 1928. The Norconian became a member of the Southern Pacific Amateur Athletic Association, meaning competitions were officially sanctioned; this attracted the best divers and swimmers in the world. The list of gold medalists who competed at the Norconian is astonishing: Richard Degener, Pete Desjardins, Eleanor Holm, Marjorie Gestring, Buster Crabbe, Dorothy Poynton, Helene Madison, Arne Borg, and Sammy Lee among others. (University of Southern California.)

JANE FAUNTZ, 1932. The roster of Olympic athletes who wore the Norconian green was impressive and included Stanley Kistler, Marion Dale, Norene Forbes, and Jane Fauntz. Unfortunately, the team was short-lived because of the Depression. By 1932, Fauntz (right, with Georgia Coleman [left] and Kathcrine Rawls) had no sponsor, making her Olympic bronze medal all the more impressive; her fame prompted a Wheaties box cover. (Los Angeles Public Library.)

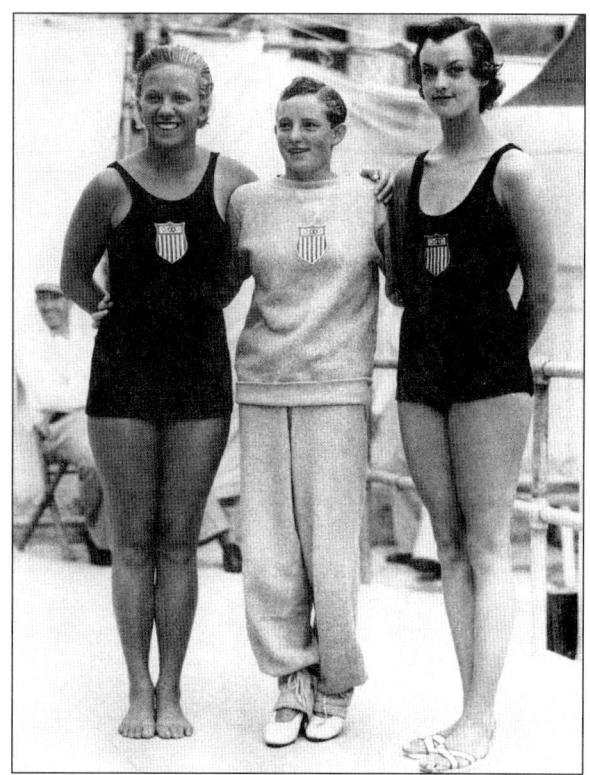

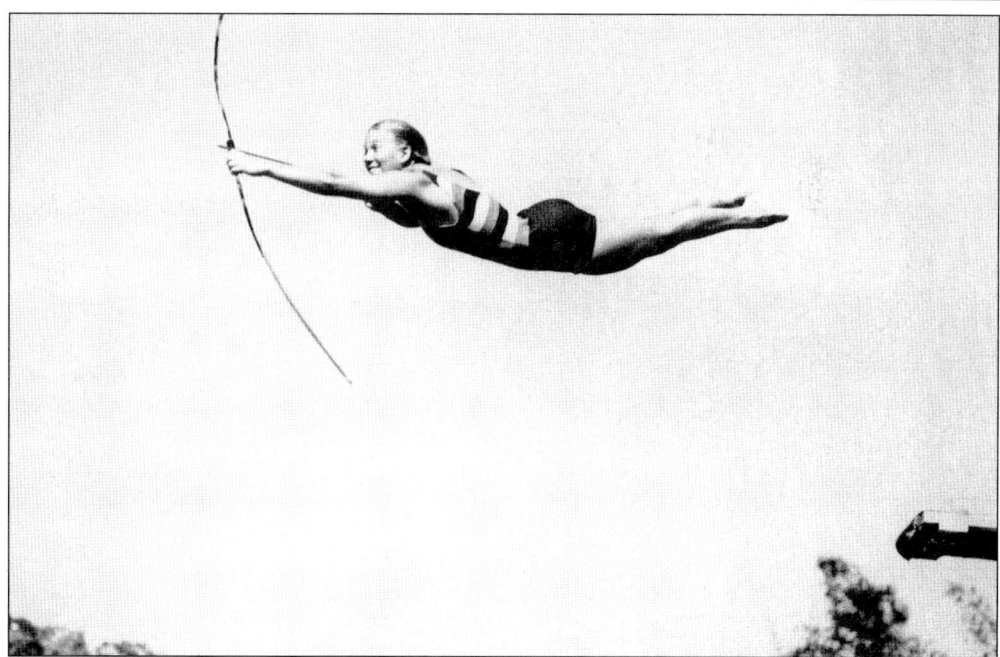

GEORGIA COLEMAN, 1932. Athletes were also expected to perform for the resort guests—comic tumbles off the high dives, skits, and even a "fire dive," a stunt whereby the diver was literally set on fire. Here four-time Olympic medalist Georgia Coleman fires an arrow at a target in midair. A Norconian favorite, Coleman died of complications from polio at age 28.

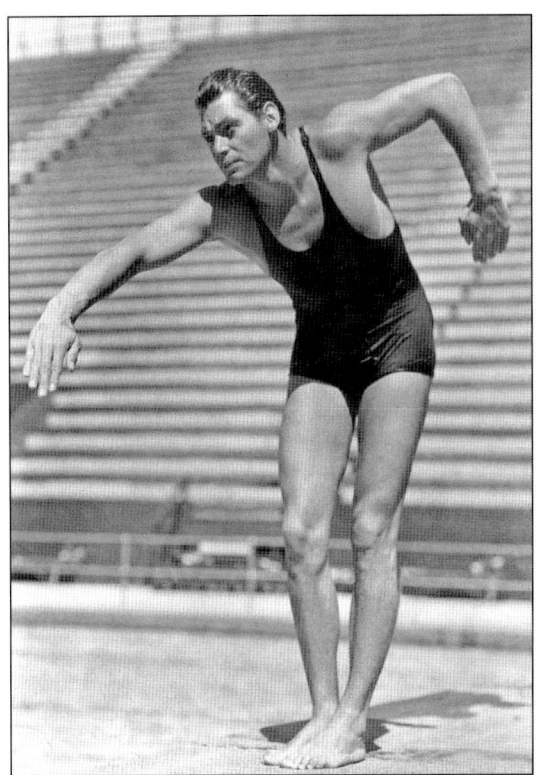

JOHNNY WEISSMULLER, C. 1935. Weissmuller, one of the greatest swimmers of all time and the winner of five Olympic gold medals, is better known today as "Tarzan." Legend has it he competed at the Norconian; unfortunately, that was not the case. He was, however, a regular guest. According to an eyewitness, in 1936, Weissmuller and Buster Crabbe, between martinis, put on a diving demonstration while fully clothed. (Bison Archives.)

THE FATHER OF SURFING, C. 1928. Duke Kahanamoku (second from the left, with fellow 1928 Olympic athletes), was a participant in five Olympic games, the winner of three gold medals and two silver medals and was enormously popular at the Norconian. Kahanamoku would demonstrate different swimming strokes in the pool and conduct surfing lessons in the lake; Duke would careen around the man-made body of water on a surfboard pulled by a speedboat.

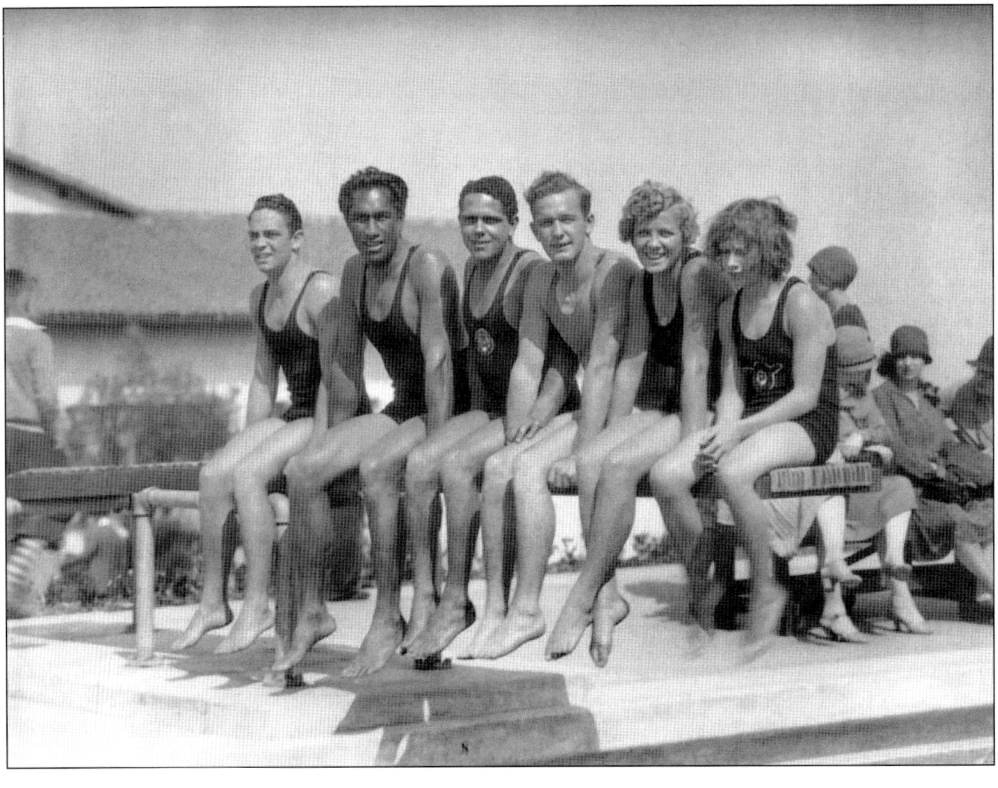

Five
THE NORCONIAN RESORT SUPREME

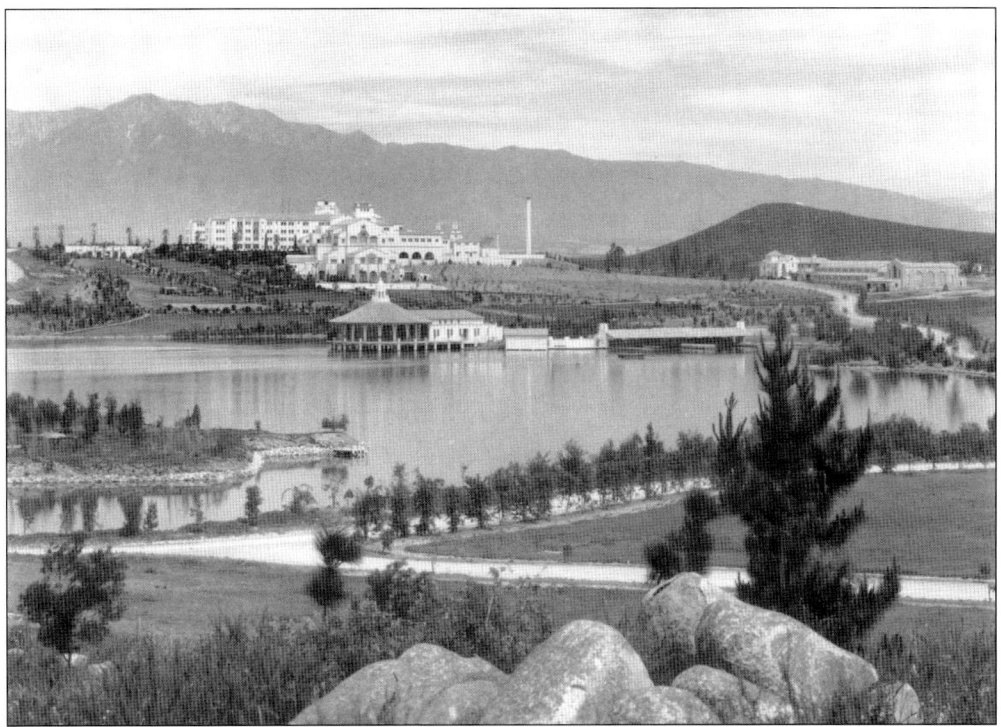

NORTH VIEW NORCONIAN, 1929. Originally the resort price tag was said to be $1.5 million, but costs may well have escalated to over $4.5 million in 1928 dollars. Rumors of financial problems dogged Rex Clark from the beginning. Nevertheless, he announced a $250,000 national advertising campaign, plans for a second hotel, and a hospital to serve "needy souls who wish to find health," none of which ever occurred.

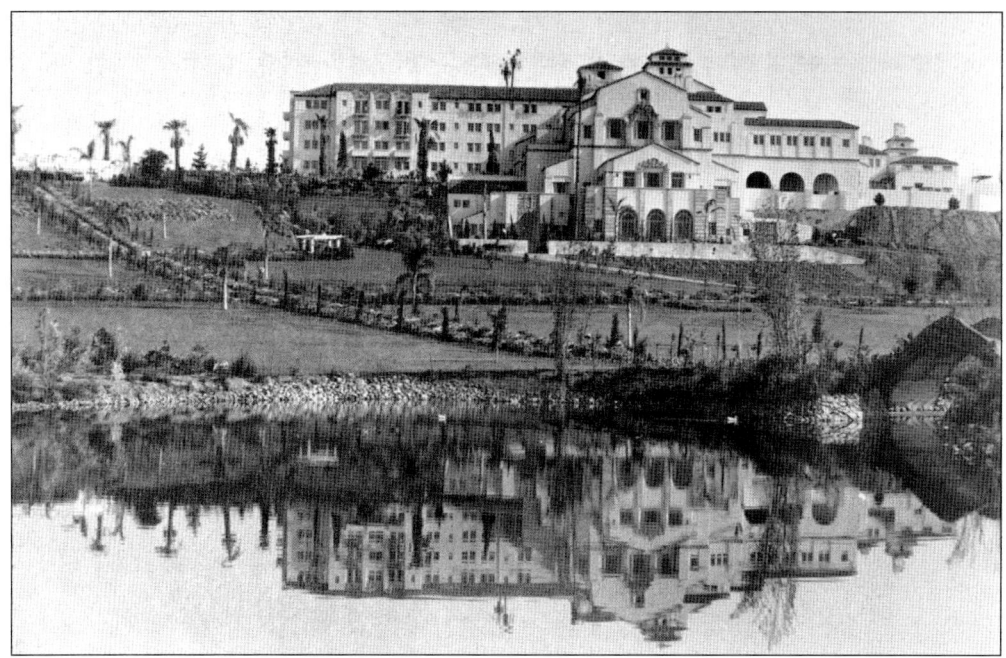

NORTH VIEW, 1929. Rex Clark made it clear his resort would welcome only the most desirable people and that was the reason his establishment was a private club. He stated, "To be open as a public place would mean we could not discriminate as to our guests." He also made it clear he was running a health resort and only healthy people were allowed—no contagious diseases!

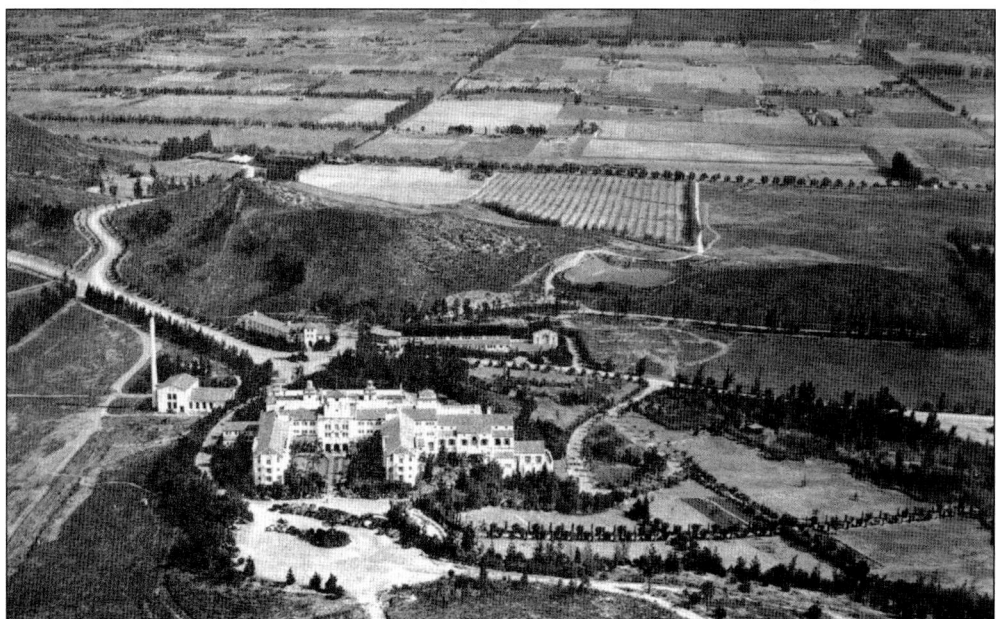

EAST VIEW AERIAL, 1929. Behind one of the great luxury resorts rests Norco. Neatly lined fields of Norco-brand melons, lettuce, onions, and tomatoes are seen in the background. Too distant to see are the prolific poultry and rabbit farms out-producing just about everyone else in the state of California. Also a fellow named Walter Knott is growing berries as big as a thumb on his first berry farm.

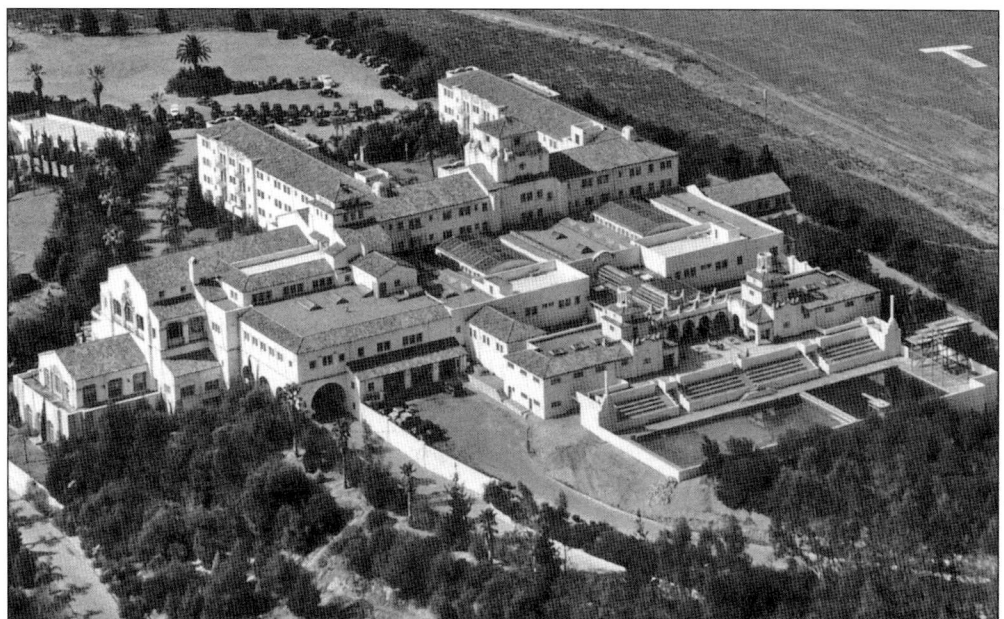

NORTH WEST VIEW AERIAL, 1931. To the top of the photograph are the U-shaped guest wings. Next is the bathhouse with its two large sunroofs, followed to the east by the sunning patios, cafe, snack bar, viewing platform, grandstands, and pools. Left of the baths are the loading dock, kitchen, and (stacked three high) the dining room, lounge, and ballroom.

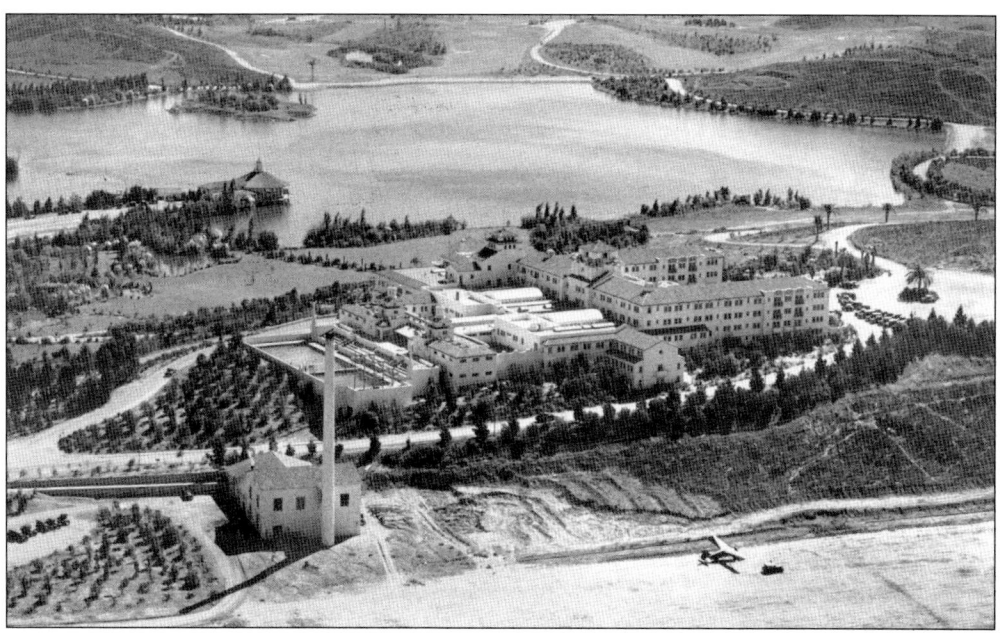

SOUTH VIEW AERIAL, 1931. In the foreground is the 2,000-foot-long airfield and powerhouse. Moving up is the inn and bathhouse, surrounded by a driveway ending in a circular parking lot. Next is the lake surrounded by yet another drive, the Pavilion, and golf course. Note the single-wing plane in the foreground.

53

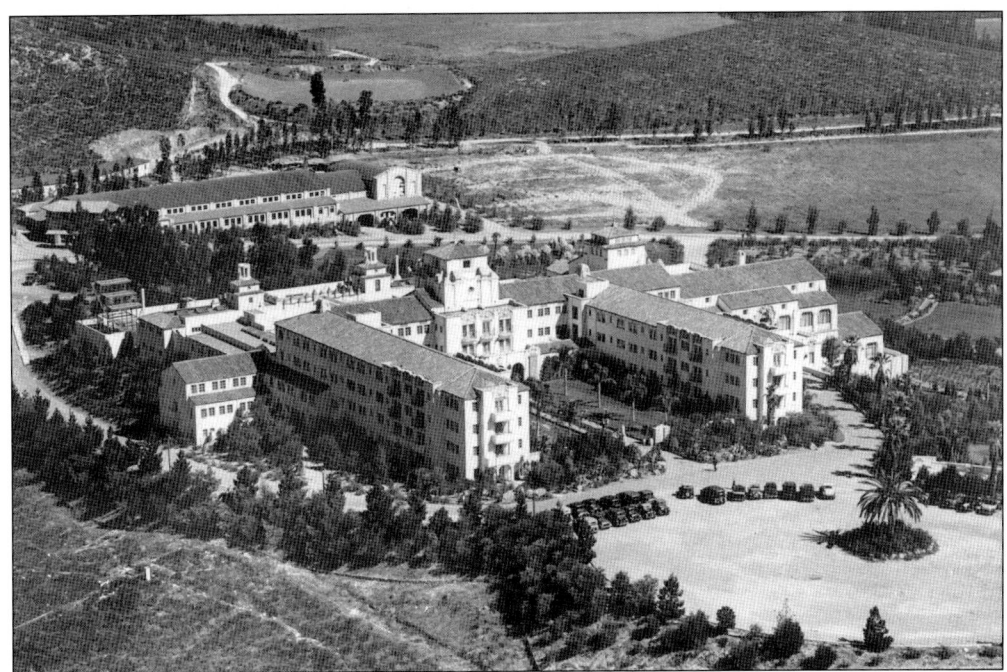

EAST VIEW, 1929. Originally Rex Clark envisioned two hotels surrounded by exclusive country homes for members of "a restricted class," complete with deed restrictions in architecture, building, commercial development, religion, and skin color. Norco already had such restrictions in place, as did Corona in certain areas of the city. As for the "palaces in the hills," they would never be built, and Clark's triumph would be short-lived.

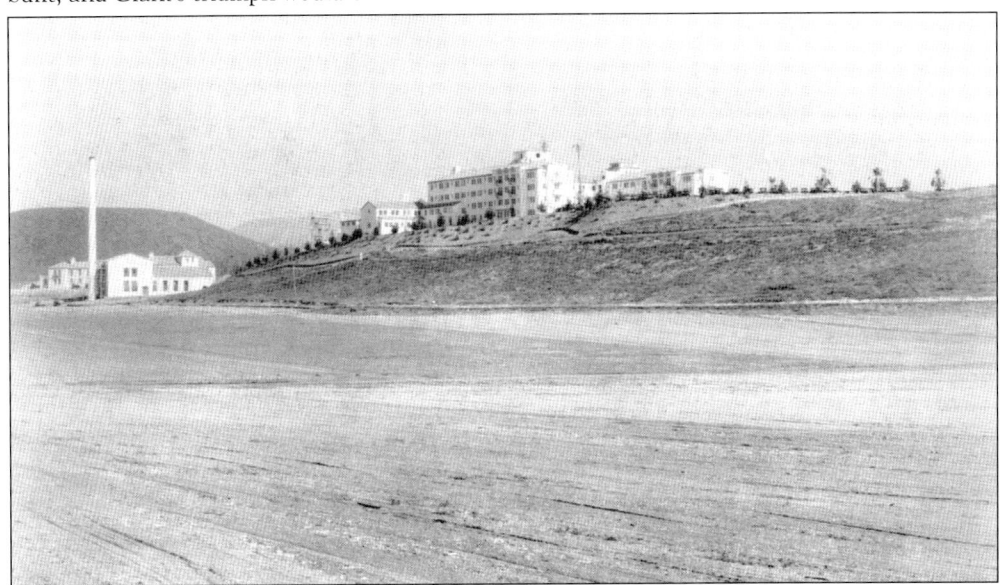

NORCONIAN AIRFIELD, 1929. Clark felt that aviation was a must for developing communities. He predicted the future was airmail, air transportation, and airfreight. His dream was to build a "Class A" airfield complete with hangers, restrooms, first aid and firefighting capability, and complete repair facilities. Clark felt that one-day guests would arrive not by automobile but by passenger plane, and he would be ready.

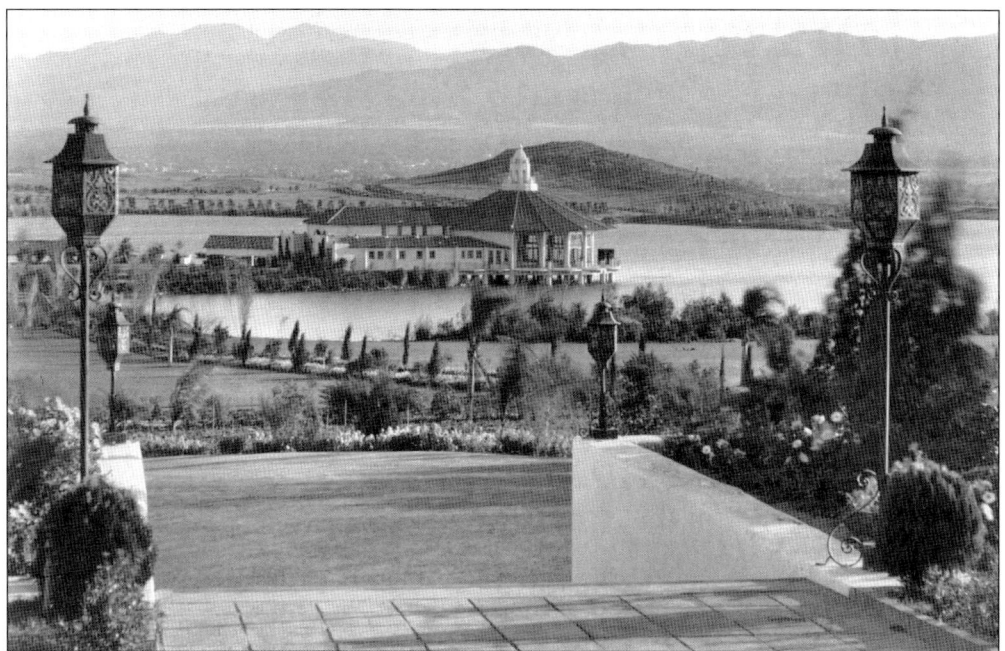

NORCONIAN GROUNDS SOUTH VIEW, 1929. This was the stunning view that would greet the hundreds attending the upcoming Lake Norconian Resort grand opening. Rex Clark would allow no dogs on this landscape and on more than one occasion asked a guest with dog in hand to leave because the canine was "raising the devil" with his flowers.

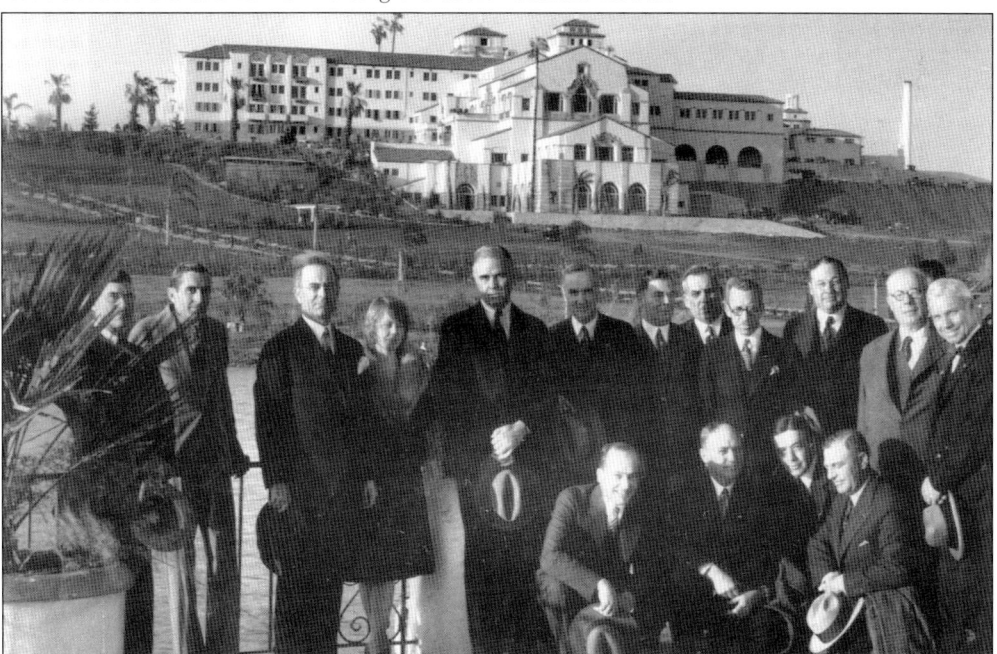

THE NORCONIAN, 1928. With the unfinished hotel as a backdrop is (third from left) Rex Clark, Norco founder and builder of the "Resort Supreme." Next to him is his mistress and future wife, Jimmie Snyder. The other men are unidentified and the reason for the gathering is unknown. This could represent a gathering of Shriners, bankers, or the Association of Undertakers.

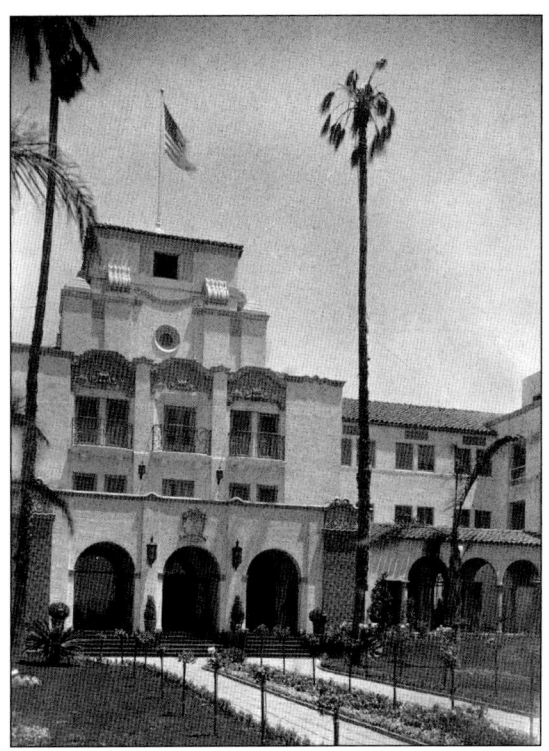

INN FRONT WALKWAY, 1929. Greeting visitors are magnificent archways and pillars in a mix of Mediterranean and Spanish mission revival styles. According to *Travel Digest*, architect Dwight Gibbs "worried that sheer size and whiteness might create an impression of aloofness and intimidate guests. . . . Using gentle curves and minimal decorative accents he worked to create a friendly, handsome luxury that would beckon and intrigue," something his creation does to this day.

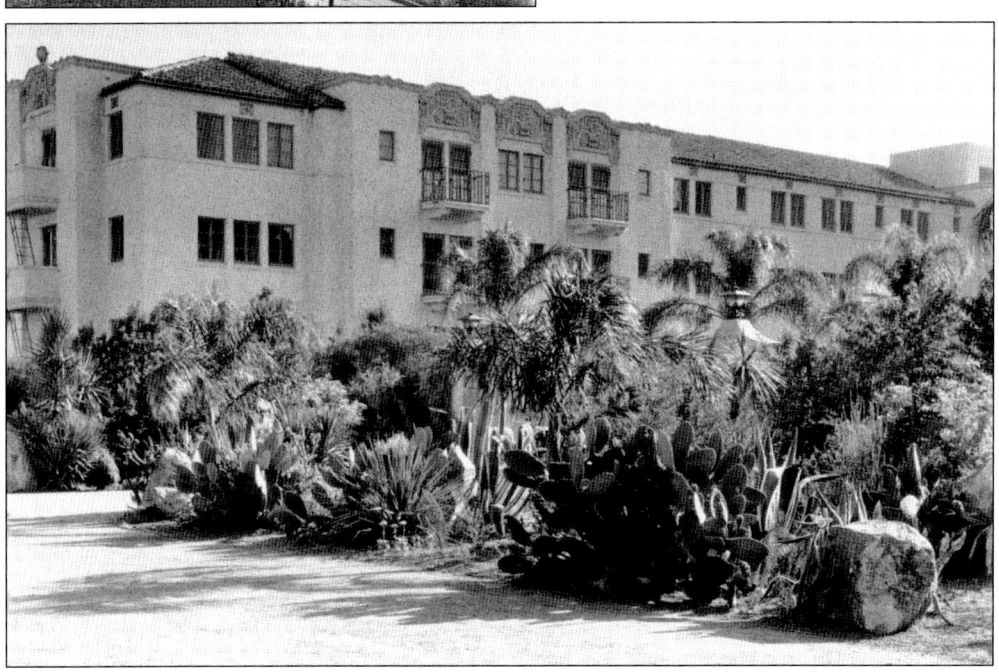

NORTH GUEST WING, 1929. Originally the entranceway into the hotel was landscaped in a Southwestern style using varieties of cactus, palms, and desert grasses, a choice pushed by Dwight Gibbs to bring out a friendly "ranch" type, wide-open-spaces "howdy." The blending of wrought iron, art deco plaster relief, and cactus was called "genius." Sadly, while some of this original foliage still exists, it is dying from lack of water.

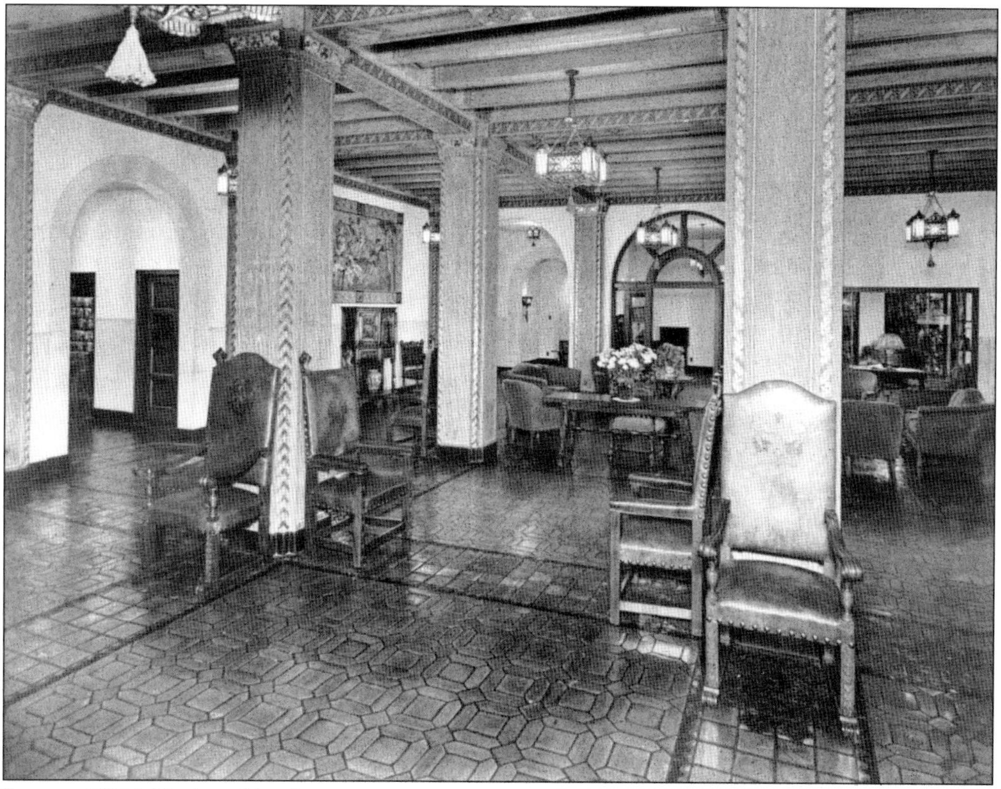

LOBBY, 1929. Designed by the legendary Anthony B. Heinsbergen, the interiors are breathtaking to this day. The floor is red tile with brilliant-colored designs running throughout; the pillar and ceiling are concrete with wood-grain finish and decorated with exquisite designs. To the center rear is a Heinsbergen painting on canvas, usually mistaken for a tapestry. The furniture was handmade specifically for the resort to Heinsbergen's specifications.

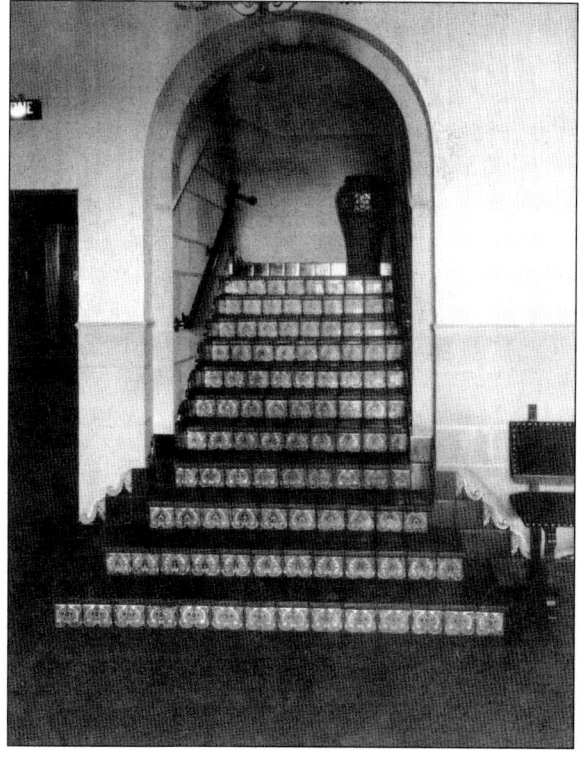

LOBBY STAIRCASE, 1929. Immediately greeting guests, this red-and-decorative-tile stairway no doubt made an impression; the colors are still vibrant after 80 years. The interior walls of the Norconian were coated with a sheen; combined with the tile, varnished wood, bright murals, and glistening fixtures, the result must have been dazzling.

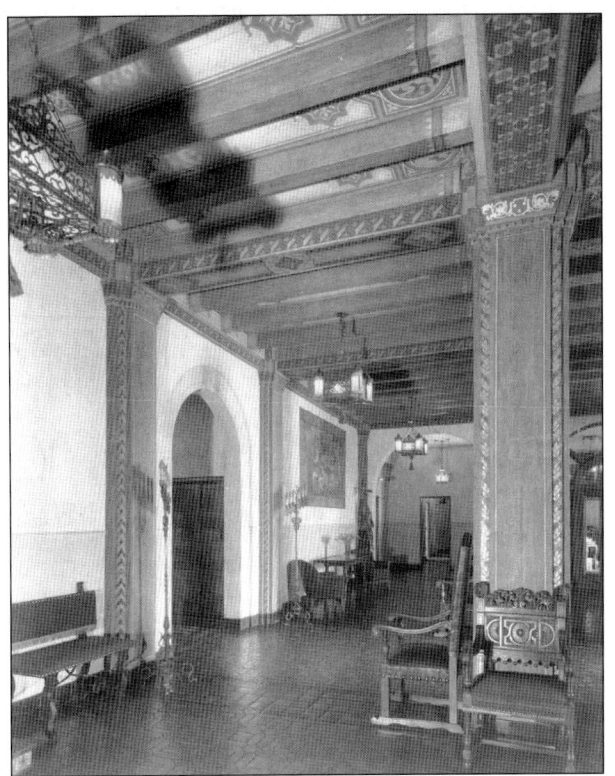

LOBBY CEILING, 1929. To create the art deco shapes and figures covering the ceiling and pillars (made of poured concrete with a faux wood-grain finish), first an apprentice would prep the surface with color, a senior apprentice would apply the handmade pieces of art, and a master artist would finish by hand the blending and intricate detail work.

CASHIER'S CAGE, 1929. Directly behind this cashier's window was Rex Clark's office. He insisted always that his door be open to the public and that his other managers and supervisors be visible and accessible to guests. On the other hand, maids, bellboys, and servants remained behind the scenes using a system of servant passages to move about the hotel.

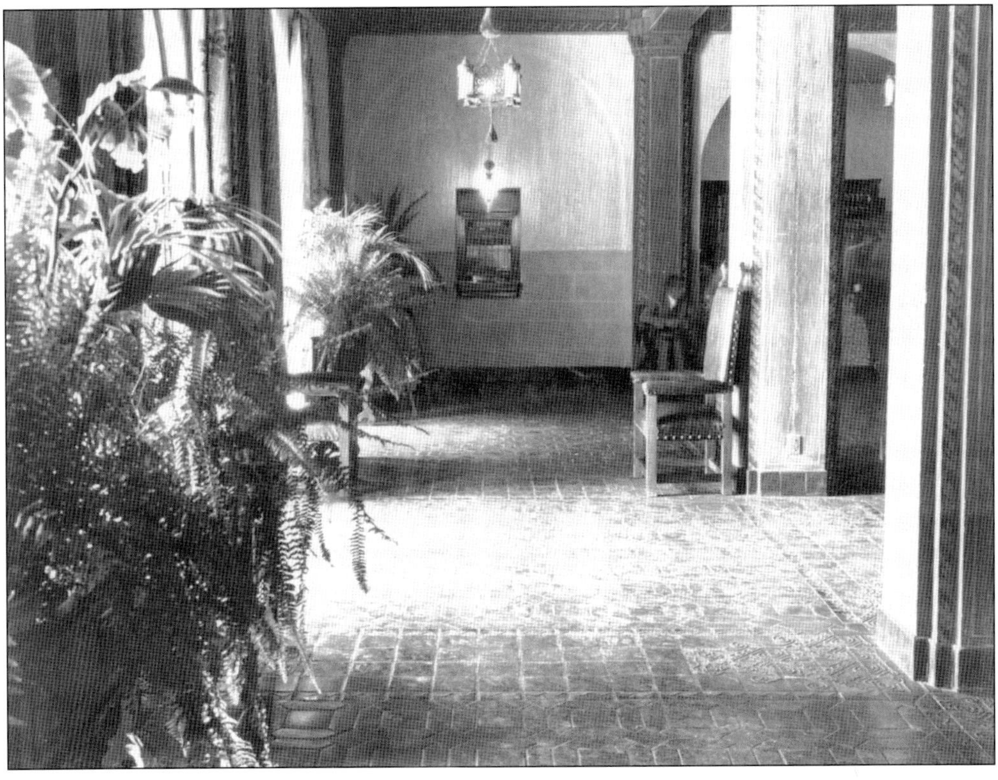

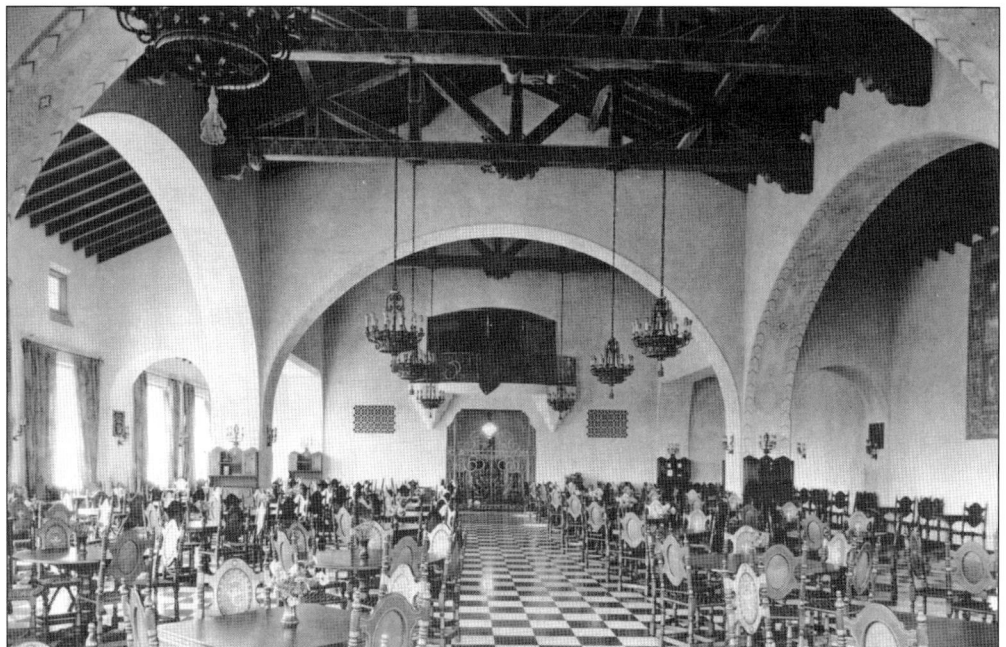

DINING ROOM WEST VIEW, 1929. One of the most impressive sights of the resort was a vast space with thick, curved pillars reaching up to meet hand-decorated wood beams and a stunning ceiling. The marble floor is a black-and-white checkered pattern; the black marble from Belgium is now extinct. The wrought-iron chandeliers, decorated with exquisite designs on a clear membrane, are simply superb to this day.

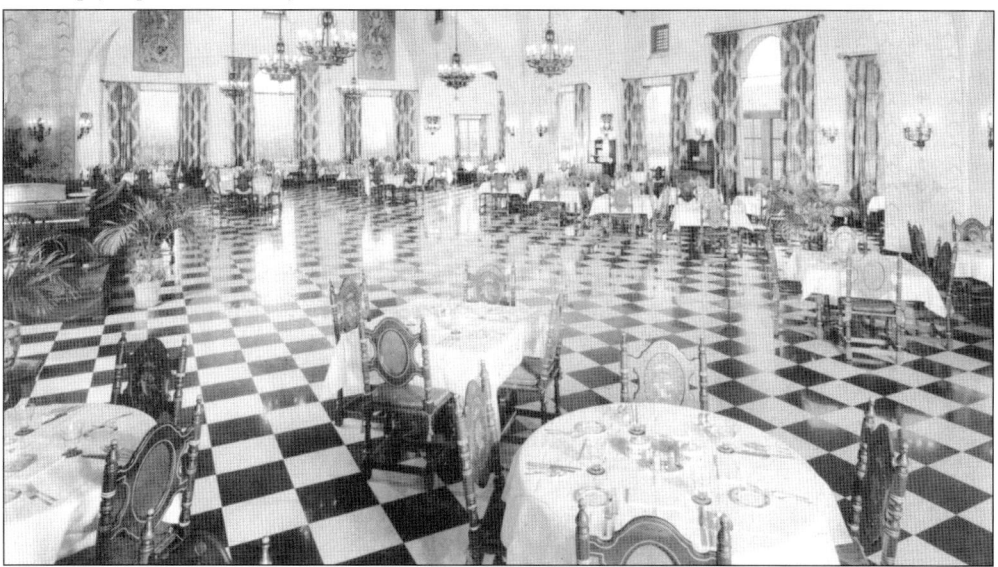

DINING ROOM SOUTHWEST VIEW, 1929. Handcrafted furniture, "Norconian" china made by "Old Ivory—Syracuse," and silverware exclusively made for the resort adorns this fabulous room. According to Norconian sales material, "Perfectly prepared food is a tradition at the Lake Norconian Club" with "super-excellent Cuisine and faultless service. . . . The most appetizing roasts, the juiciest steaks and the plumpest chickens [are] served in that restful atmosphere which is Southern California's heritage."

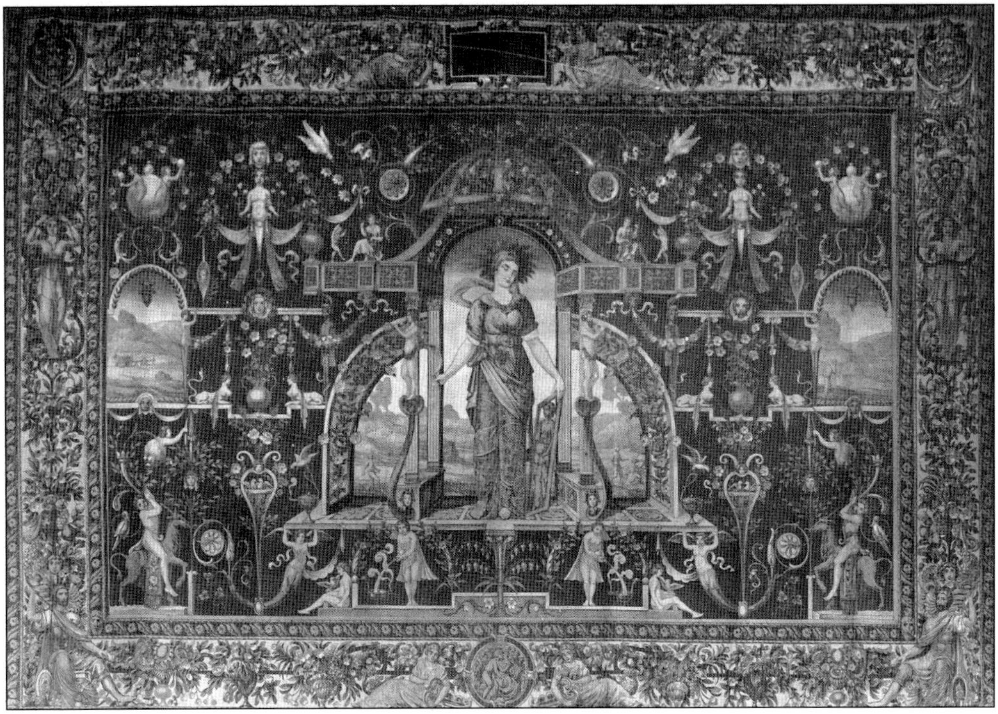

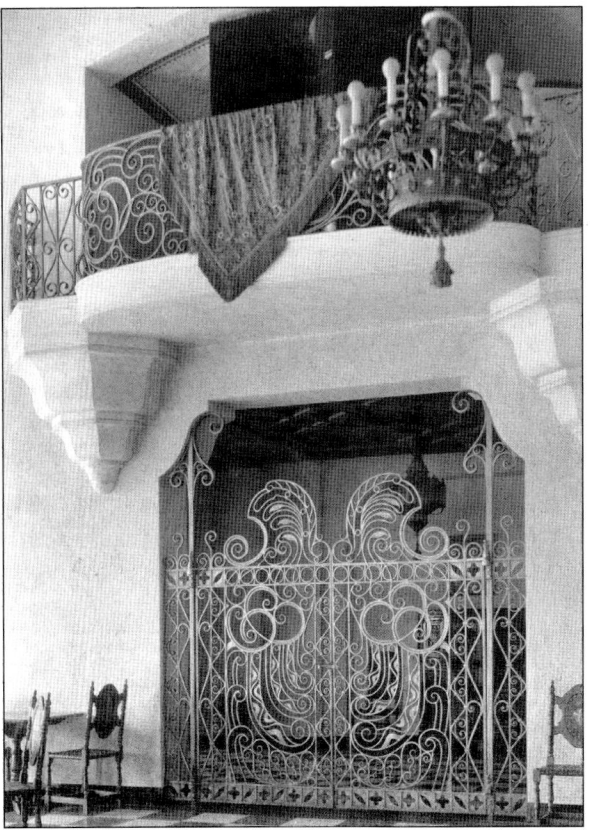

PAINTING ON CANVAS, 1929. A. B. Heinsbergen, acclaimed Dutch muralist, worked with the finest architects mixing American and European traditions to create hundreds of art deco interiors, including the Wiltern Theatre, Beverly-Wilshire Hotel, Roosevelt Hotel, 750 Pantages Theatres nationwide, and the 1928 Los Angeles City Hall. These fabulous Heinsbergen paintings were hung throughout the resort; unfortunately few survive today except in photographs.

DINING ROOM ENTRANCE GATES, 1929. Throughout the Norconian, one will find gates, railings, grills, vents, and all manner of handcrafted wrought iron. Literally dozens of exquisite pieces still exist with each thought to have been crafted on-site. The gates shown are a stunning example of a lost art, complete with art deco curves and classic Heinsbergen designs all hand strapped and pinned together; and they are still there.

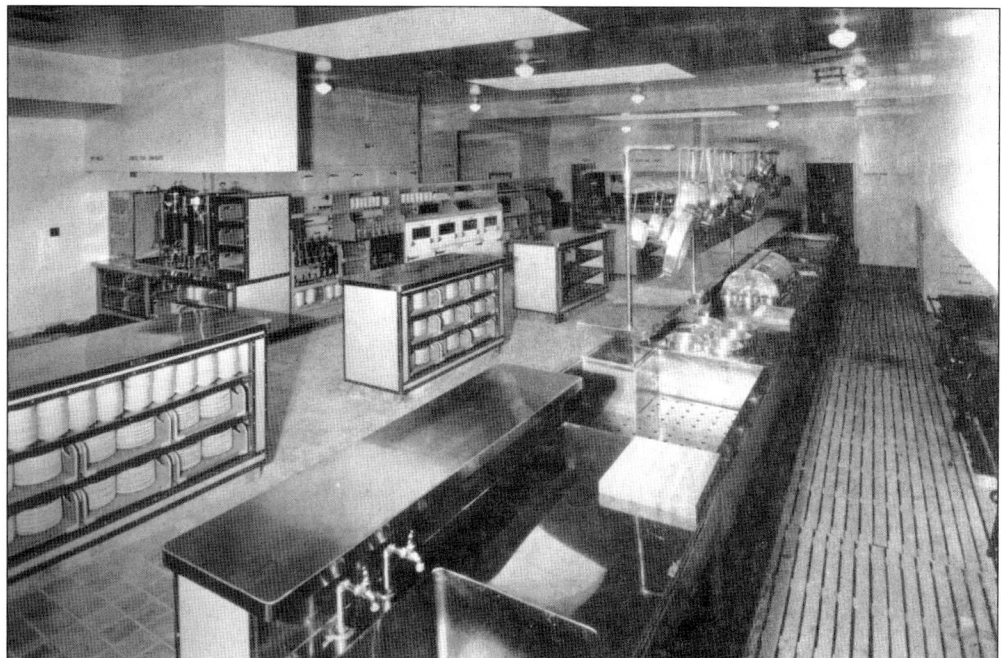

KITCHEN, 1929. Rex Clark insisted on cleanliness and regularly led guests on spontaneous tours through his electrically powered culinary center complete with every modern commercial grade appliance. This kitchen served the dining room and, via behind-the-scenes hallways, the ballroom, hotel rooms, and for special occasions both the tea room and the Pavilion. Rex Clark was quite proud that his kitchen could serve several hundred at a single sitting.

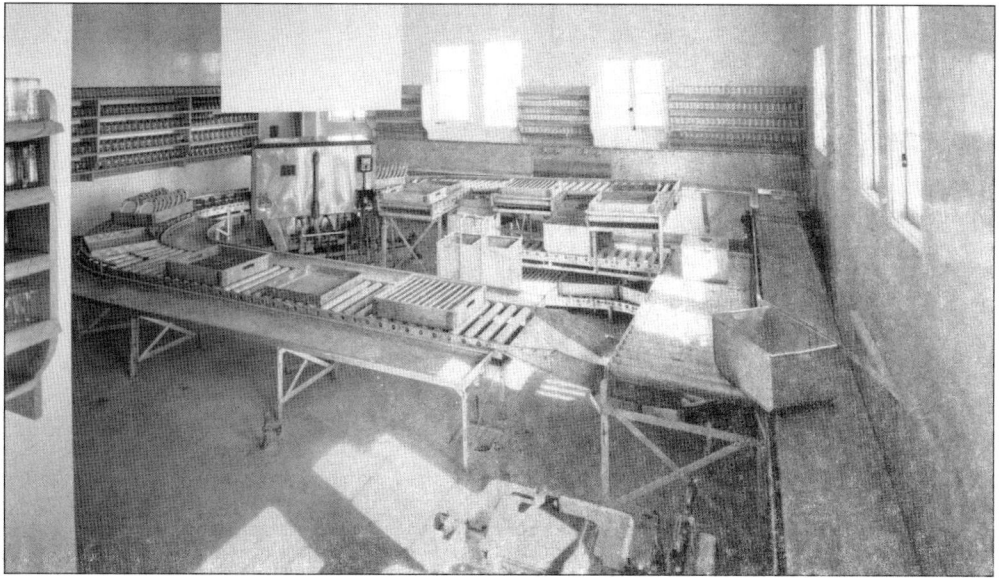

DISHWASHING BAY, 1929. Even dishwashing was made an art and modeled after Henry Ford's automobile assembly line. According to Rex Clark's daughter, her dad could not tolerate dirty dishes. A sales brochure proclaimed, "Soiled dishes are removed instantly from all tables in specially designed covered dish wagons," a 1929 model of efficiency. This was one of the first electrically operated dishwashing conveyance systems in Riverside County.

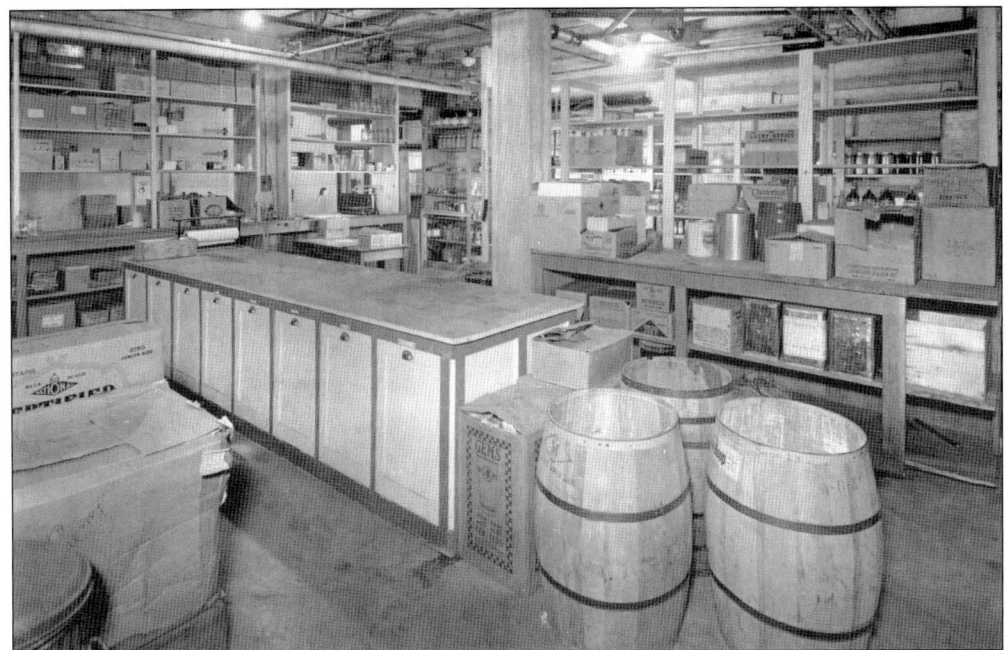

STORAGE AREA, C. 1930. The room pictured above demonstrates use as a food storage area and presents a bit of a mystery. At the end of the counter is a box of distilled gin, leading one to believe the photograph was taken after the lifting of Prohibition. However, the date on the back of the photograph reads 1930, indicating a violation of the Volstead Act; you dog, Rex Clark!

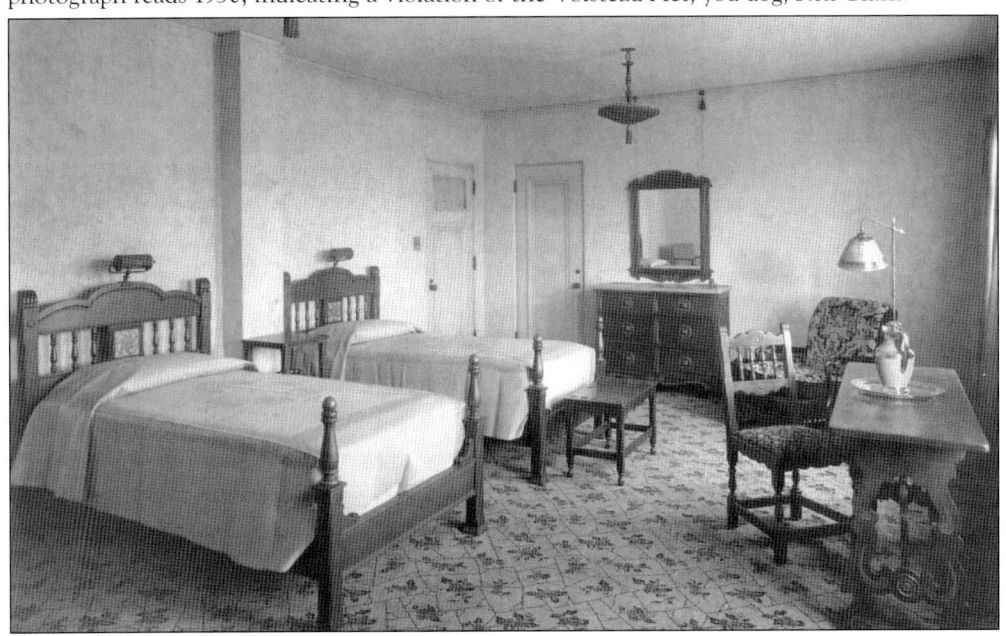

BEDROOM, 1929. There is always surprise at how small the bedrooms are for such a luxury hotel. Jeffrey Greene, one of the leading restorers of Heinsbergen interiors, says this was not unusual and was in fact common in the grandest resorts built around the 1920s. Nevertheless, photographs from the period indicate the rooms were comfortable and complete with adjoining baths (with five color schemes), electricity, and heat.

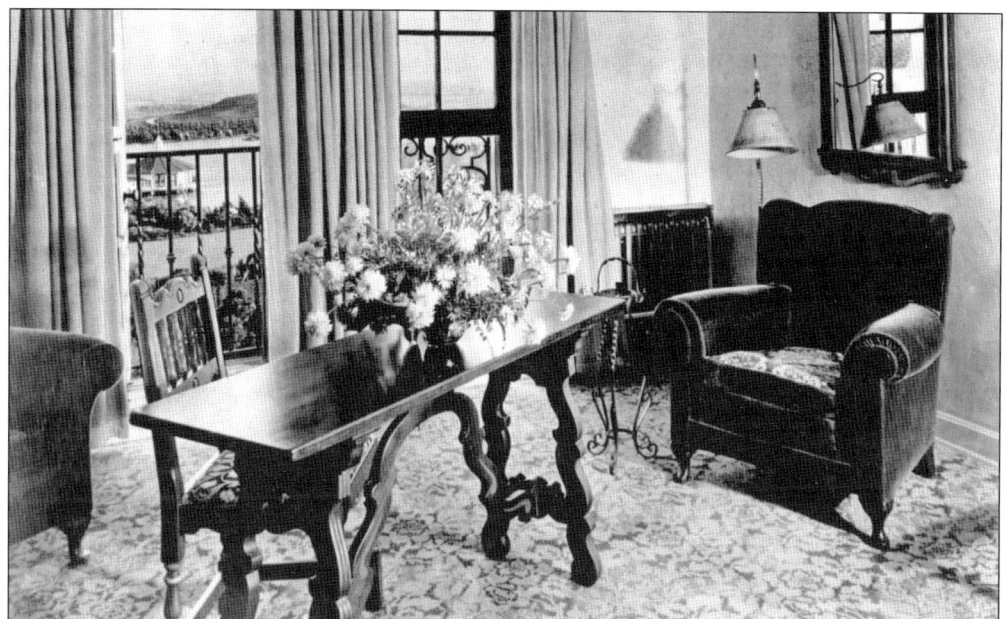

SITTING ROOM, 1929. A mix of room options were available: single, double, and what might be considered a suite (two rooms connected by a short hallway). Corner rooms appeared to be the largest; however, all bedrooms were quite narrow. The furniture was "exclusively designed Spanish style mahogany with colorful tile tops on the tables and dressers." Maid, laundry, and room service were available, with coffee served on silver platters.

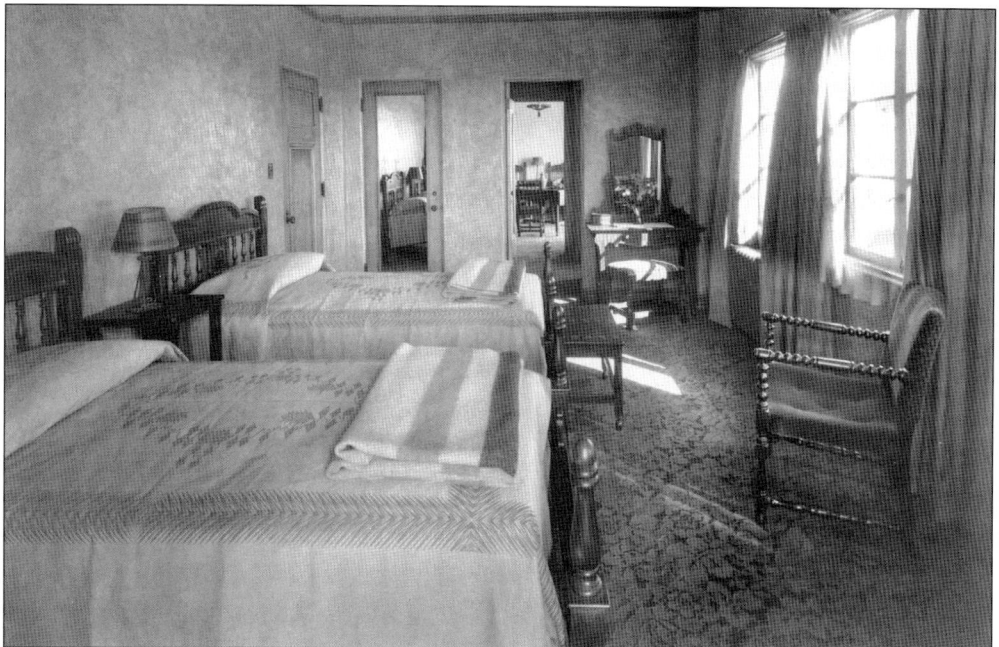

BEDROOM, 1929. Opening day, rates were $12 and up for a single to $22 and up for a double, depending on the size and location of the room. Rooms were available to club members, but temporary cards could be issued to "discriminating" visitors without joining the club. By 1935, in the midst of the Depression, a double room could be had for $7.50 a night and $3 for a single.

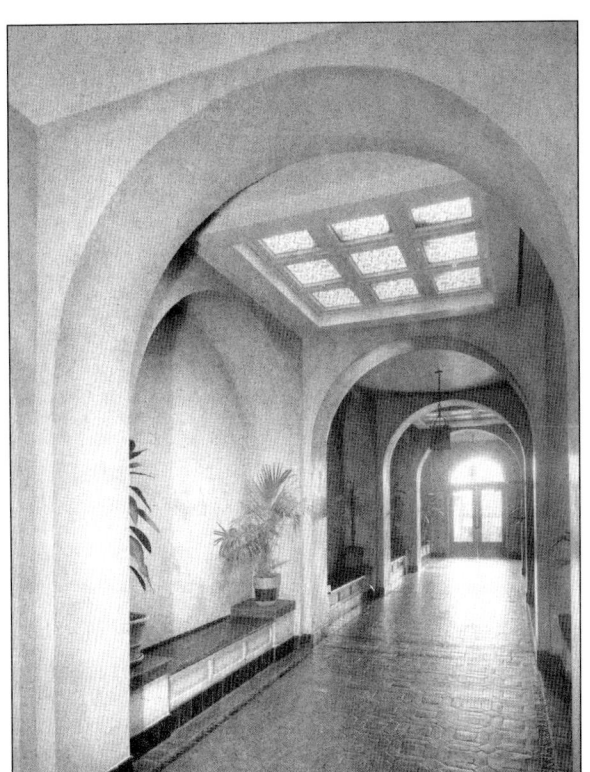

LOST HALLWAY, 1929. In 1932, Clark made renovations to the inn and bathhouse, altering two major hallways. The navy later made huge changes, carving new passageways to accommodate office and patient space. The result is an unbelievable and spooky maze of crisscrossing passageways, which twist and turn in such a way that getting lost in the seven-storied structure is a real possibility. The hallway pictured likely vanished in those renovations.

GIFT SHOP, C. 1930. Clearly Asian was the theme: kimonos, ornamental jars, knickknacks, paper lamps. This is another mystery room in that it is unclear where this shop was located. Likely it was to the right side of the lobby and later converted to the warden's office. Almost nothing is known about this gift shop or what they sold as old-time Norco residents couldn't afford to buy anything.

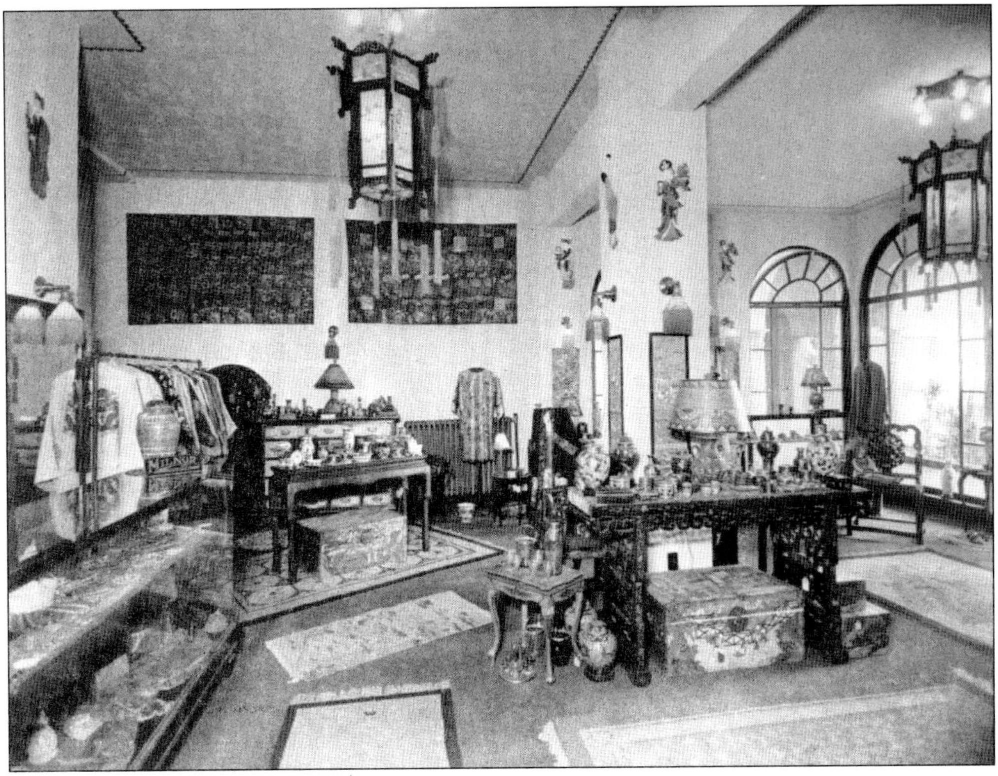

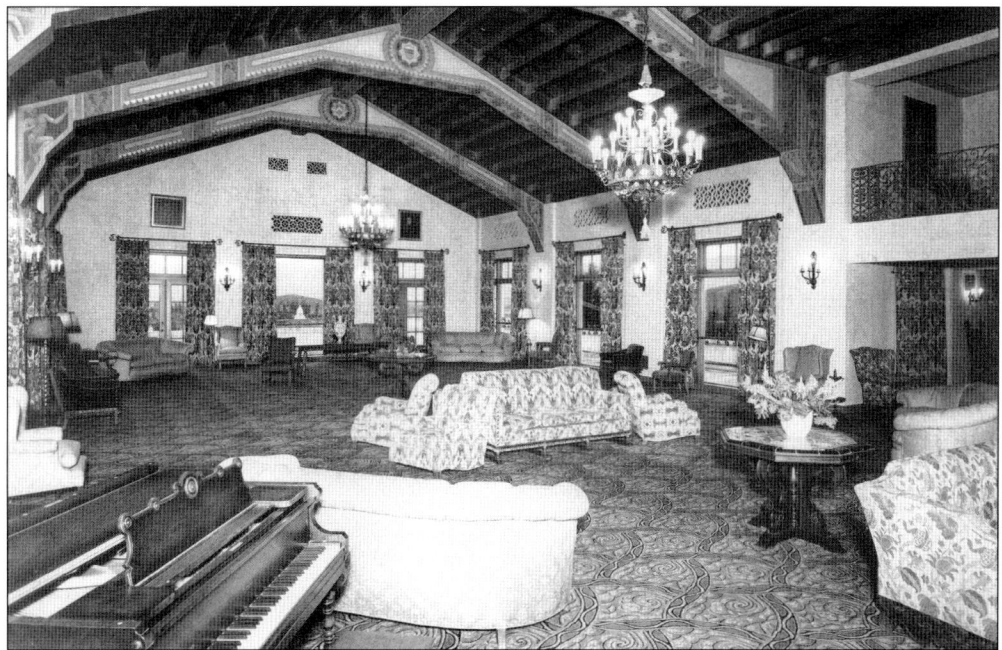

LOUNGE SOUTH VIEW, 1929. Rex Clark said it best: "The Lounge expresses the delicate finesse and nobleness of proportion that characterized the salons of Paris in the reign of Louis the Magnificent. Here one may read, write, smoke and leisurely while away the hours in an atmosphere of undisturbed tranquility." Well, maybe he didn't say it best; the room to this day, despite many changes, is spectacular.

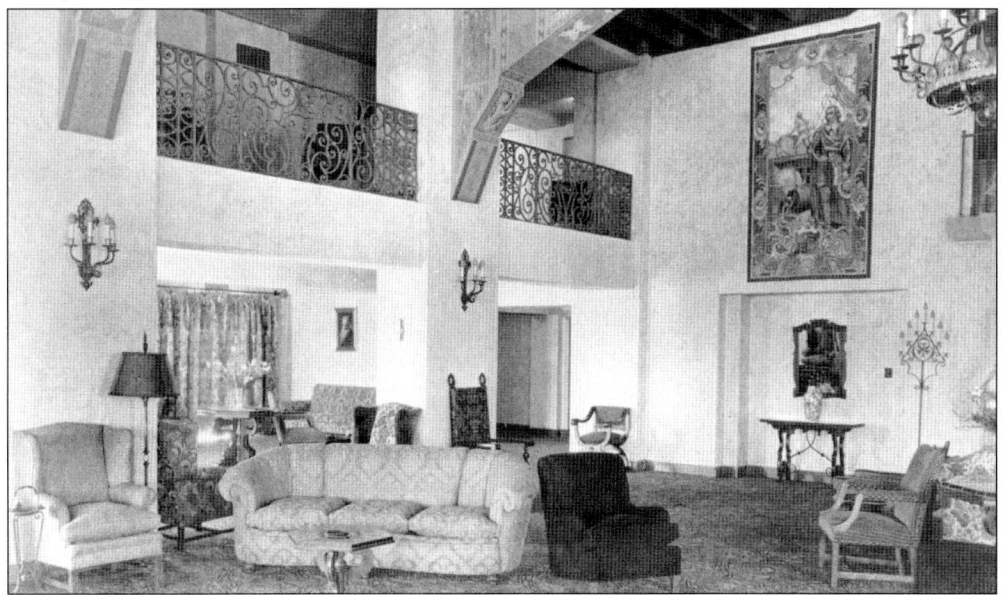

LOUNGE NORTHWEST VIEW, 1929. Adorning the ceiling are fabulous, richly colored paintings depicting ships, lions, elegantly attired (and un-attired) people, and bold geometric patterns. European- and American-style furniture mixed with Spanish wrought-iron railings and chandeliers made this room special. Today the room is cut in half and the view blocked with air-conditioning ductwork and a projection booth. The artwork and chandeliers, however, still remain.

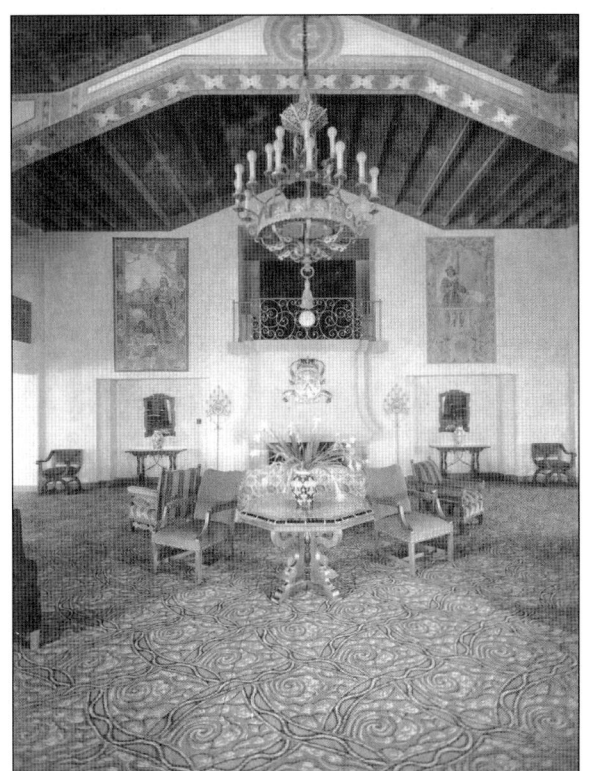

LOUNGE NORTH VIEW, 1929. A fireplace, viewing balconies, and gigantic chandeliers, all of which still exist, dominate the room. Long gone is the Norconian Crest on the fireplace, and the rugs have been replaced with navy-issue linoleum. The film *Top Speed* used an almost exact replica of this room to film a scene where a bevy of beautiful girls surround comedian Joe E. Brown.

BALLROOM FOYER NORTH VIEW, 1929. Colorful decorative tile, almost iridescent textured plaster walls, red tile floor, magnificent hand-painted canvas ceiling covering, beautiful Spanish chandelier, and an A. B. Heinsbergen mural made this room another masterpiece. Even more amazing, the room still exists as you see it, except for a major exception. The canvas ceiling covering has been cut to allow rainwater to pass through.

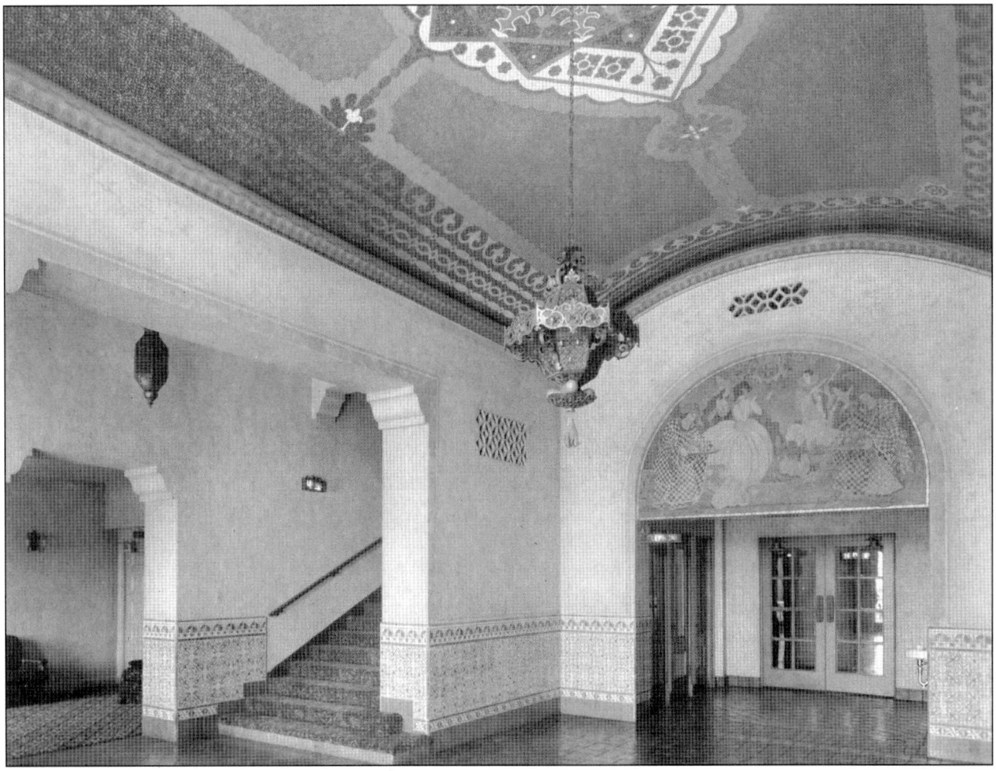

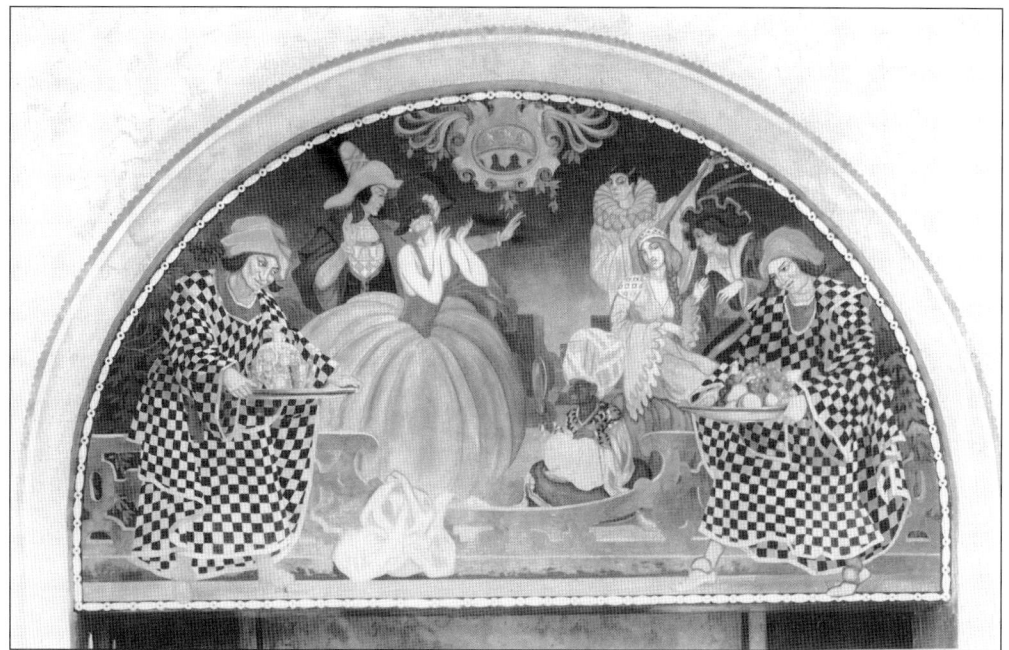

A. B. Heinsbergen Painting, 1929. After 80 years of collecting grime, the colors of this marvelous Heinsbergen masterpiece are still wonderfully vibrant; gorgeous reds, blues, and greens dominate this piece. Unfortunately, as of this writing, like so many of the hundreds of other pieces of art located in the old Norconian, rainwater and neglect may well destroy this one-of-a-kind painting.

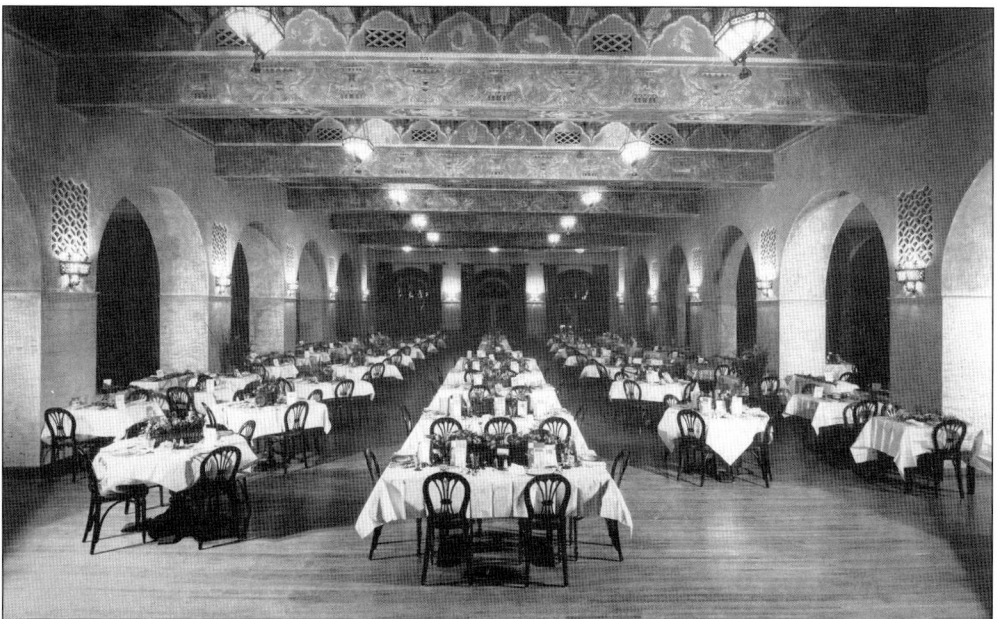

Ballroom South View, 1929. This view almost exactly exists today. Fabulous paintings cover the gigantic cross beams and ceiling. Notice the art deco geometric air vents on the pillars; gigantic swamp coolers blew water-cooled air throughout the main rooms of the hotel. After the building became a prison, basketball was played on the specially designed dance floor.

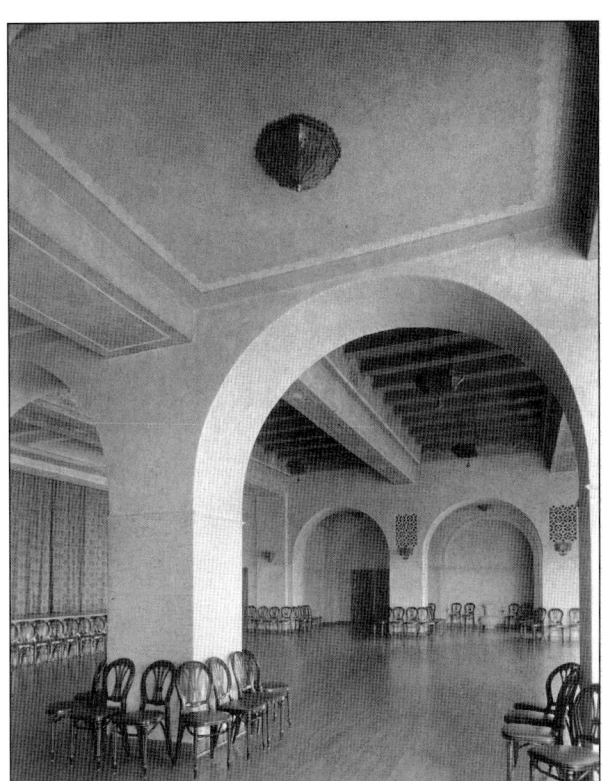

BALLROOM EAST VIEW, 1929. To the left is the mid-sized stage, complete with overhead stage lighting, footlights, and dressing rooms. Small- and big-time bands played the resort. Spike Jones, just out of school, was the drummer for the first Norconian house band. The ceiling, including the lighting fixture, at the top of the photograph is unchanged today, except water damage is destroying the plaster.

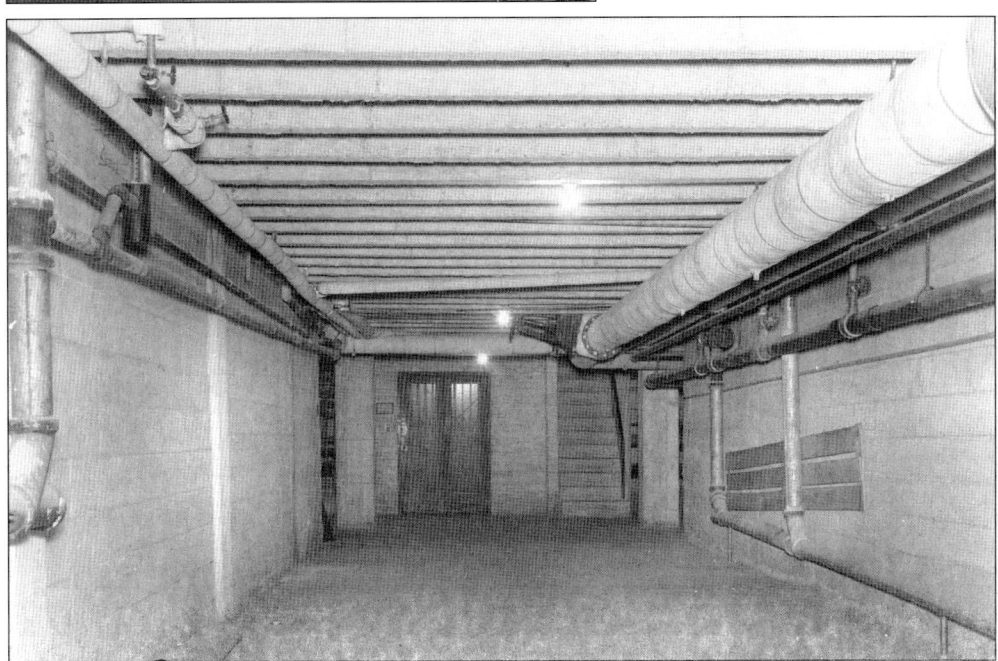

ENTRANCE TO SERVICE TUNNEL, 1929. Legend has it that Al Capone and "bootleggers" used the 450-foot tunnel to move about unseen. It was unlikely Capone would hide from anyone, and tracks from the inn to the tea room were likely used for carts carrying food not booze. It is said that an elevator repairman died in the pictured service elevator and now haunts the old prison.

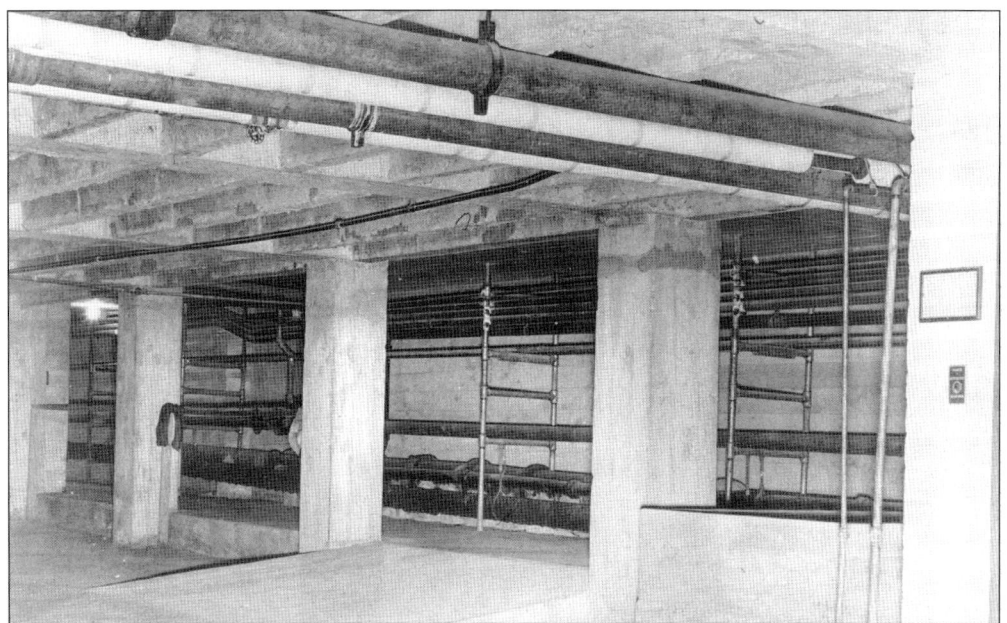

SERVICE TUNNEL TO TEA ROOM, 1929. A single tunnel runs from the tea room to the laundry. One intended purpose was to carry service pipes and wires for the resort buildings. Clark felt that if one day a new method of heating by sunlight was found or television perfected he could run the necessary apparatus into the Norconian through the service tunnel without disturbing hotel operations.

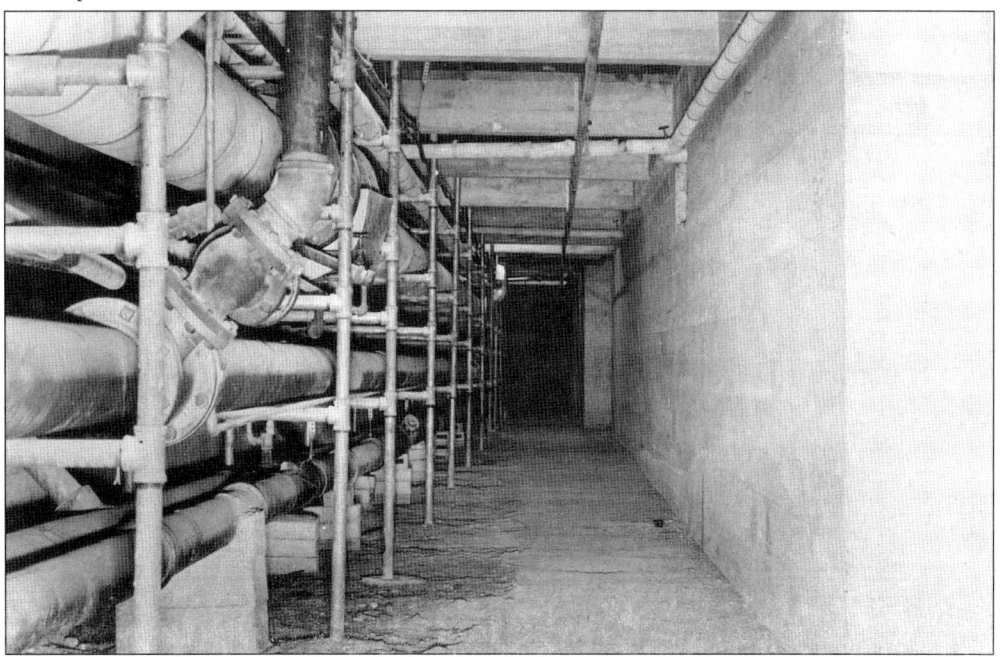

TUNNEL TO LAUNDRY, 1929. Almost unchanged today, the tunnel narrows in places and, because of newly added piping and wiring, is at times almost impassable. An iron gate was added at the powerhouse some years ago. It seems, after the site became a prison, several inmates used the tunnels to escape, forgetting that on the other end was the U.S. Navy.

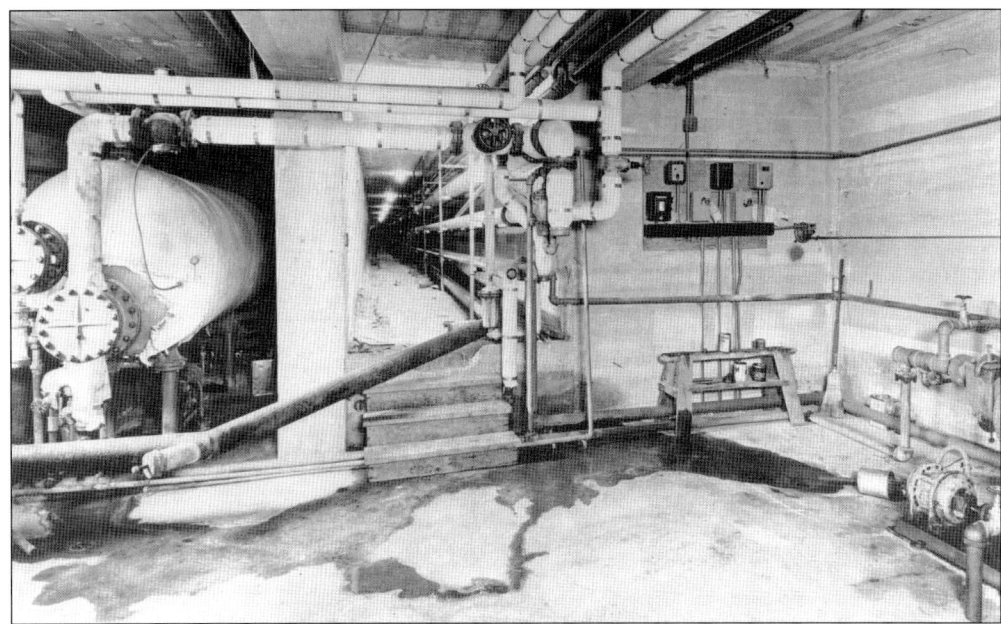

TUNNEL LAUNDRY ENTRANCE, C. 1930S. George Milner, former navy security guard, told of a smell coming from this tunnel entrance in the late 1940s. Investigating, he entered and found that the deeper he went in, the stronger the smell became until finally he was gagging. Turning a corner, he found a young sailor, rope around his neck, hanging from the low ceiling, another of the ghosts who supposedly walk the resort grounds?

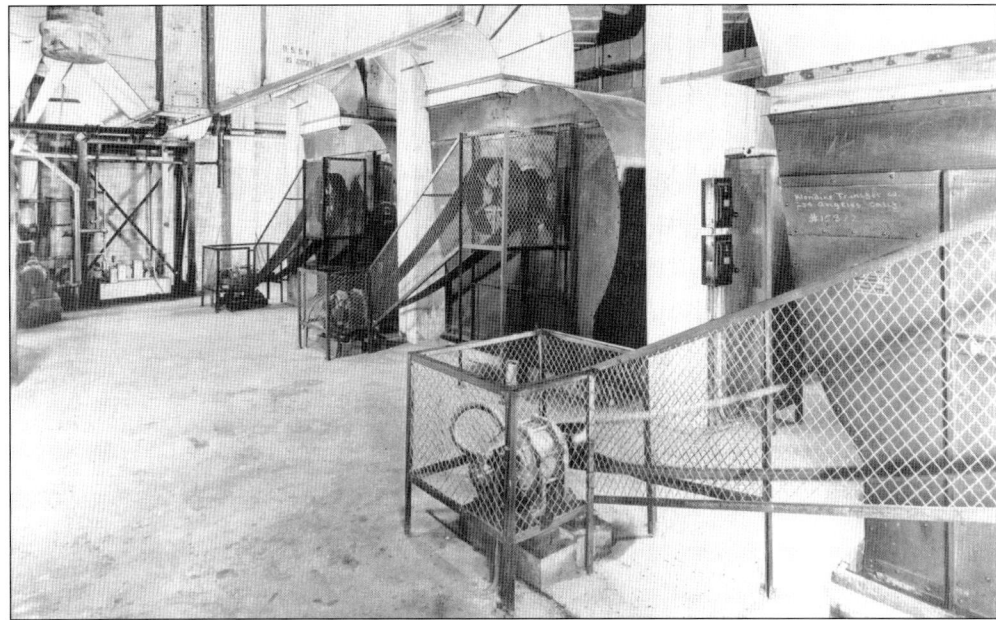

AIR COOLING SYSTEM, C. 1930S. Gigantic, state-of-the-art, evaporative coolers moderated temperature in the main gathering rooms of the inn (lobby, dining room, and lounge). A huge intake tunnel supplied fresh air as water was pumped into giant pans at the base of the coolers, which chilled the air that was then captured by huge cylindrical fans that in turn blew the "conditioned air" through elaborate ductwork.

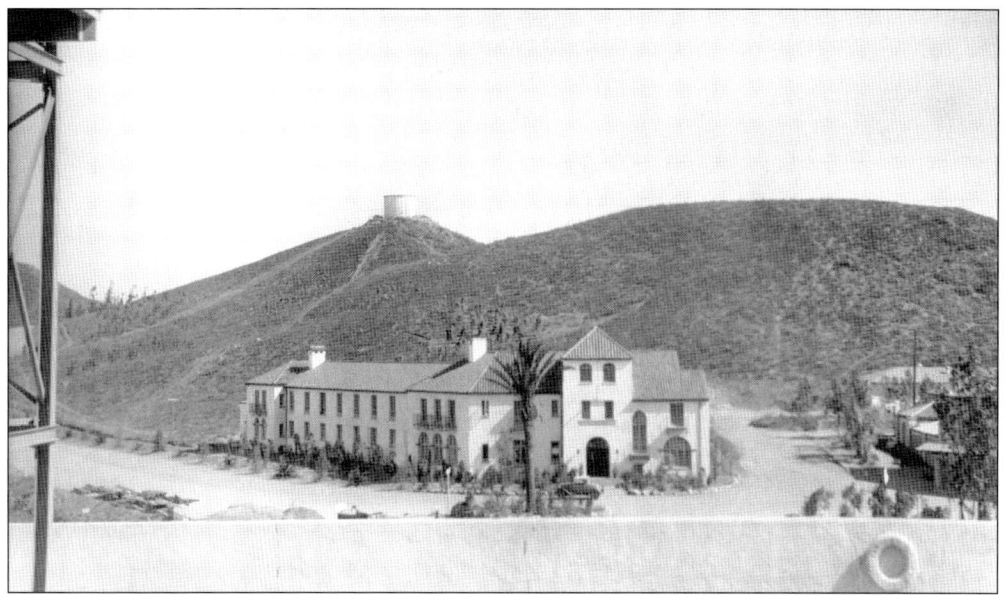

CHAUFFEURS' QUARTERS, C. 1930. The chauffeurs' quarters were designed by famed Californian architect G. Stanley Wilson as a mini hotel for guests' drivers; today the exterior is virtually unchanged but the interior is another story. Unfortunately, despite placement on the National Register of Historic Places, this gorgeous landmark may soon be torn down. Note the hills behind there is a tank holding the water supply for Norconian guests and the former site of several Easter Sunday services.

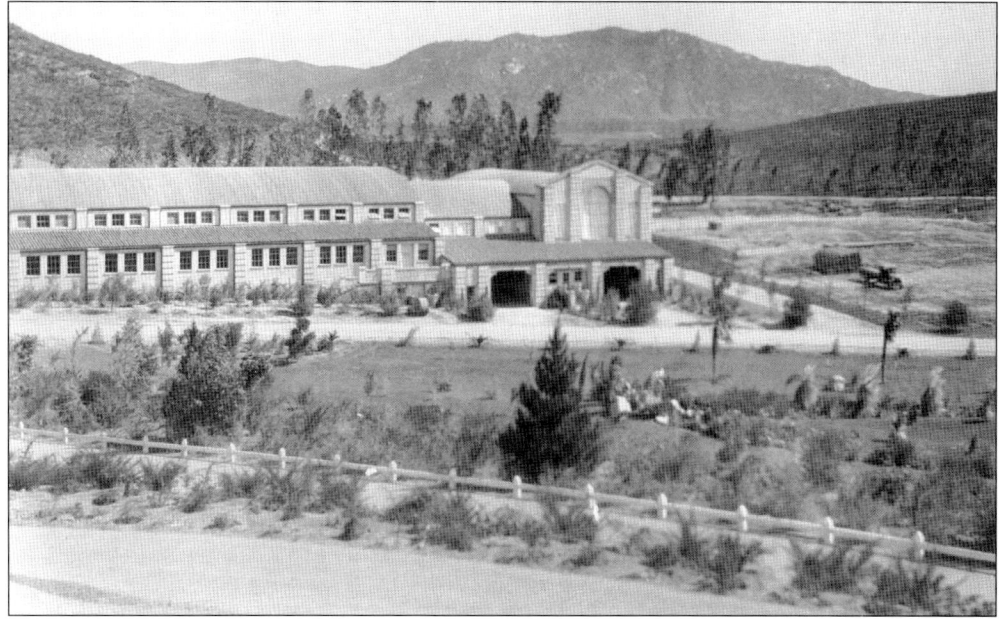

GARAGE/LAUNDRY BUILDING, C. 1930. Designed by G. Stanley Wilson, the garage was completed in 1929 and contained the greatest ground-floor space of any such building in Riverside County. The dimensions were 350 feet by 150 feet, translating to 52,500 square feet. Wilson himself directed the construction, overseeing a crew of 150 men. The building was constructed of steel and concrete at cost of $150,000 in 1929 dollars.

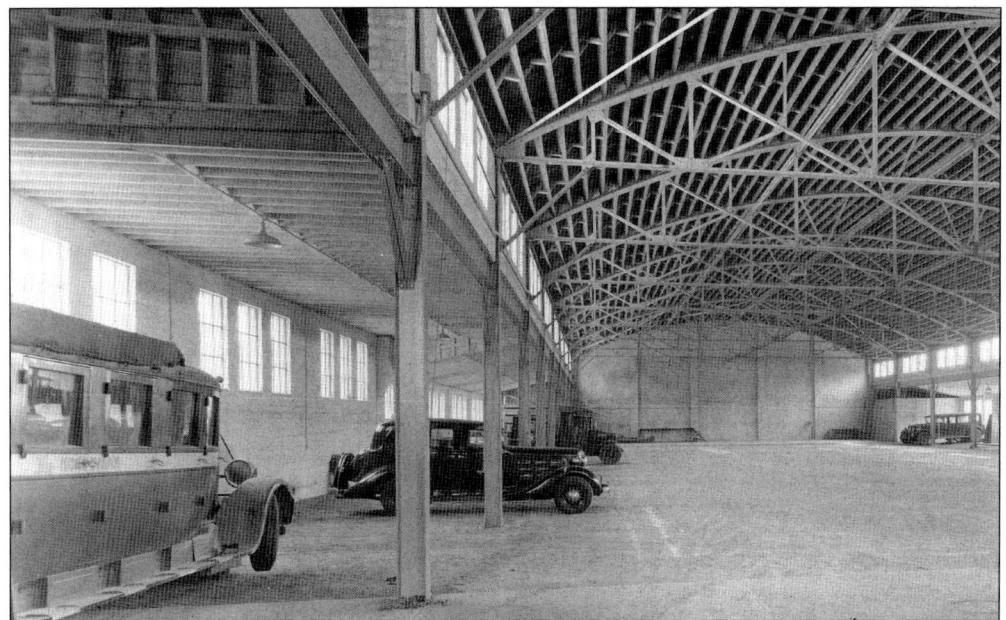

GARAGE INTERIOR, C. 1931. The structure was designed to be "fireproof" and held 150 cars, three service bays, a detailing area, and a complete gas station right at the front door. Many tales are proudly told of a father, uncle, or grandfather who tuned-up, tinkered-on, or just plain washed Clark Gable's car. For a star who could afford the best, he must have driven one filthy lemon after another.

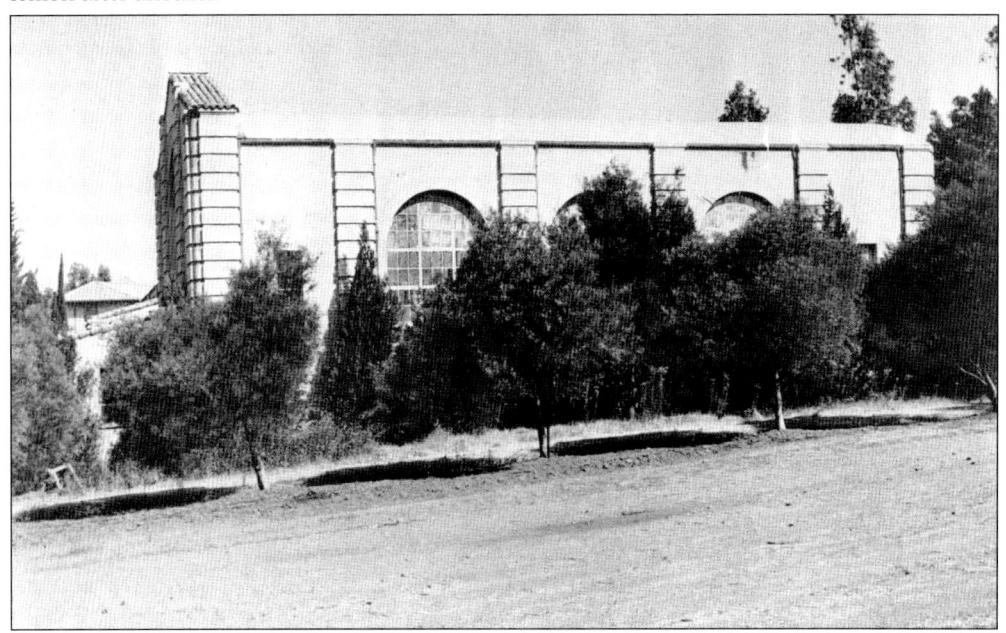

LAUNDRY NORTH VIEW, C. 1931. The building is of concrete and steel construction, a mix of art deco and Mediterranean architecture utilizing huge, sectional-plate windows, sectioned pillars, and ornate, red-tiled facing. Though in perfect condition, it was torn down in 1996 and was one of only two buildings not to survive from the original resort operation. Oddly, it was thought to be intact in 2000 and listed on the National Register of Historic Places.

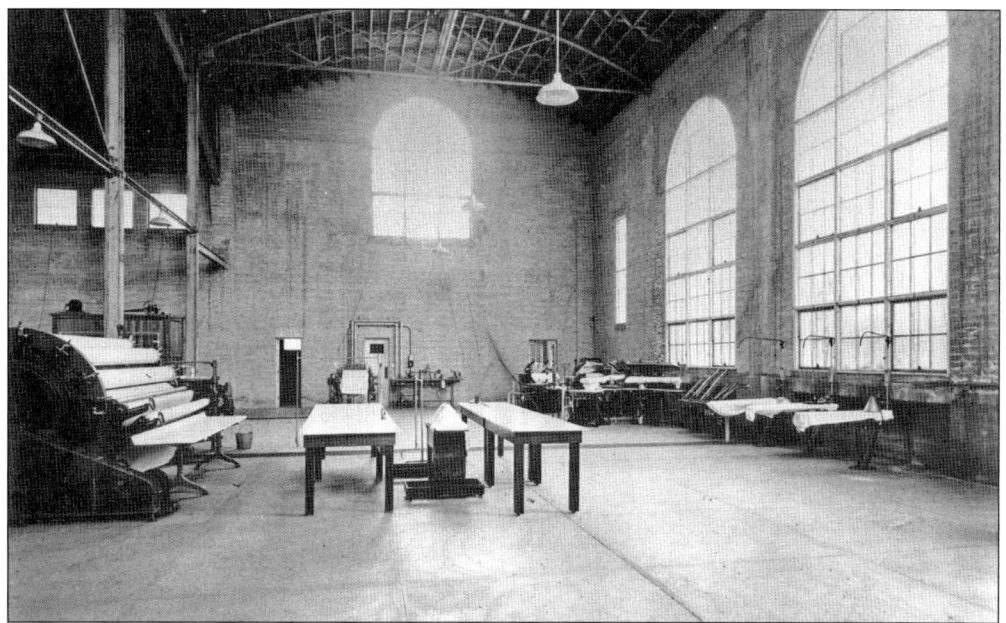

INTERIOR LAUNDRY EAST VIEW, C. 1930. Built with high ceilings and huge windows as heat relief devices and employing state-of-the-art Troy Manufacturing equipment, the laundry provided washing, pressing, dry cleaning, and folding services to guests as well as servicing the hotel-owned linens. A lone news article indicates that the underground service tunnel was a means to transport laundry to and from the hotel.

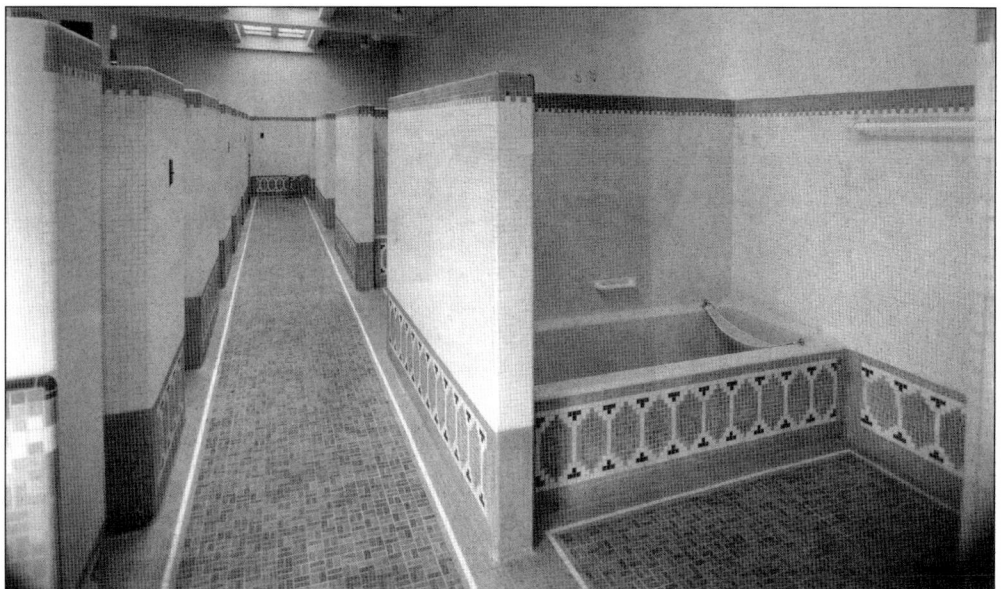

NORCONIAN BATHS, 1929. Advertising Roman, Turkish, and Russian baths for the discriminating guest, Rex Clark offered a simply immaculate and unbelievable complex. The above treatments (depending on the one purchased) required air- and steam-heated rooms; mineral baths; cold, cool, warm, and hot rooms; private massage rooms; gymnasium; sun rooms; and finally a cold, pure water plunge. Seen here are the still-existing, though non-operational, individual mineral tub chambers.

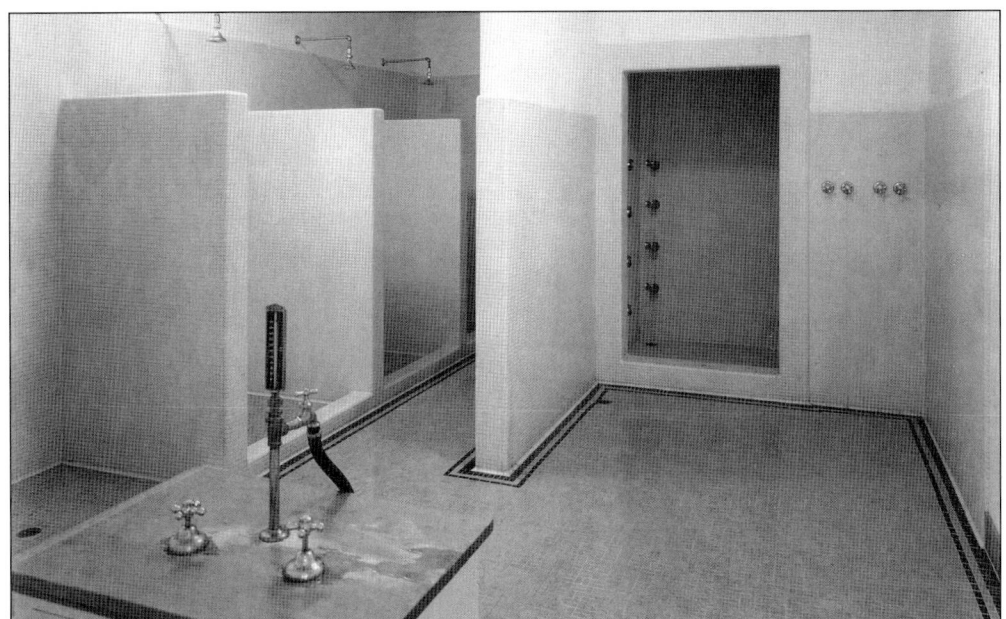

SHOWER ROOM, 1929. Rex Clark's daughter pointed out that perhaps a factor in the resort's failure was the mandate that entrance to the bath area required a deluge under the pictured 17-head shower—all under the supervision of an attendant. The bathhouse was separated into two identical facilities: a department for men and another for women. Amazingly, the shower is still there.

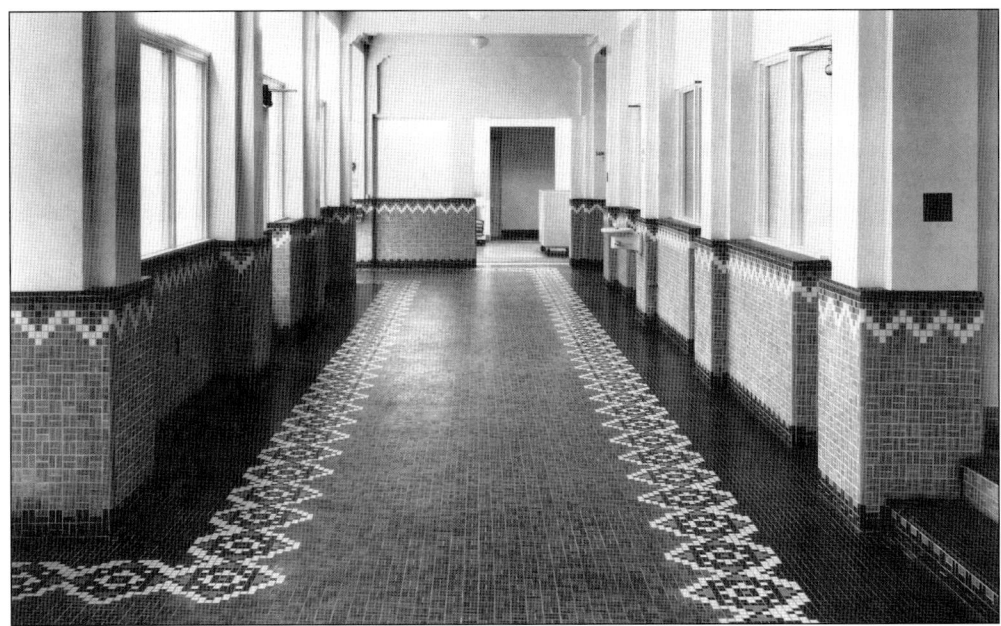

BATHHOUSE HALLWAY, 1929. In the finest tradition of Turkish baths, the Norconian employed exquisite tile work to decorate and keep sanitary the bathhouse. Each department had a single freshwater indoor plunge in the center (left) and was surrounded by "eight tiled Roman (sunken) tubs, eight tiled raised tubs, Russian vapor cabinets, leg baths, sitz tub, electric steam cabinets, massage tables, etc."

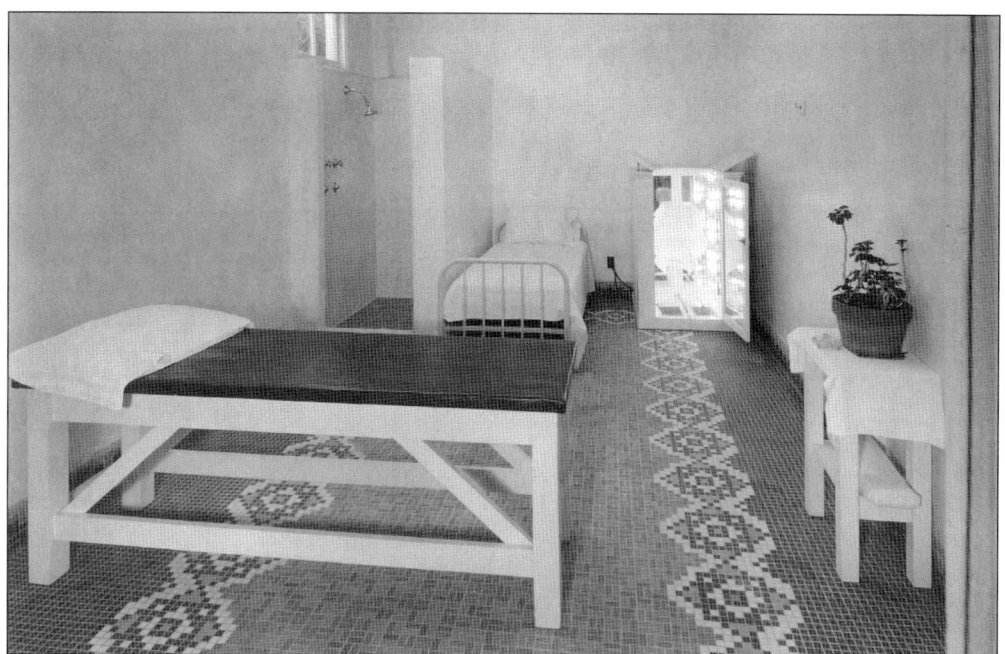

PRIVATE ELECTRIC CABINET ROOM, 1929. A guest would take a hot shower, dry, and seat themselves in the dry-heat electric cabinet; after sweating profusely, another hotter shower and a massage followed. Finally came a cold or hot shower (depending on the style of bath purchased) and a relaxing rest on the bed to the rear of the room. The cost—$1.

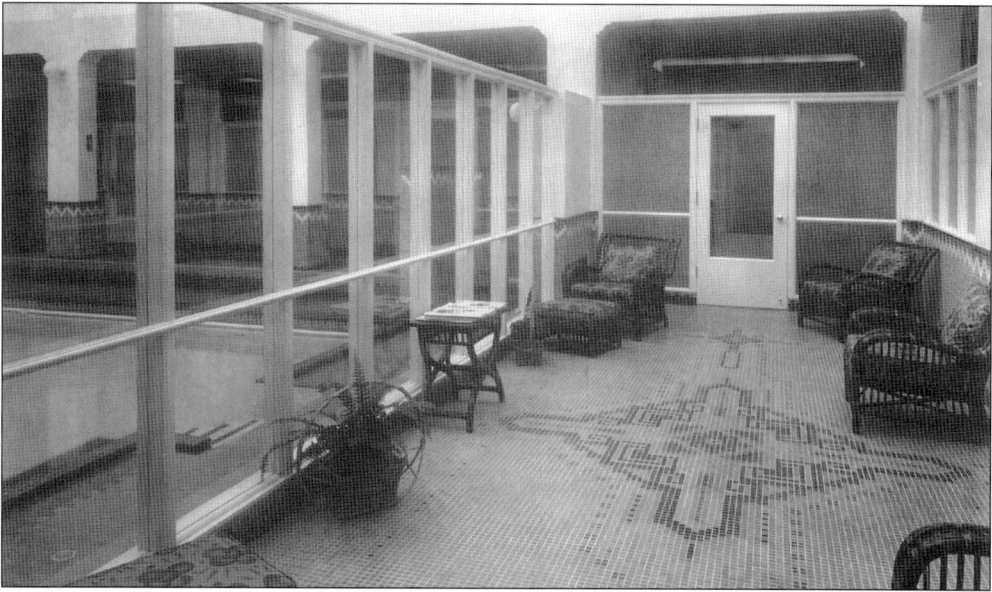

GLASS-ENCLOSED LOUNGES, 1929. A brochure description reads, "Restfully furnished lounges immediately adjoin the fresh water pools in both departments . . . a popular gathering place for guests to read or discuss the topics of the day." Rex Clark offered the latest rejuvenating "hydro-therapy techniques," stating that his mineral waters had received the "highest praise from medical authorities" and asserted the "indisputable fact that his hot springs were superior to those in Europe."

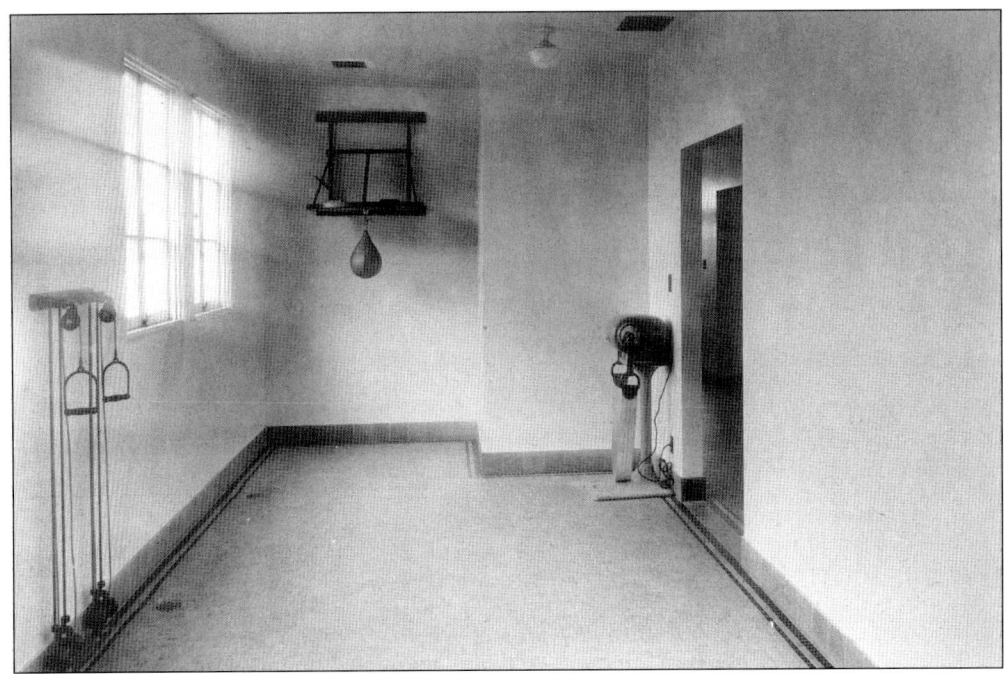

NORCONIAN GYMNASIUM, 1929. No reputable resort would be without a state-of-the-art gym, complete with wall-mounted pulley weights, a speed bag, and a machine, called a "slendorizer" designed to shake any excess weight right off the body. Clearly, exercise equipment of the 1920s was less sophisticated. It is interesting to note that there are many stories of the wonderful exercise facilities available at the Norconian.

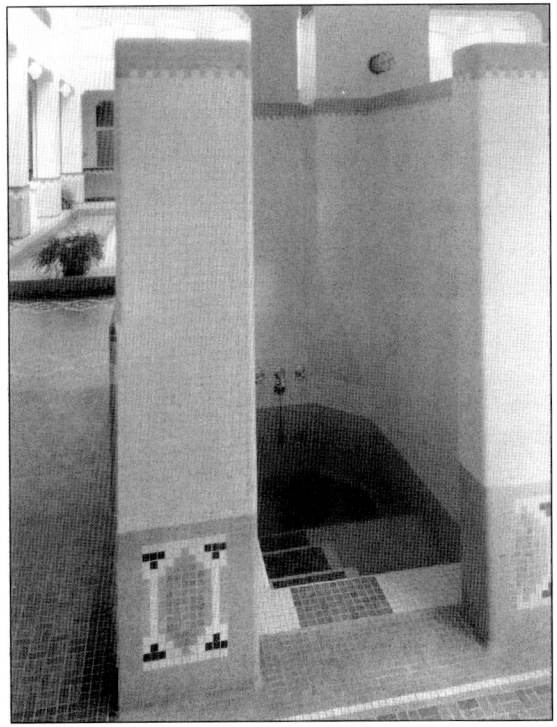

POOLSIDE HOT TUB, 1929. Patrons could alternate between a hot poolside bath and the cold, freshwater plunge, all under the supervision of patron health specialist Dr. Harris Garcelon, later of the Arrowhead Springs Hotel. Initially, the bath operations were entrusted to Mr. and Mrs. W. N. Russell (formerly employed by the largest bathhouse in Hot Springs, Arkansas) and later Axel Springborg of Glen Ivy Hot Springs fame in Corona, California.

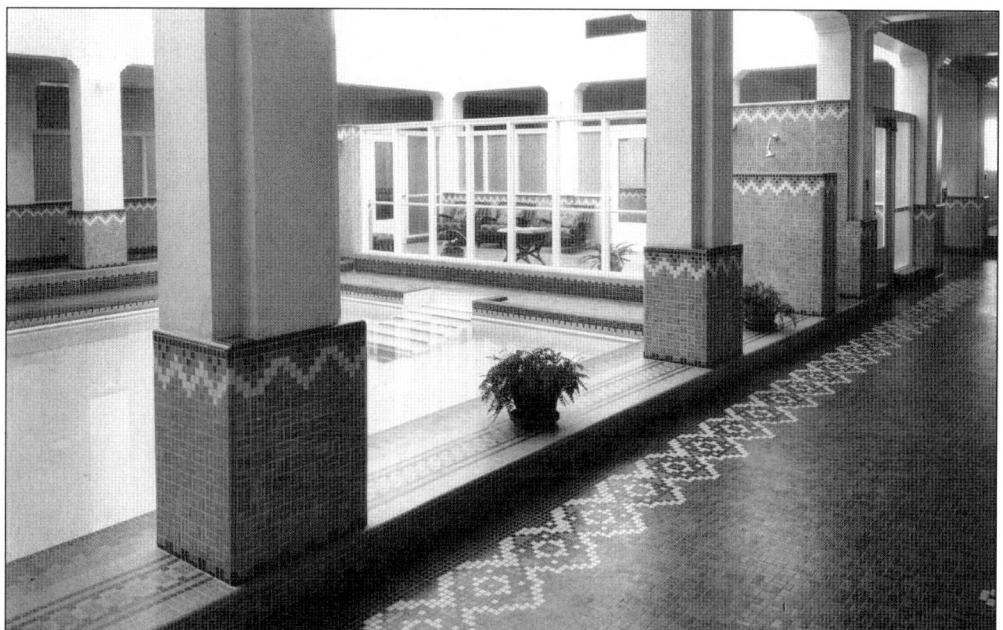

INDOOR FRESHWATER PLUNGE, C. 1929. According to sales material, after undergoing the therapeutic, heated by nature, 126 degree "Natural Hot Sulfur Baths—Superior to Any in the World" and becoming "super endowed with wonderful recuperative energy," a guest would end the experience with a cool, refreshing dip in the indoor freshwater plunge.

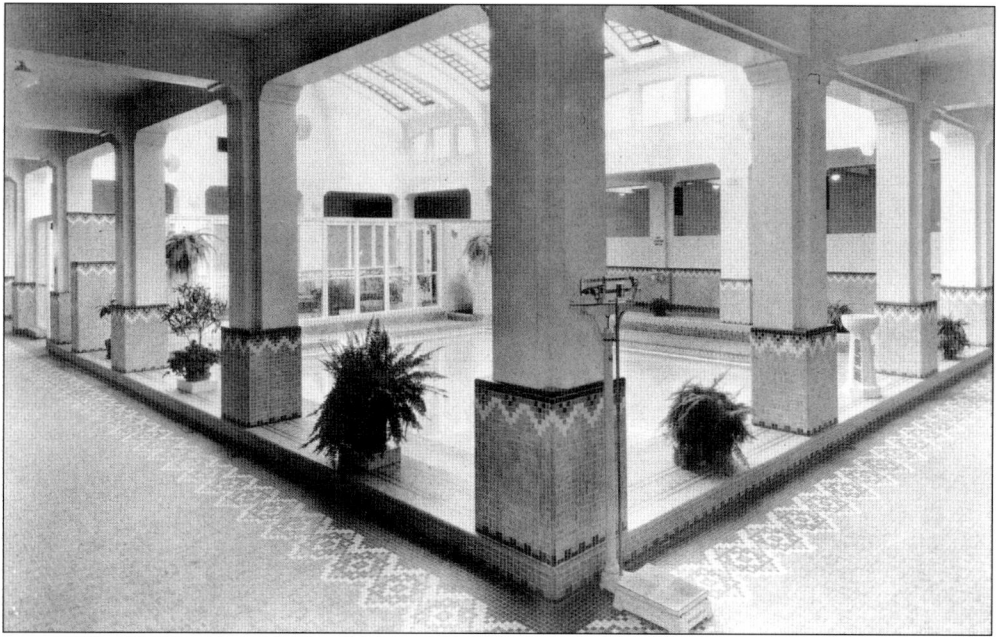

INDOOR POOL, 1929. An advertising brochure stated, "The natural hot alkaline sulphur water which gushes forth from Mother Earth possesses properties of the utmost desirability," and all departments use "our famous radio-active hot mineral water, which has no free carbon dioxide (Radioactivity 3.8 Mache units per liter)." A "complete Smith-Emery chemical analysis" was available upon request.

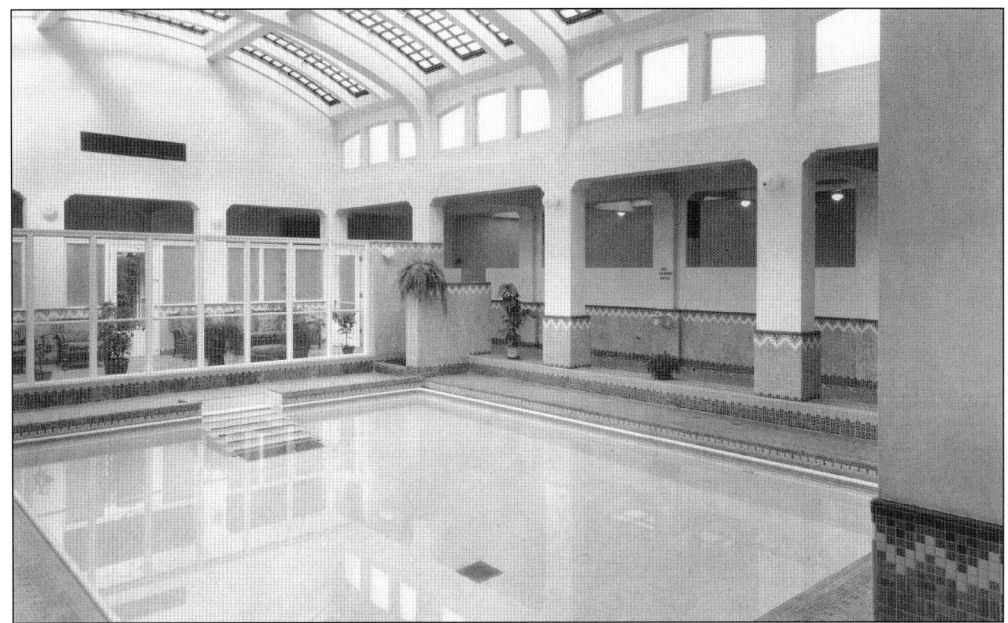

INDOOR FRESHWATER PLUNGE, C. 1929. Up until the early 1990s, prison officials enjoyed the indoor pools. Today the glass ceilings have been painted over, walls have been erected, and the pools covered to make floors. Surrounded by stunning tile work, majestic arches, and sun lounges, two new rooms were created for various functions of a prison. But, underneath it all, the pools are still there.

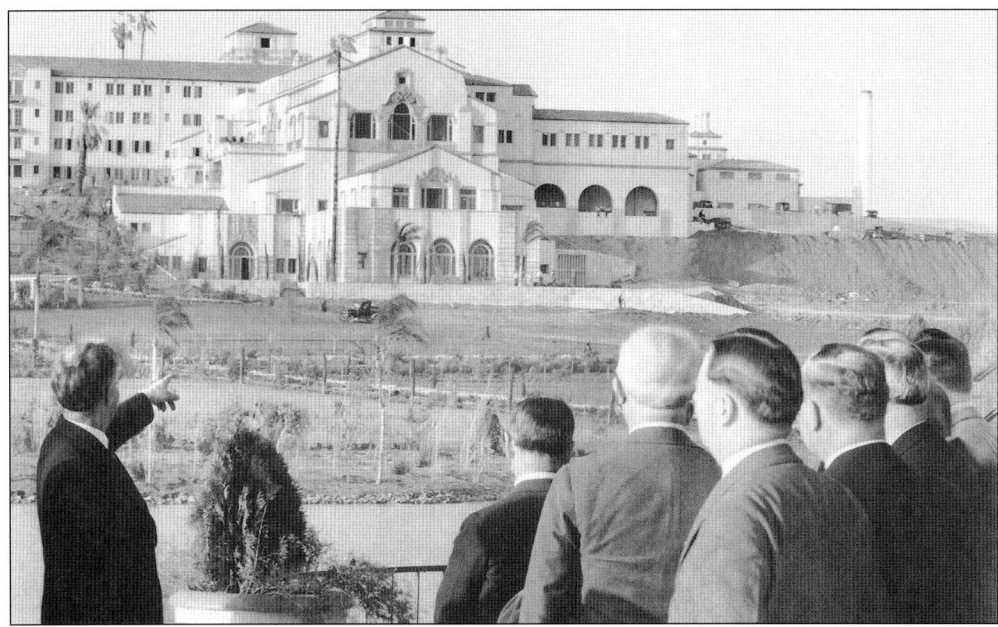

THE UNVEILING, C. 1929. Rex Clark points at his almost-finished masterpiece: the Norconian. Millions had been spent to create what was considered at the time to be an architectural wonder and likely one of the finest full-service resorts on the West Coast. Mere months after this photograph was taken, Rex Clark's world would be rocked by the Great Depression and his "monument to health" labeled "Rex's Folly."

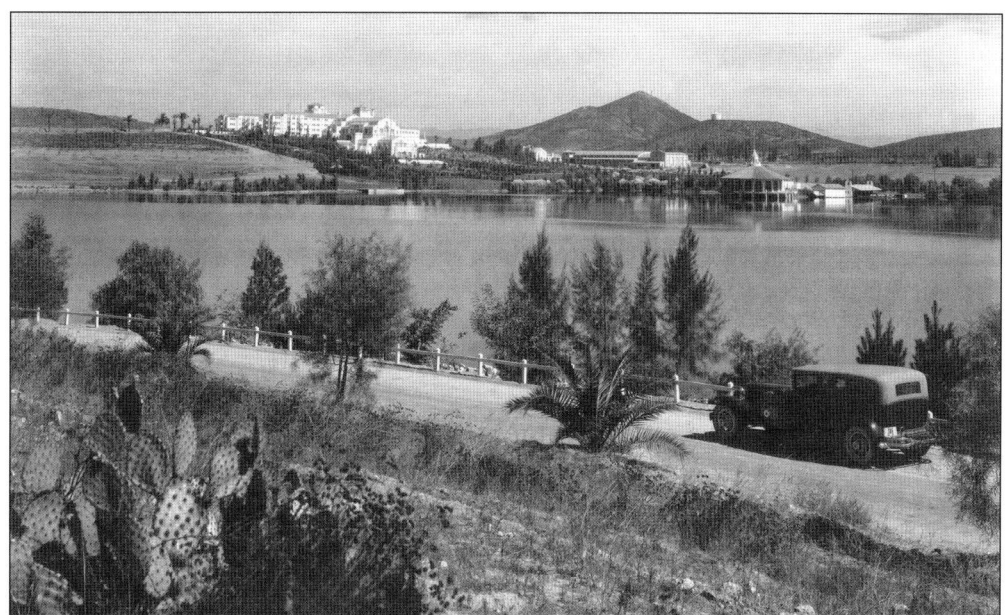

THE LAKE NORCONIAN CLUB, C. 1930. Press releases heralding the "grand and glorious unveiling" were issued in newspapers from San Diego to Los Angeles, 6,800 invitations were sent, and politicians, business leaders, movie stars, and just about all of Riverside County's best and brightest had made reservations. The Resort Supreme after much anticipation was about to open in the middle of the poultry capital of California.

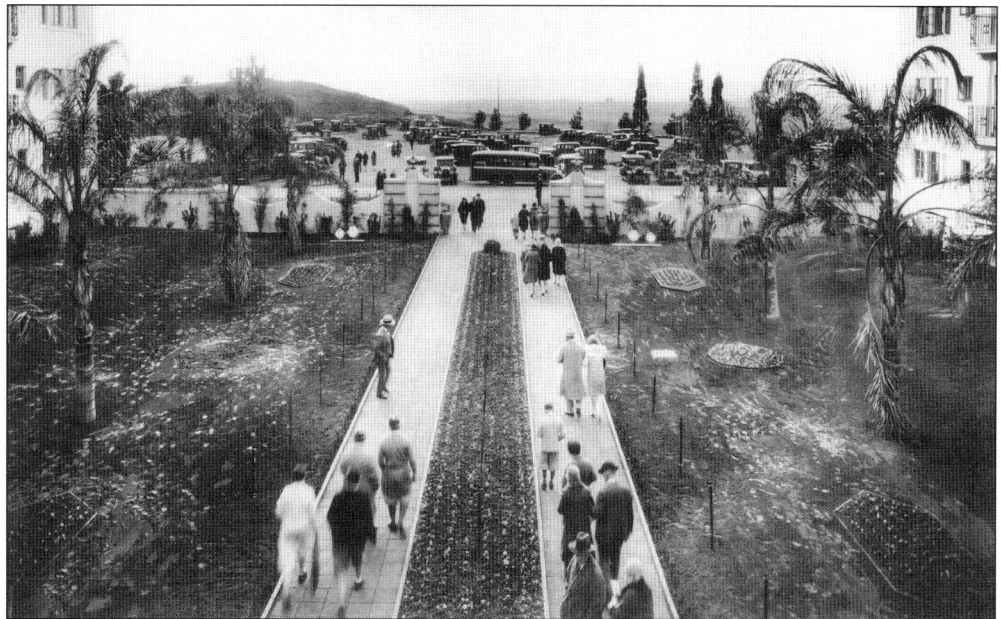

HOTEL MEN'S ASSOCIATION PREVIEW, JANUARY 1929. The first to see the completed resort were fellow Californian hotel owners. "Large motor transit busses" transported over 100 lodge owners from Los Angeles. First stop was the Fuller Rancho, where Transport Company owner O. B. Fuller himself showed the guests the string of riding horses to be used at the resort; later was a dinner of duck in the Casino and a grand tour.

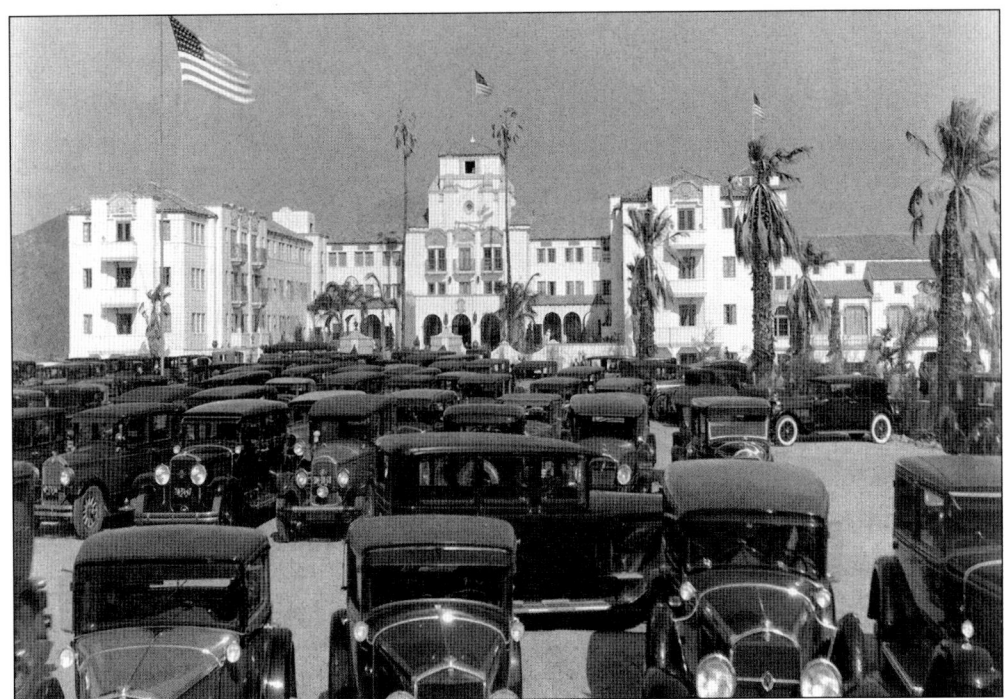

GRAND OPENING, FEBRUARY 2, 1929. Though this photograph shows not a cloud, according to the *Los Angeles Times*, rain kept opening day guests to around 1,000. However, the *Corona Independent* reported, "Thousands of awestruck guests were in attendance." One attendee 80 years later stated, "After I couldn't eat anymore me and my friends played hide and seek around all them cars."

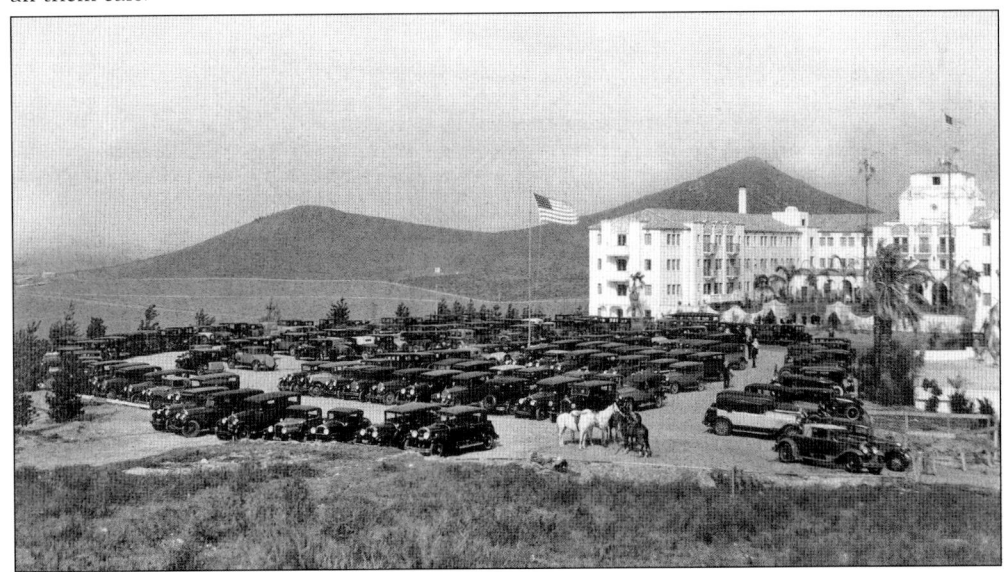

OPENING DAY, 1929. Note the horses hitched toward the front of the parking lot. Initially, as mentioned before, the Fuller Rancho was to provide a string of horses to quench the equestrian appetites of guests. However, by the early 1930s, longtime Corona resident Sam Markowitz was furnishing horses from his small ranch. A vivid memory was Rex Clark's lack of payment, not unusual, it would seem.

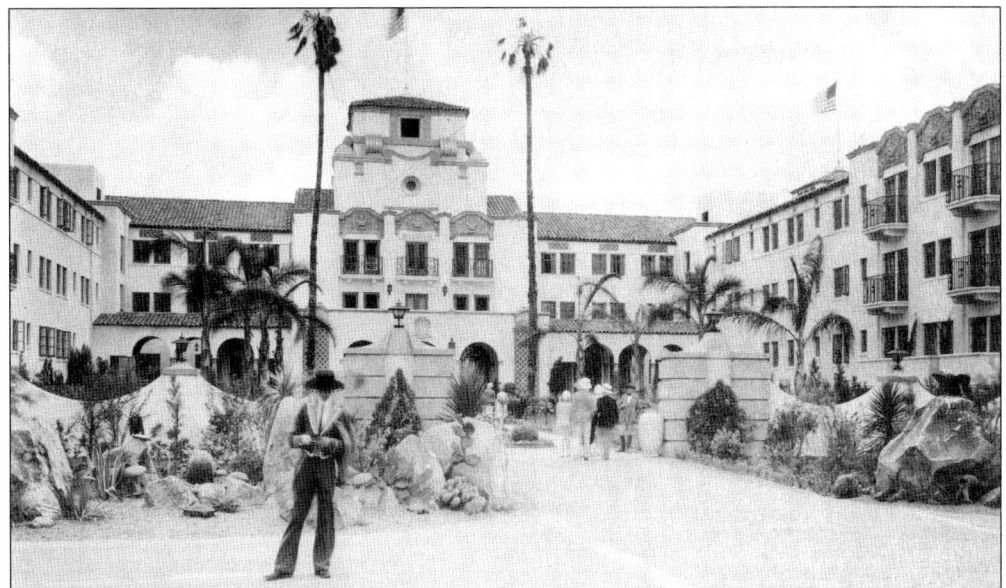

NORCONIAN FRONT ENTRANCE, 1929. The *Daily Independent* reported, "People were dazzled and amazed at the splendor of the magnificent structures, the acres of beautiful flowers and the surrounding country which has made a setting for the most delightful and unusual resort in the West, where climate, scenery and hospitality are the best." Longtime Corona resident Ray Harris said, "We'd never seen anything like it; it was unbelievable."

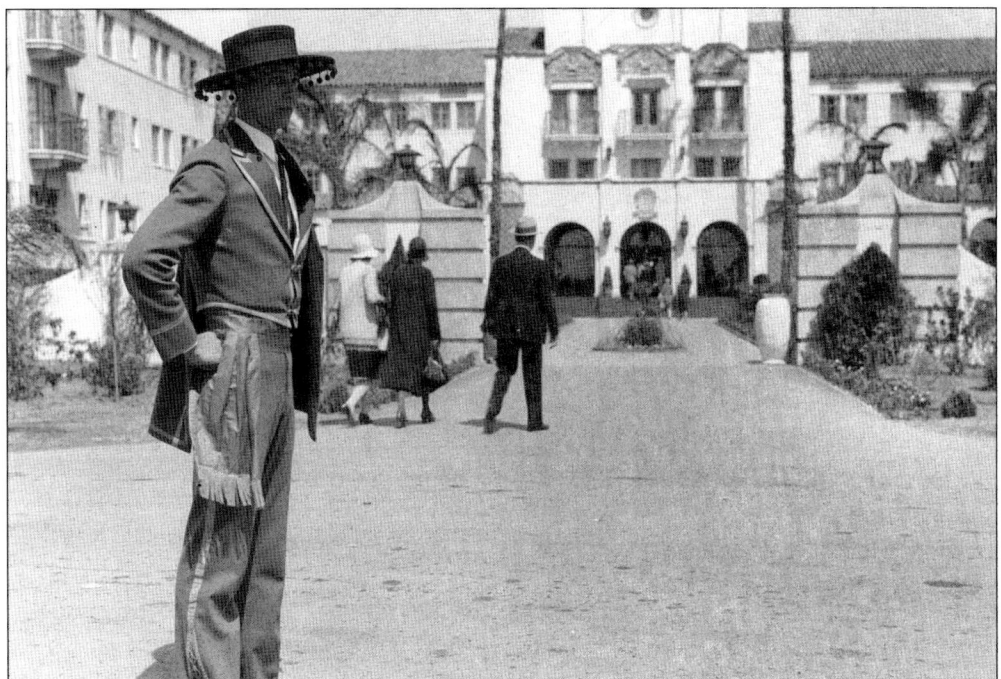

PARKING ATTENDANT, FEBRUARY 2, 1929. Larry Key, longtime Corona resident, attended the opening with his parents. "I remember those hats with tassels, not much else, but I remember those hats," he said. Southwestern mixed with Mediterranean was the theme of the day. Guests were entertained by strolling Spanish troubadours and beautiful girls in Spanish attire.

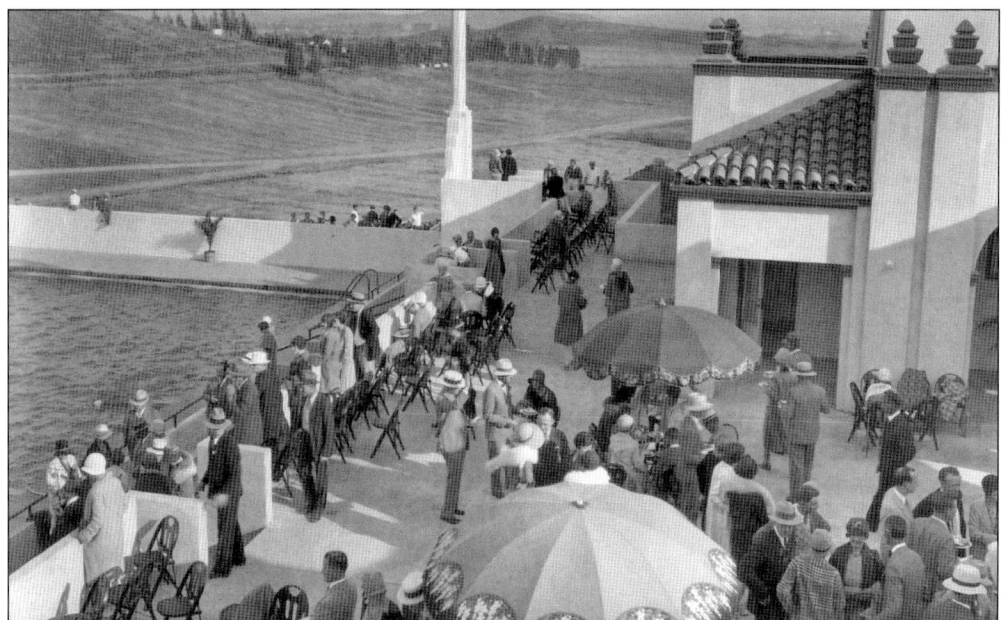

OPENING DAY, PLUNGE PATIO, C. 1929. Members of the Los Angeles Athletic Club, many of whom were recently returned members of the U.S. Olympic team, treated guests munching on yet another buffet to diving and swimming exhibitions. On the golf course, some of the finest golfers in California were demonstrating their prowess with exhibitions of putting and driving. Buster Keaton, Stan Laurel, and Hal Roach were all reported in attendance.

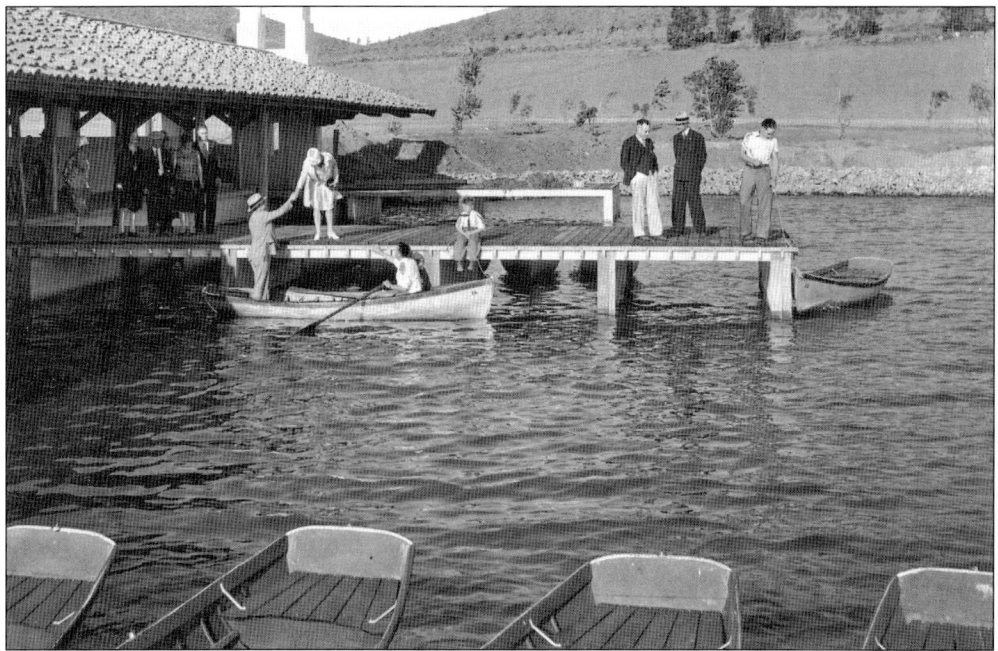

BOAT DOCK, C. 1929. Guests were invited to row about the lake in either a canoe or rowboat, putt about in a motorboat, take in the hydroplane races, and watch water board and skiing demonstrations. Of course, one could simply take a stroll around the 60-acre lake as the music from one of two orchestras hired for the day wafted across the water.

Furs, Pearls, and Girls, 1929. Rex Clark always saw to it that beautiful young ladies were in attendance at all Norconian functions. On opening day, Mack Sennett was said to have supplied several "bathing beauties" to liven things up. Behind this lovely lady is the main doorway leading into the hotel, looking exactly as it does today.

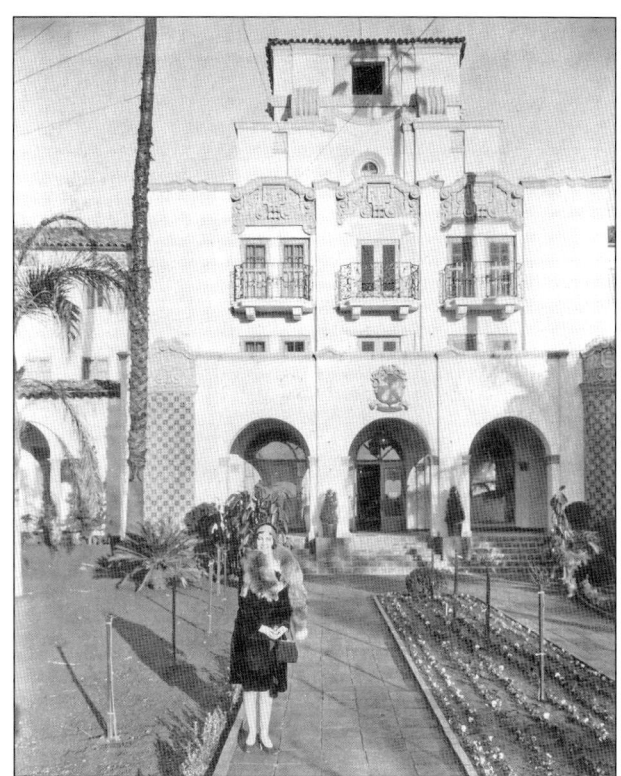

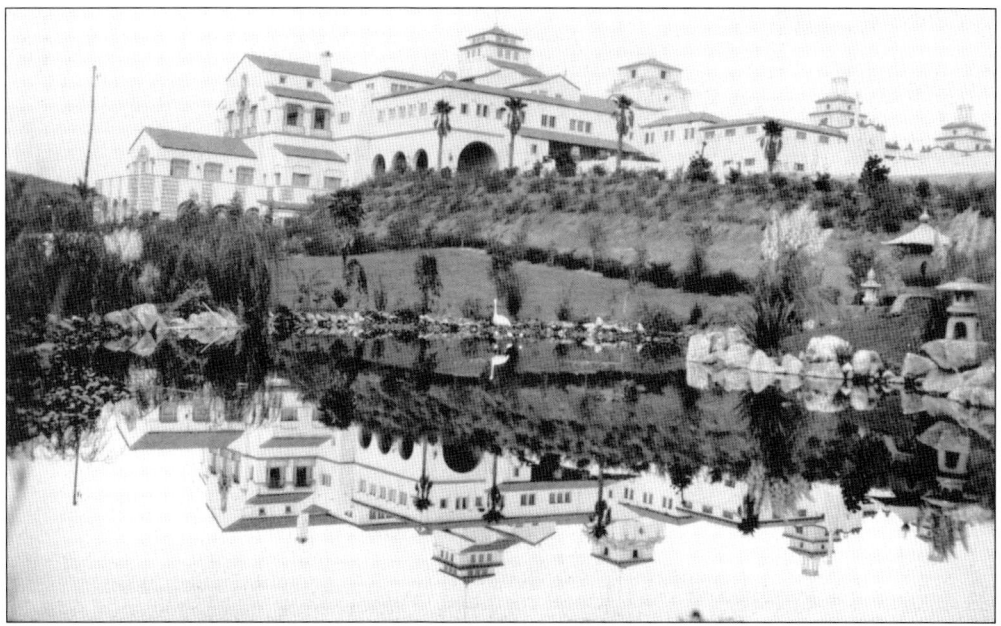

Northwest View, 1929. This view shows the Norconian exactly as architect Dwight Gibbs envisioned the hotel: pure white and gleaming from atop the hill. Over the years, geese and ducks began to include the ponds and lake in their migration patterns. A favorite pastime of old-time residents was blasting one's auto horn while driving through the circular tunnel (center left) that led to the hotel entrance.

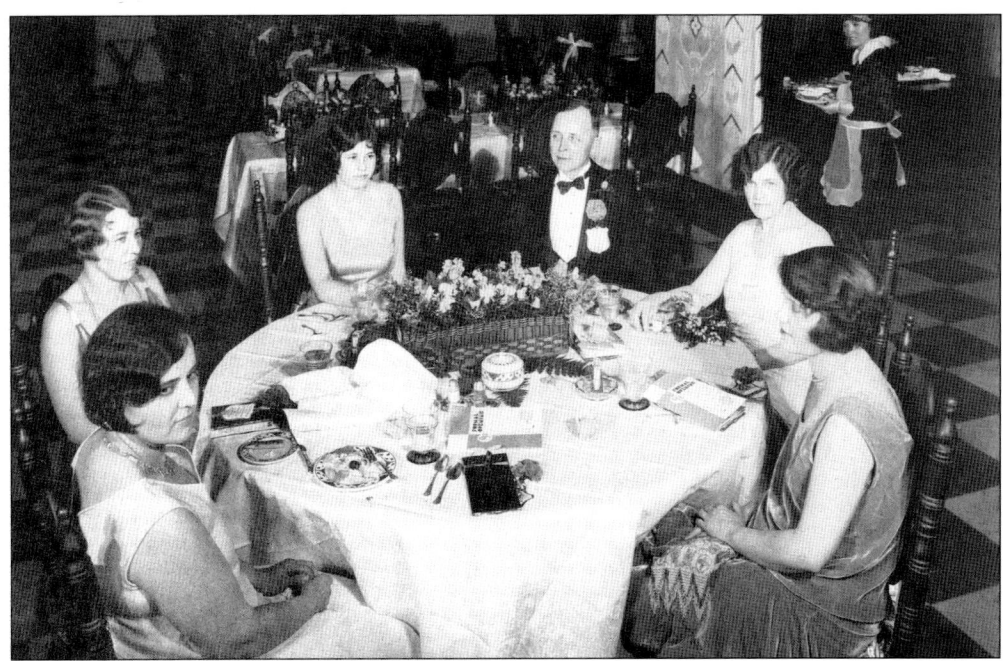

OPENING NIGHT DINNER, 1929. Tuxedoed, bejeweled, be-gowned, and fur-covered attendees were served dinner in both the dining hall and ballroom. Pictured are unidentified guests seated in the middle of the dining room with opening night programs in front of them. Strolling troubadours, entertainers, and dancers weaved between tables and passed out party favors to every guest.

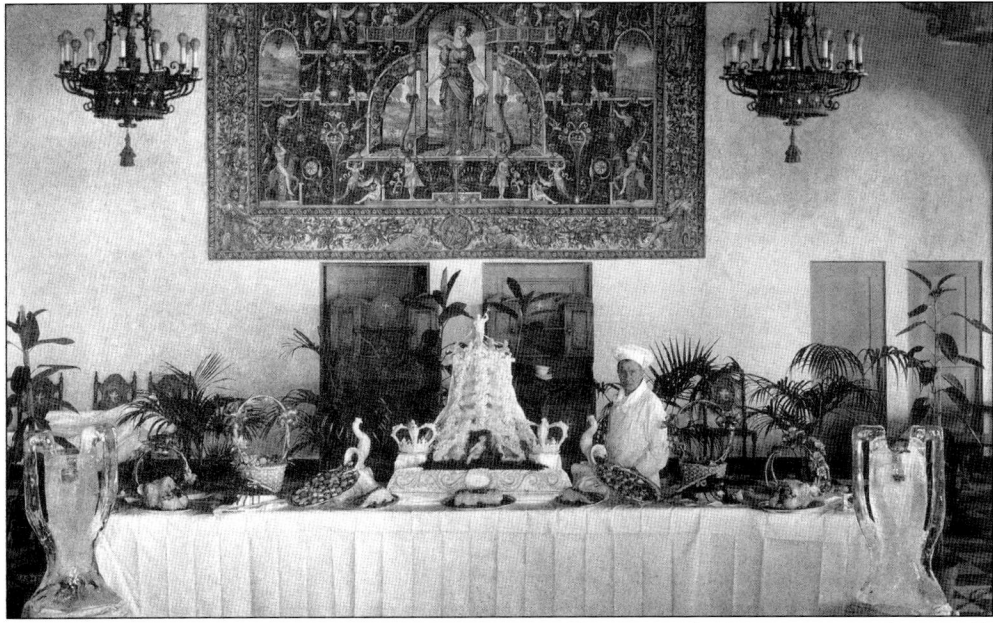

OPENING NIGHT FEAST, 1929. The menu, as prepared by master chef Harry Massey (pictured), was spectacular with dishes from Germany, France, Sweden, and Spain. Rex Clark's joke was that the menu was also written in those languages and a prize was offered to the guest who provided the "correct translation" of the "gustatorial demonstration." Guests dined on lobster, chicken, and Café "Moka."

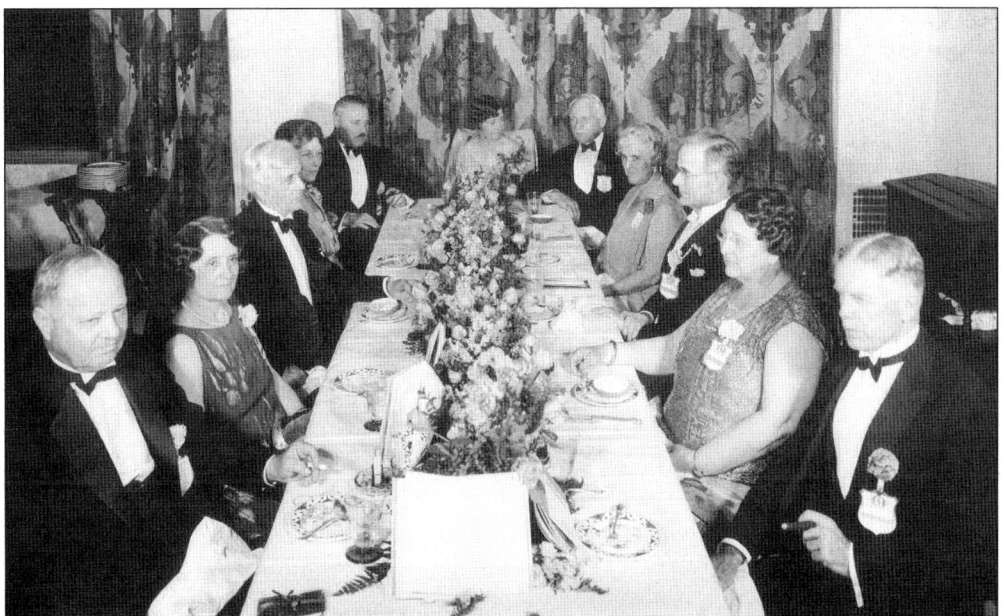

REX CLARK OPENING NIGHT, 1929. Pictured on the right is Captain Gully, to his right is his wife, Edna. Next is the proprietor of the Norconian, Rex Clark. At the head of the table is Grace Clark, apropos as it was very likely her money and connections that financed the entire venture. The other male guests appear repeatedly in early Norco photographs; unfortunately, to date they are unidentified and their moment in the sun forgotten.

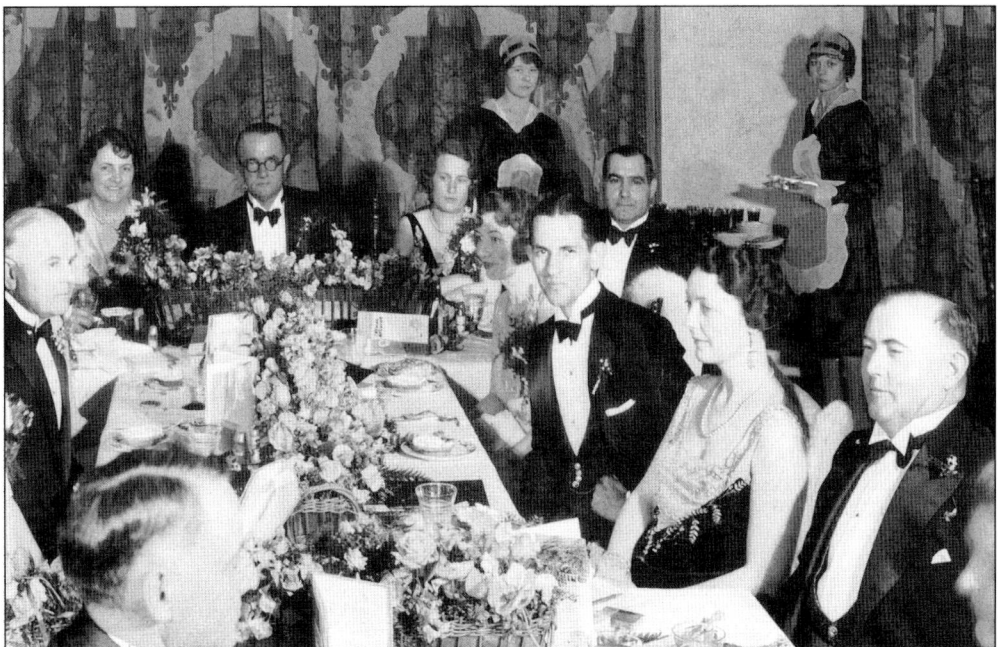

ON TOP OF THE WORLD, 1929. Rex Clark planned for a community of luxury homes built to accommodate the "restricted class" to surround the Norconian. However, it was not to be, as the nation was about to be tumbled into the worst economic pit of its history, Rex Clark was getting a divorce, and the resort was already in financial trouble.

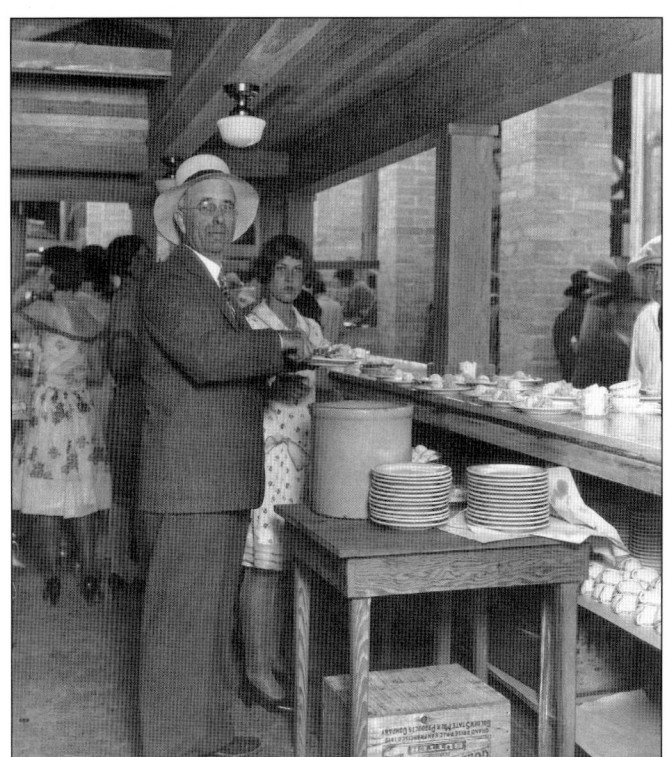

REX CLARK, C. 1930S. Ellen Revelle stated, "Dad was very concerned that guests were having a good time and while in the dining room, would make a point of going to every table to say, 'hello.'" Here Clark dishes up pie and ice cream in the snack bar area above the pool. Behind the scenes were lawsuits, mechanics liens, the IRS, and little cash.

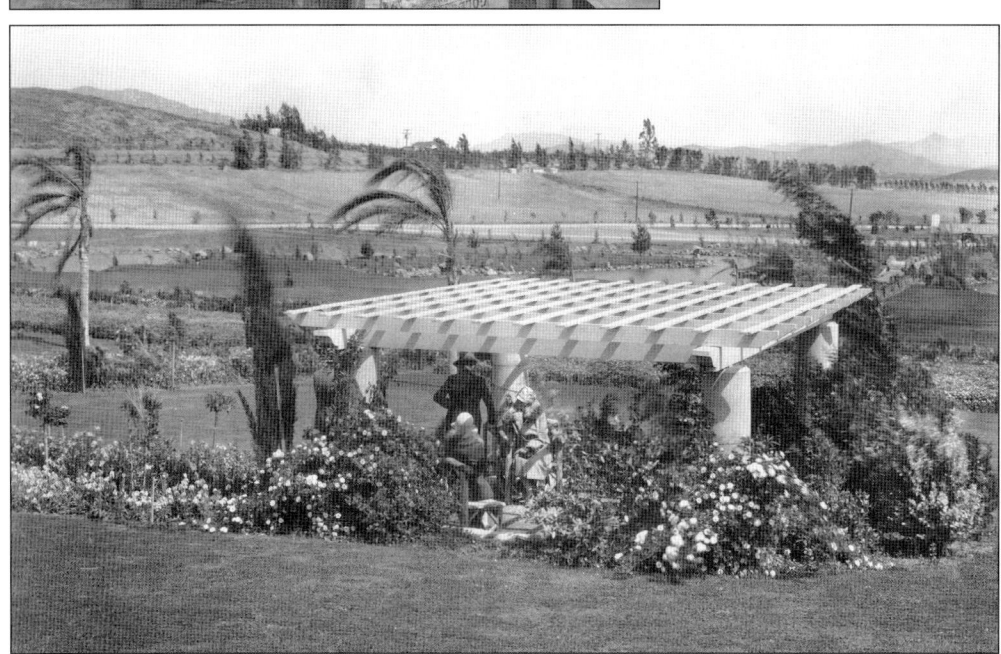

NORCONIAN GROUNDS, C. 1929. Strategically placed on trails throughout the grounds were gazebos and airy structures where strolling guests could rest while enjoying the rose gardens and hundreds of different kinds of shrubs, plants, and terraced ponds. Surprisingly, two of those structures still exist, as does much of the original landscaping, trail markers, bridge, and ponds—a little worse for the wear but still there to enjoy.

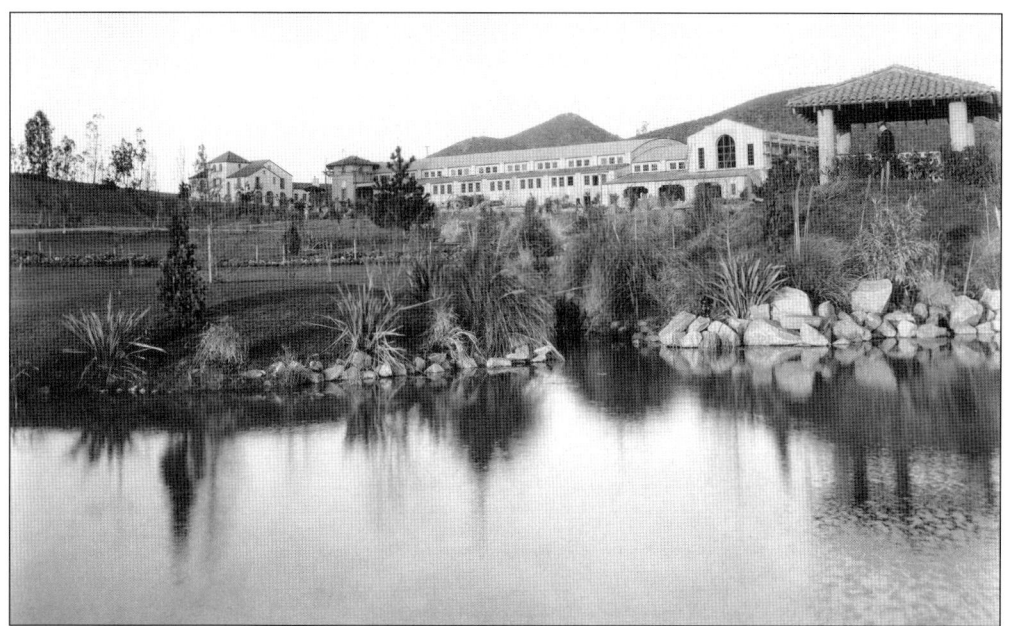

LAUNDRY/GARAGE COMPLEX, C. 1930. Rex Clark stands in a gazebo looking at the almost completed laundry and garage in the background. From the beginning, rumors circulated about Clark's financial situation, and there was curiosity about where his money came from. In December 1929, Clark vigorously denied he was closing his club or that he was selling out to chewing gum magnate William Wrigley.

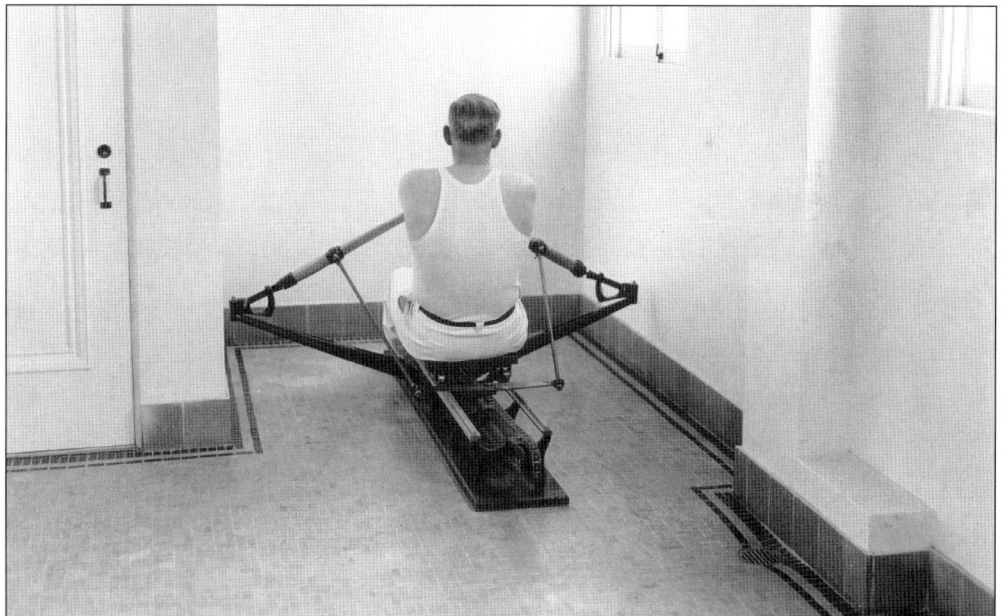

GUEST WORKING OUT, C. 1932. By today's standards, the Norconian gymnasium was quite primitive, but in 1932, it was right in line with Rex Clark's dream to build a resort devoted to good health and fitness. An interesting mystery, tennis is mentioned frequently in brochures, newspapers, and speeches by Clark, but no evidence of courts can be found. Where did tennis greats Bill Tilden and Helen Wills play?

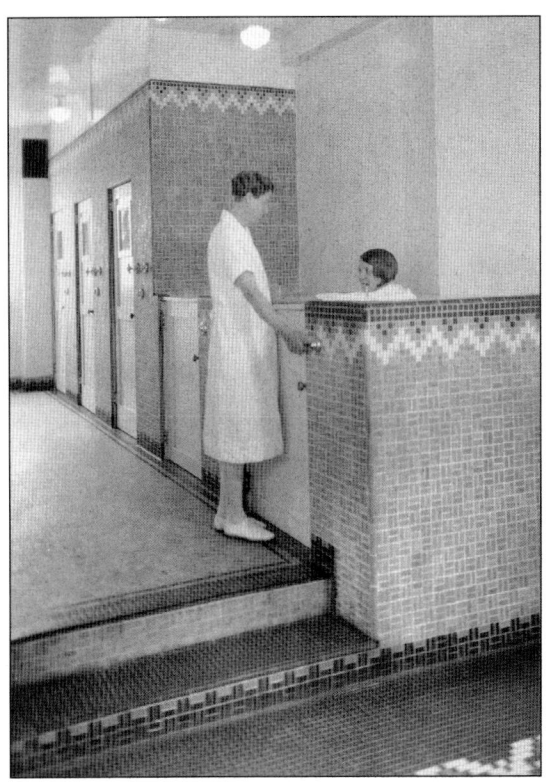

TILED STEAM CABINET, C. 1930. Attendants were specifically trained to apply hot packs and wraps and give massages, as well as see to it that guests had towels, drinking water, and other necessities. Here a patron sits in a "sweat box." The three booths to the back are private steam saunas. After becoming a navy hospital, these facilities were utilized to treat wounded soldiers. Though not operational, these baths still exist.

SOUTH VIEW, C. 1929. Through a dining room window can be seen the Pavilion and as far as Corona. To this day, every window of the inn has a view of either mountain ranges, the lake, or courtyards that at one time were stunningly kept. Rex Clark insisted on daily fresh flowers and plants directly from his own nursery to be displayed at all times throughout every building in the resort.

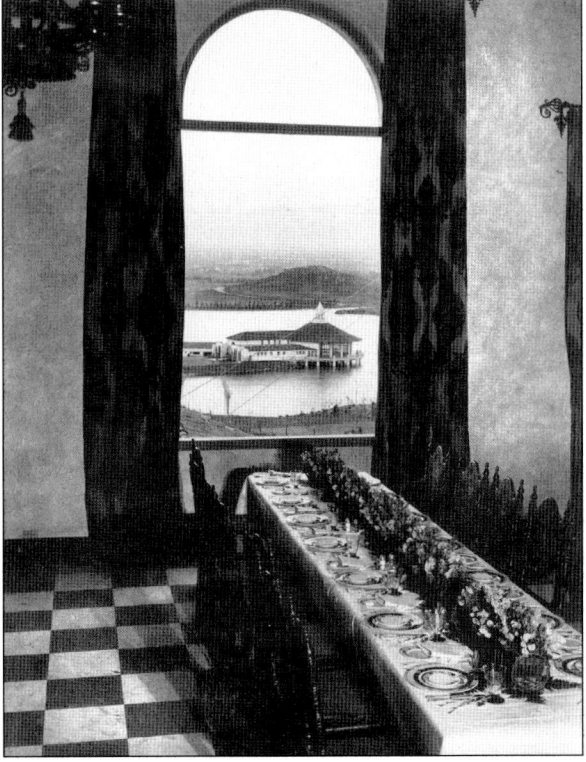

88

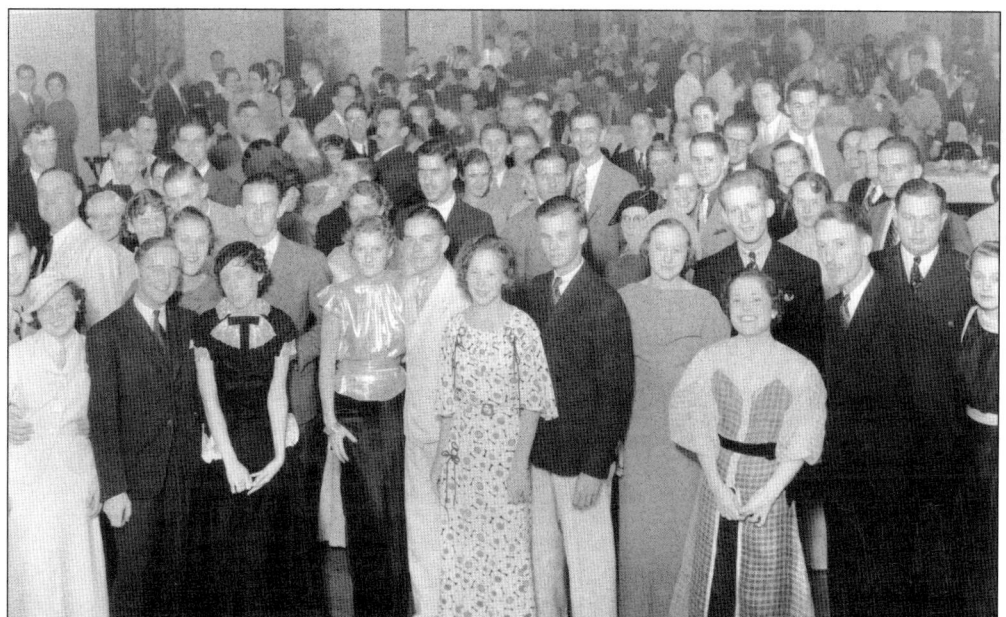

RIVERSIDE COUNTY BANKERS, 1935. Secretary associations, Lions Clubs, Corona Dunkers, Shriners, various law enforcement agencies, law associations, and medical groups rented, at one time or another, portions of (dining room, Pavilion, ballroom) or the entire facility to hold all manner of parties and celebrations. This particular dinner/dance is being held in the Norconian ballroom. (Los Angeles Public Library.)

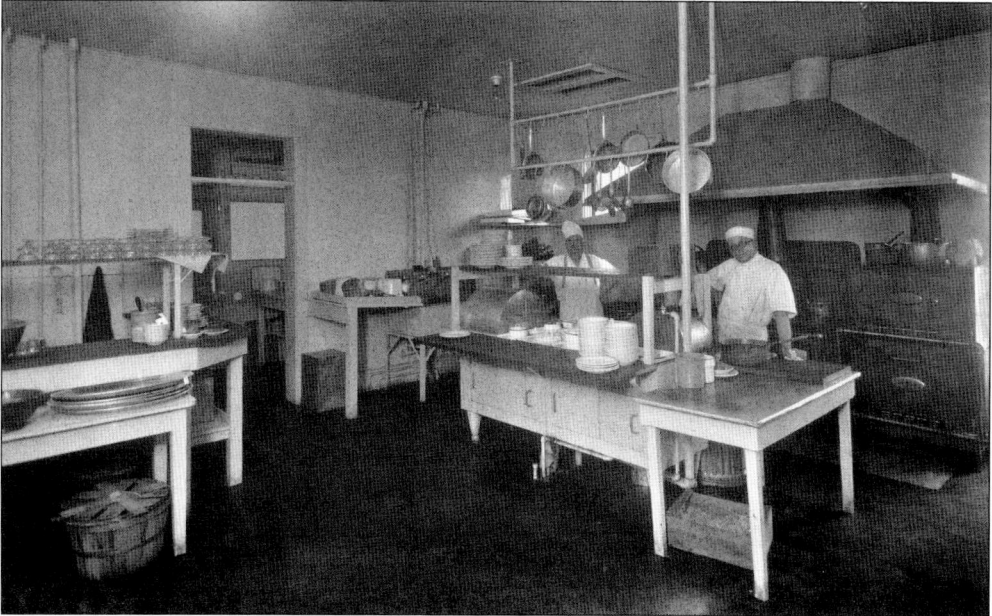

KITCHEN HELP, C. 1930. In the late 1930s, Clark would employ primarily cheap Filipino help to do behind-the-scenes labor and grunt work. However, that was not the case during the first years of the resort. Here two gentlemen pose in their spotless culinary "preparatory"; it appears this was a pastry kitchen where Norco's famous apple pies were prepared for the "discriminating guest of the Norconian."

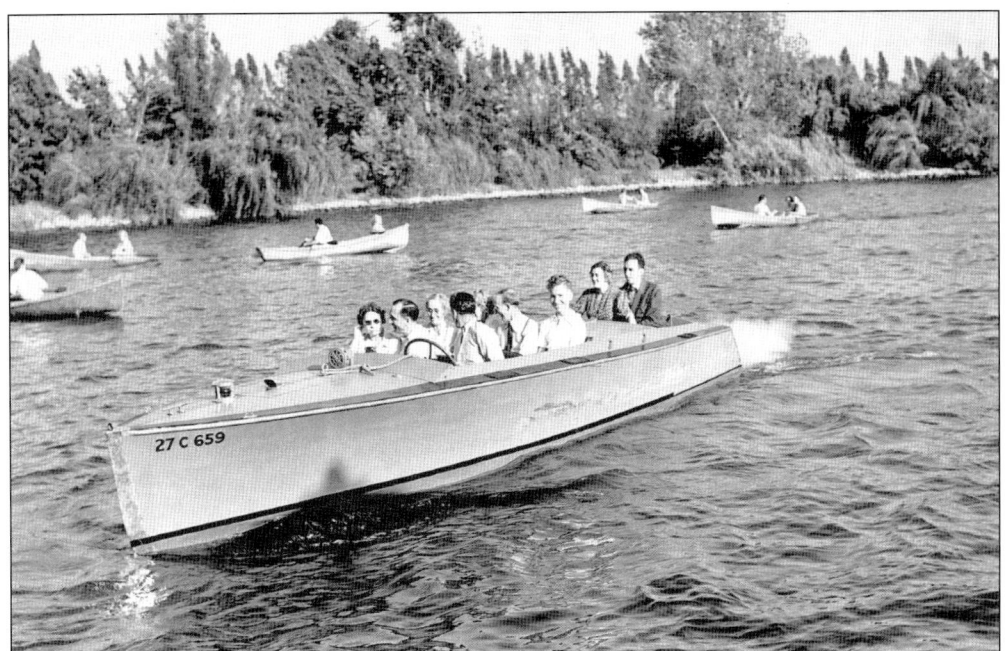

MOTOR BOATING ON THE NORCONIAN LAKE, C. 1938. In the opening days of the resort, William Clark, youngest son of Rex, was in charge of all activities at the lake. When the Norconian closed, he ran a water taxi service transporting passengers to the off-shore gambling ships on the California coast, participated in several yacht races, and later had a successful career in the coast guard.

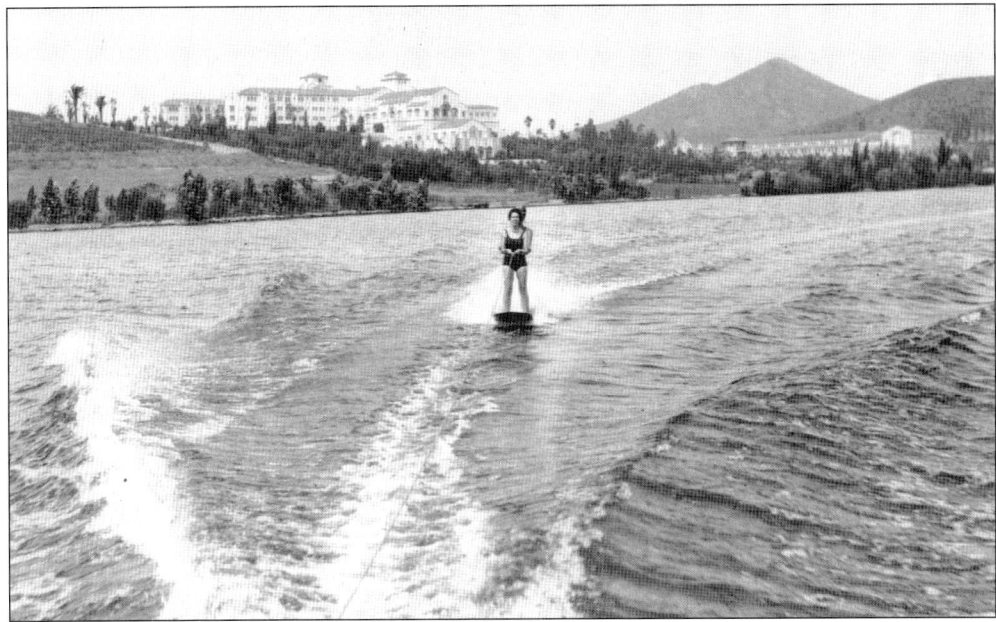

WATER BOARDING, EARLY 1930S. William Clark was not only adept at water sports and boating, but also the photographer who took this picture. Mike Nugent, a one-time caddy at the Norconian, described Clark as follows: "very slender, heck of an athlete and very popular with the ladies" and "he always made a point to say hello; real nice fellow."

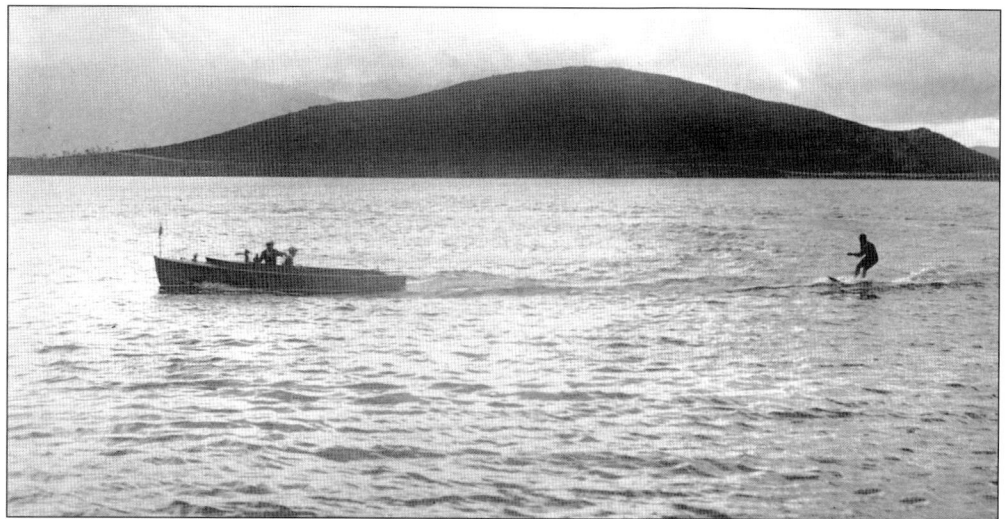

WILLIAM AND REX CLARK, C. 1929. This is purported to be one of a series of photographs of Rex Clark operating a speedboat with his son William in tow. Of all the three children, William stayed closest to his father, though the relationship, as with the other two children, was strained. Eventually father and son owned large cattle ranches side by side in the Santa Barbara area, but they rarely spoke.

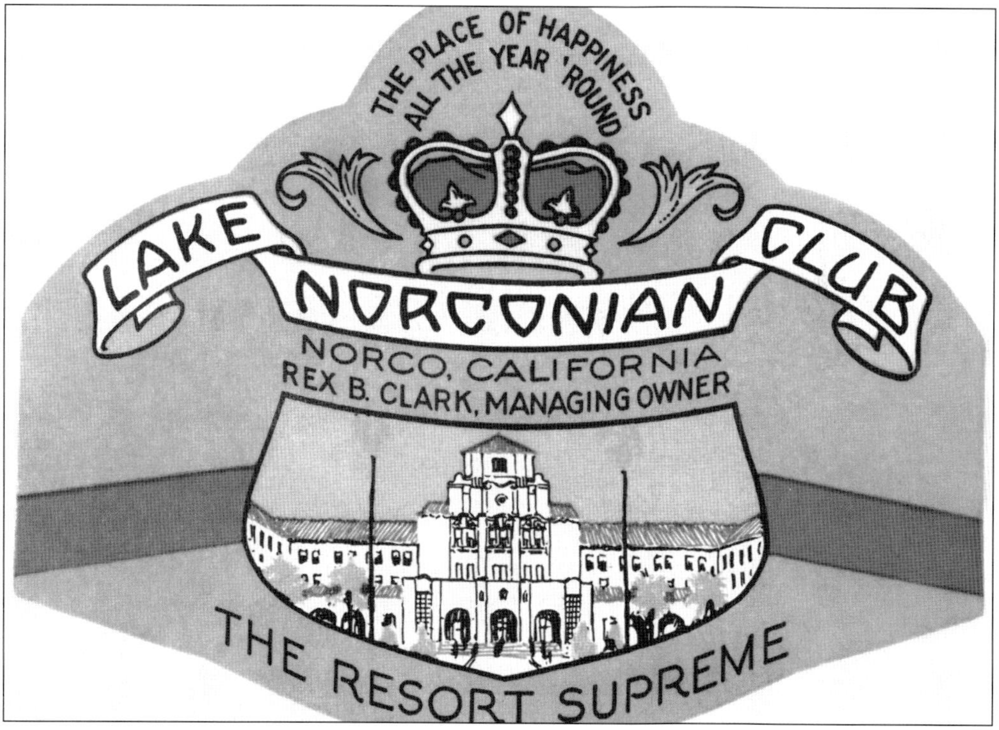

A PLACE OF HAPPINESS, C. 1929. Rex Clark used a wide variety of advertising venues to publicize his resort: newspaper articles, advertisements in theater programs, magazines, and so on. Here is a bumper or luggage sticker, which notes the Norconian is "The place of happiness all the year around." From the beginning, rumors circulated that the resort was in trouble and would become a seasonal retreat; despite Rex Clark's denials, the rumors proved correct.

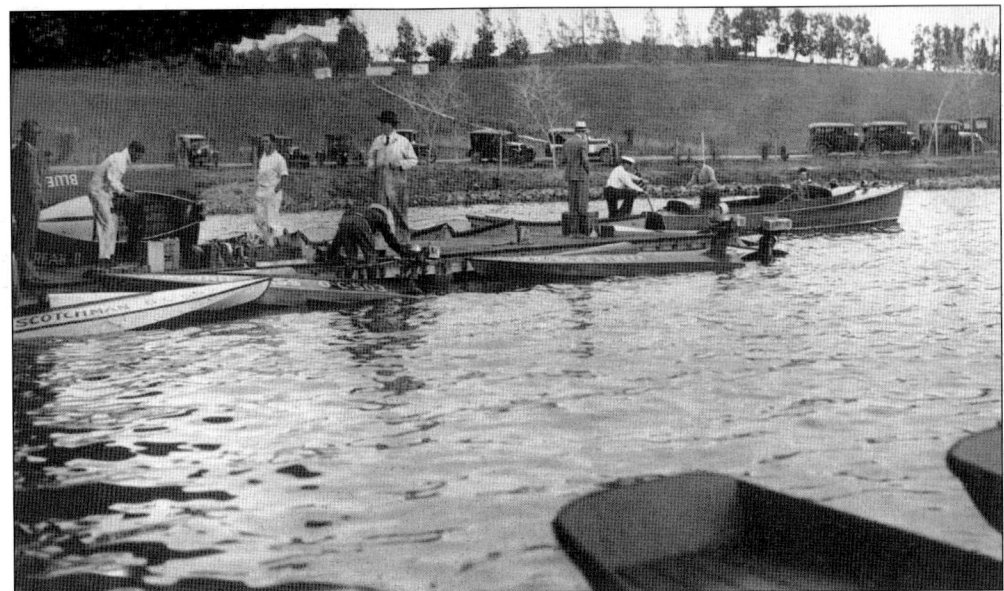

NORCONIAN DOCKS, C. 1928. Speedboat exhibitions and races were regularly held on the Norconian Lake one-mile water speedway oval. The Outboard Motorboat Association sanctioned competitions, and many of the fastest outboard motorboats in the world flew across the 60-acre lake in Norco. Charlie Holt's *Fire Fly*, the holder of the American speed record at 38.43 miles per hour, and Johnny Graham's *Bonnie Lass* five-mile world record holder appeared frequently at the resort.

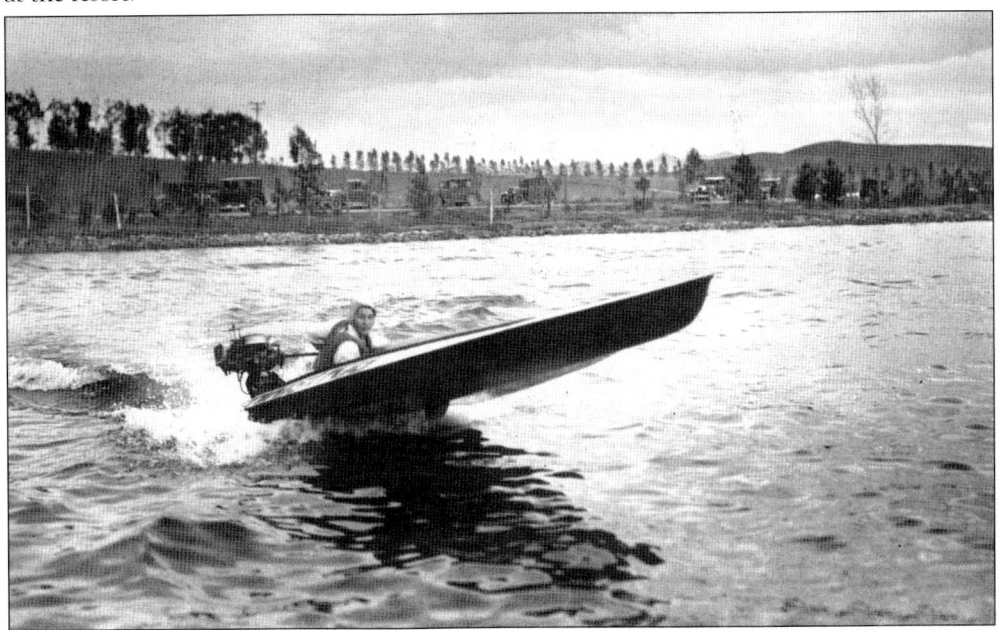

THE SUNKIST KID, 1928. Teenager Loretta Turnbull in this photograph on Lake Norconian was not yet world champion or known as the "Queen of the Seas," but she was fast nevertheless. A pioneer in women's speedboat racing, Turnbull helmed the above *Sunkist Kid* to beat the best male racers in the world, with three feet to spare, on Lake Guarda in Italy to become world's best outdoor motorboat racer—male or female!

BATHING IN LIQUID MOONLIGHT, C. 1928. In August 1928, Rex Clark opened his outdoor pools to the public. He also devised a publicity gimmick using neon, waterproof lighting in the pool itself. It is unknown how he did this or whether the lights were permanent or temporary, but one longtime resident remembers not being allowed to go swimming with her friends because her mother was afraid she would be electrocuted.

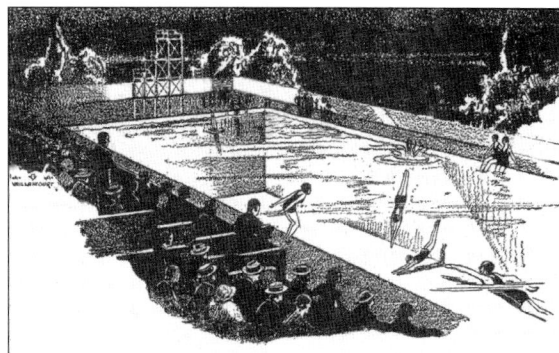

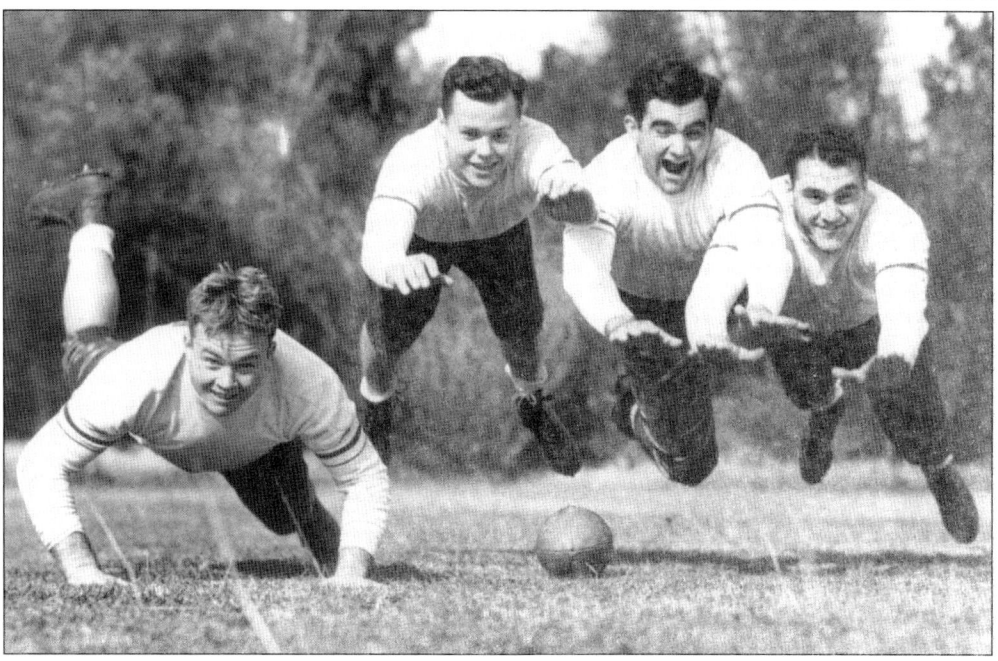

UNIVERSITY OF PITTSBURGH, 1935. The Panthers visited the Norconian in 1932 and again in 1935. One of the greatest collegiate dynasties of all time swam, golfed, went to the Corona Theatre, and played tough Pittsburgh football. Here, from left to right, Bill Glassford, Ave Daniel, George Delich, and Tony Matise practice on the Norconian Resort lawn. (University of Pittsburgh.)

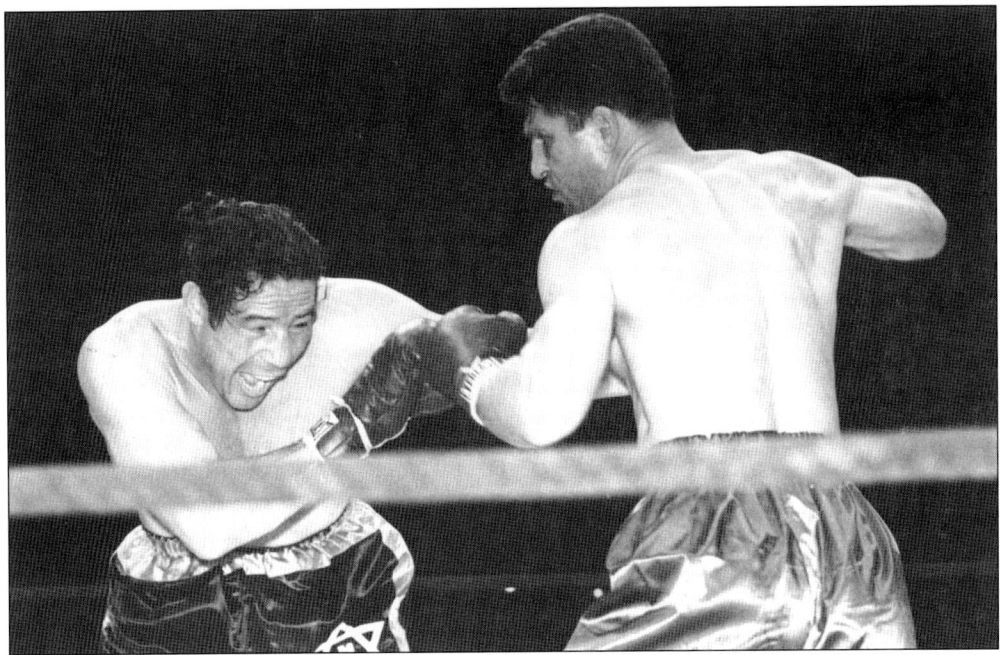

MAX BAER AND LOU NOVA, 1939. After beating Max Baer (left) in the first televised fight in history, Lou Nova rested and trained at the Norconian. He ran trails, ate "mush and vegetables," practiced yoga headstands, golfed, played tennis, and worked out in a temporary boxing ring for his next fight with Joe Louis.

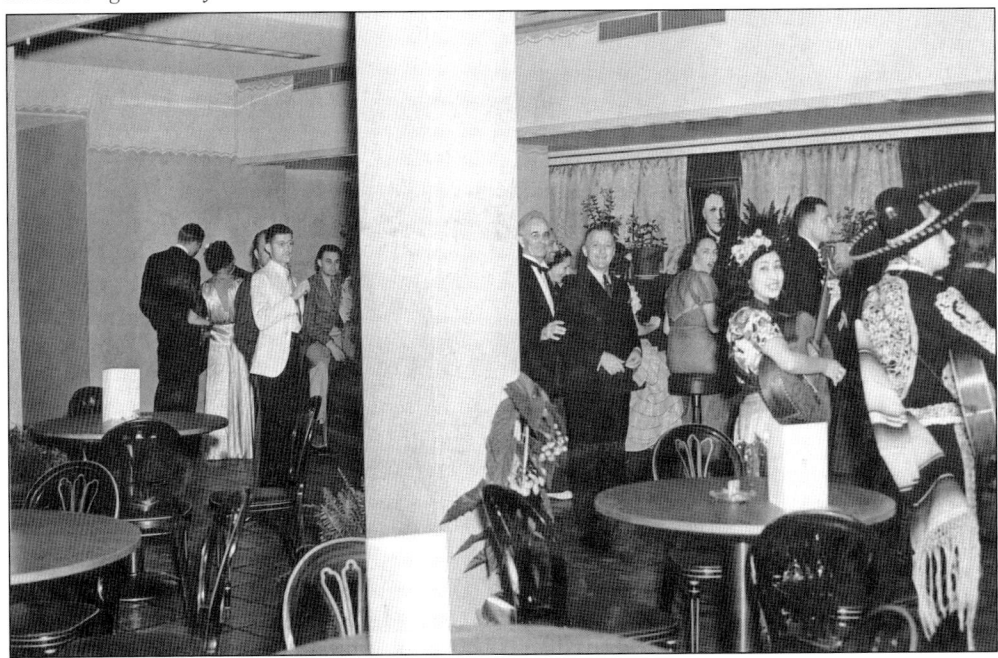

BAR/CAFE, C. 1939. Rex Clark, in tuxedo next to the pillar, was a die-hard Republican, and his resort was used on several occasions in the late 1930s to promote candidates for various offices. Thus far the man in front of Clark is unidentified; however, we know he is probably the guest of honor at this shindig as his picture hangs above the bar.

NORTH VIEW, C. 1934. Sometime in 1932, the resort closed and remained closed until 1935. The once-manicured grounds quickly became overgrown with minimal maintenance being performed. Old-time resident Phil Newhouse remembers finding golf balls and broken clubs in the drained ponds. In a 1933 letter, Rex Clark writes of seeking funds and investors, being cash strapped, distrusting banks, and delinquent taxes.

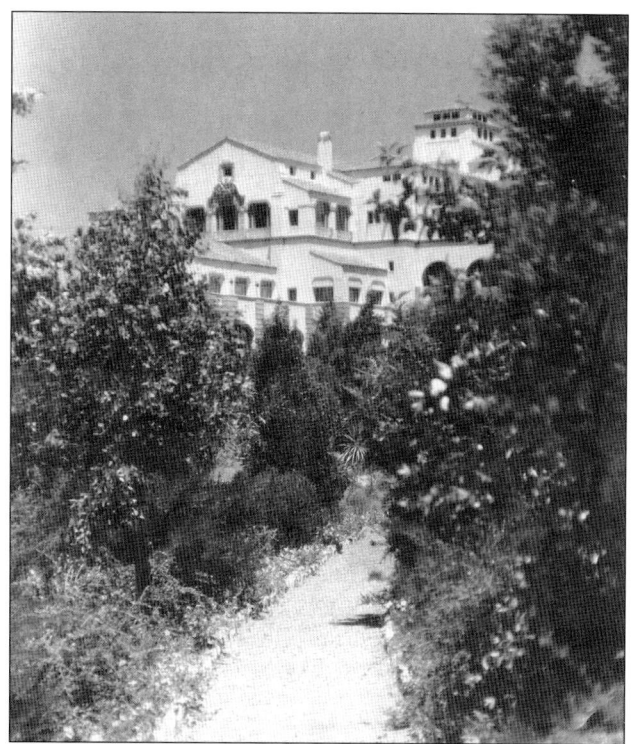

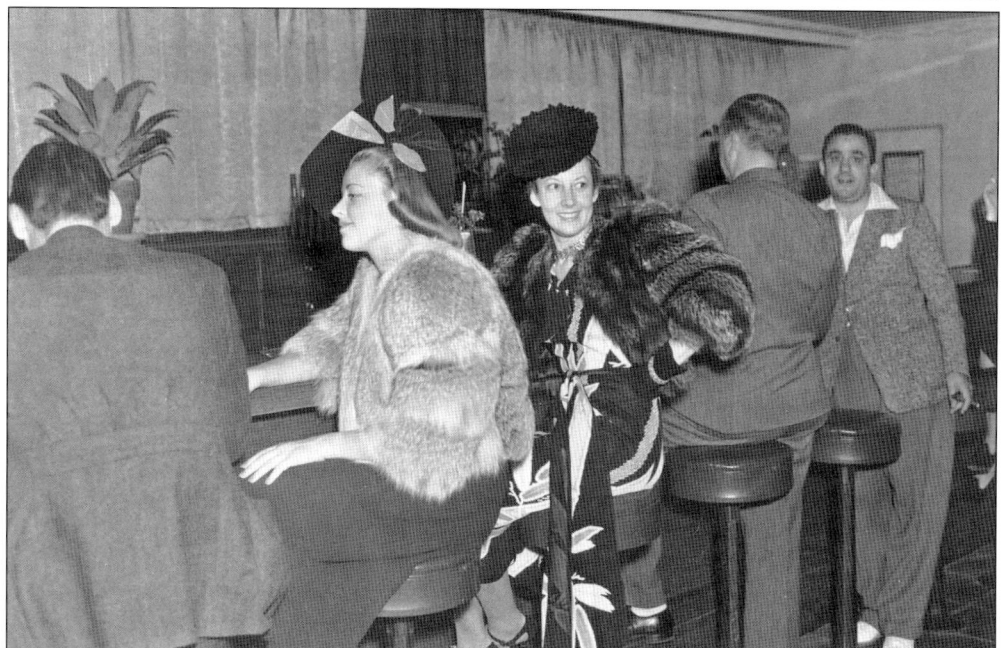

NORCONIAN BAR, C. 1934. While there are conflicting stories as to whether or not Rex Clark allowed alcohol during Prohibition, most certainly he was one of the first to petition for newly legal liquor licenses in 1933. The photograph above depicts the spanking new renovated bar with happy patrons drinking legal booze for the first time at the resort. Unfortunately, booze alone was not enough to completely reopen the Norconian.

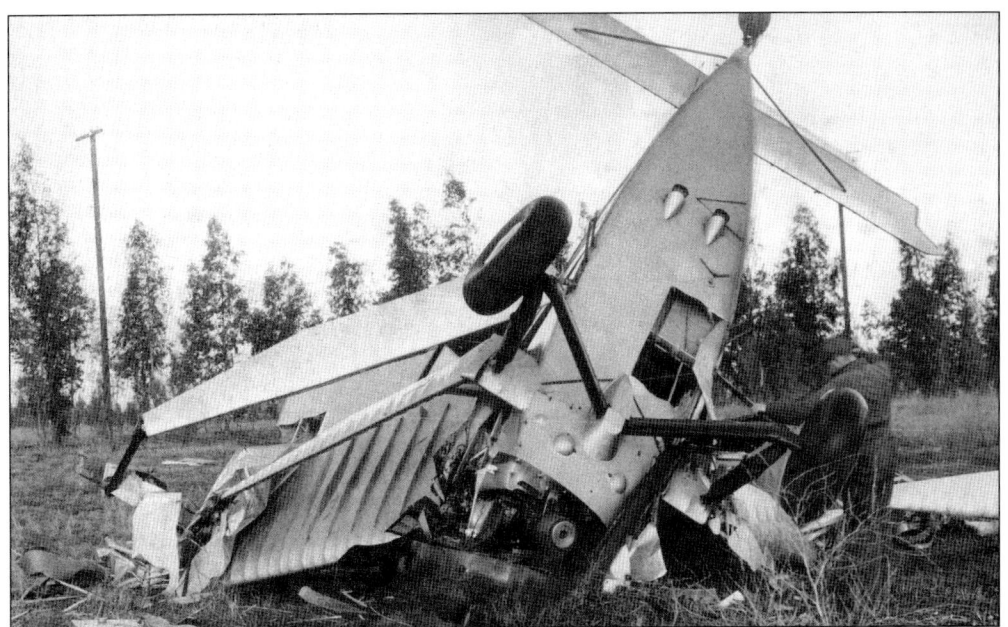

THE DEATH OF MARSHALL S. BOGGS, 1933. This photograph depicts the only known Norconian Airfield fatality. Boggs, who in 1931 made history by piloting "the first blind landing made entirely by radio signals," was testing radio beacons and mistook an unlit field for the Norconian airstrip. He died a short time later at the Corona Hospital while his two female passengers, though seriously injured, survived. (Los Angeles Public Library.)

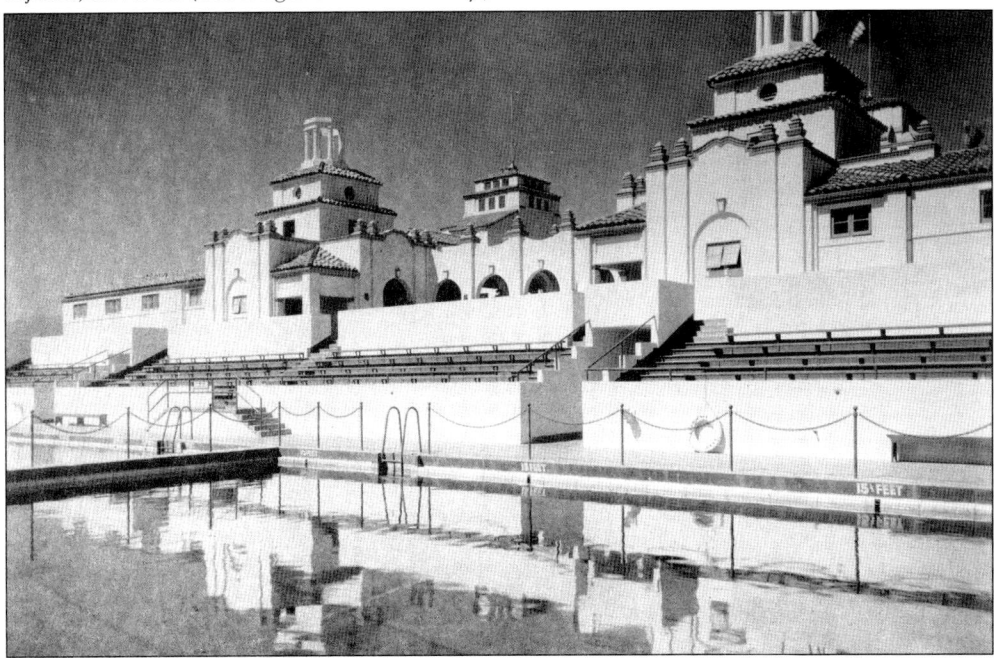

A FISHY TALE, C. 1934. With the resort closed, Rex Clark converted his outdoor pools into trout ponds, installing rockeries and aerating apparatus. Unfortunately, the 1,000 trout died in a single night. Clark refused to pay for the fish and the supplier sued; Clark was victorious and received $150. Phil Newhouse saw the fish with his own, somewhat disbelieving, eyes.

ESTHER ANN WALKER, 1938. After winning the one and only "Miss Norconian" contest, this beauty represented the resort and brought home third place in the 1938 Miss California pageant. Initially, three local girls, including Shirley Gilbraith, were announced the resort finalists, but a week later, Esther suddenly appeared and was declared the winner. Shirley stated, "It was a put-up job, they were outsiders." Esther Ann Walker was a ringer.

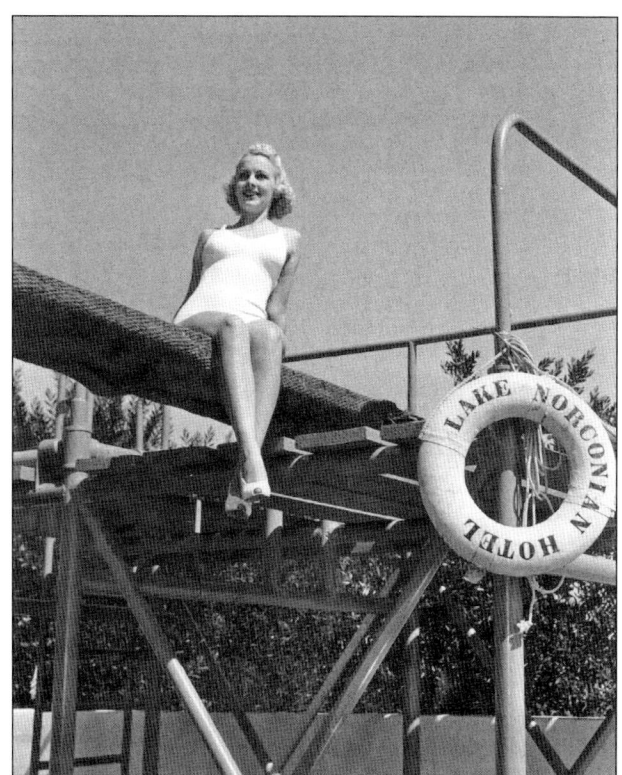

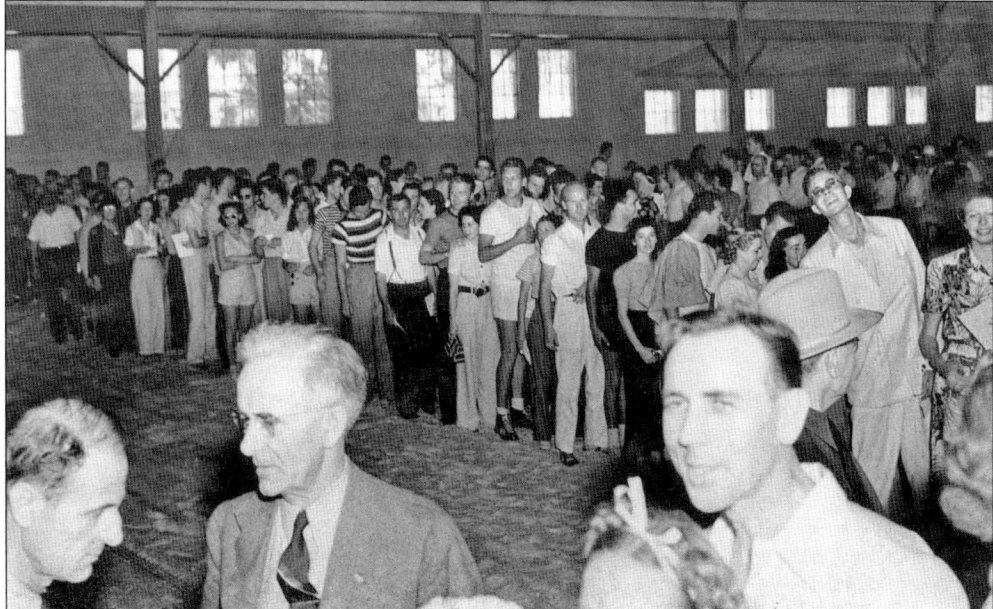

GARAGE INTERIOR, 1940. By 1932, Rex Clark, lower center, was divorced from his longtime wife, cut off from that avenue of cash, and desperately fighting off creditors and a federal government suit for back taxes. However, in 1935, the Norconian suddenly reopened, perhaps because of a cash infusion from his ex-wife's trust fund. The opening was not so grand as before, but the Norconian was back in business.

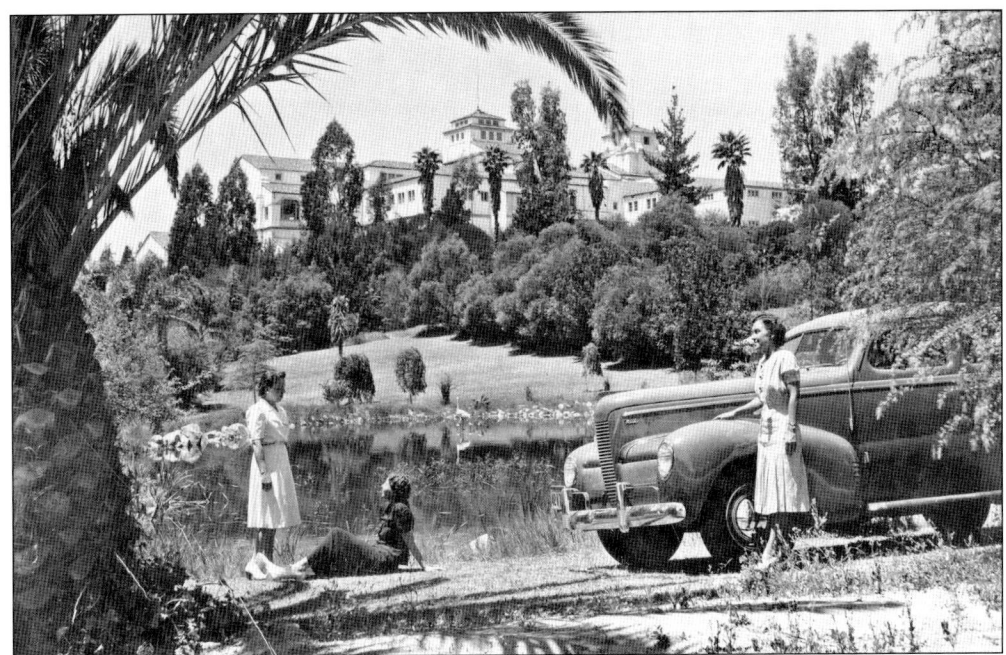

THE NORCONIAN, C. 1940. In May 1940, the Norconian became the Clark Hot Springs Resort, and the best room in the inn could be had for a mere $3. In November, citing "threatened labor trouble," the resort closed for good. Rex Clark's daughter, Ellen Revelle, perhaps said it best, "It was just too big." (Los Angeles Public Library.)

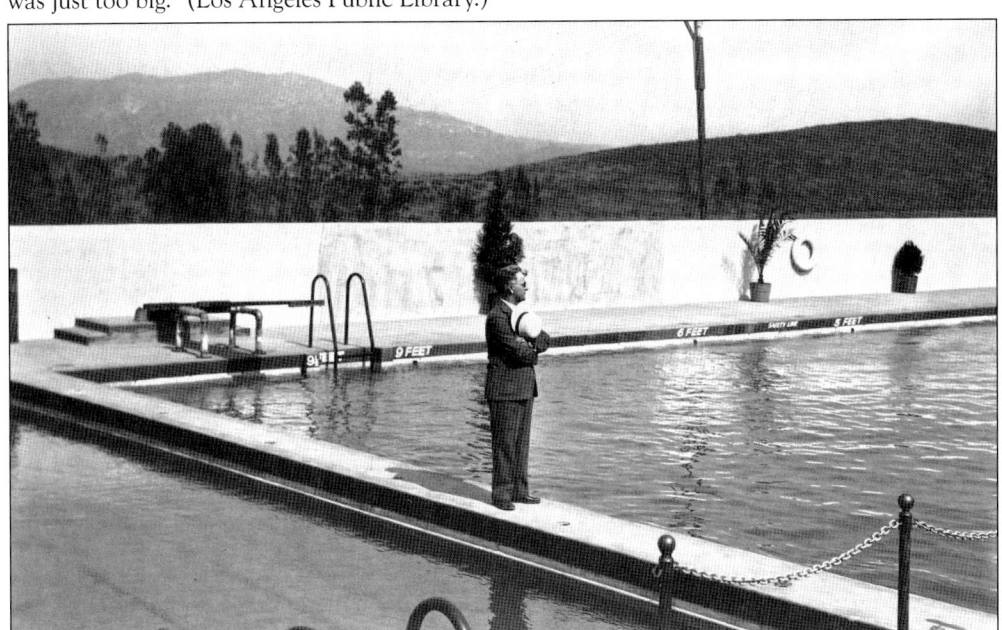

HIS KINGDOM, 1928. Rex Clark surveys his magnificent Olympic pools, not knowing he is on the verge of wild success and crushing defeat. Clark eventually married his longtime mistress, accumulated millions in California real estate, and lived in as large a residence as one could find in Beverly Hills. He died August 31, 1955, and rests in an exclusive and private courtyard at Forest Lawn Cemetery in Glendale, California.

Six

HOLLYWOOD IN NORCO

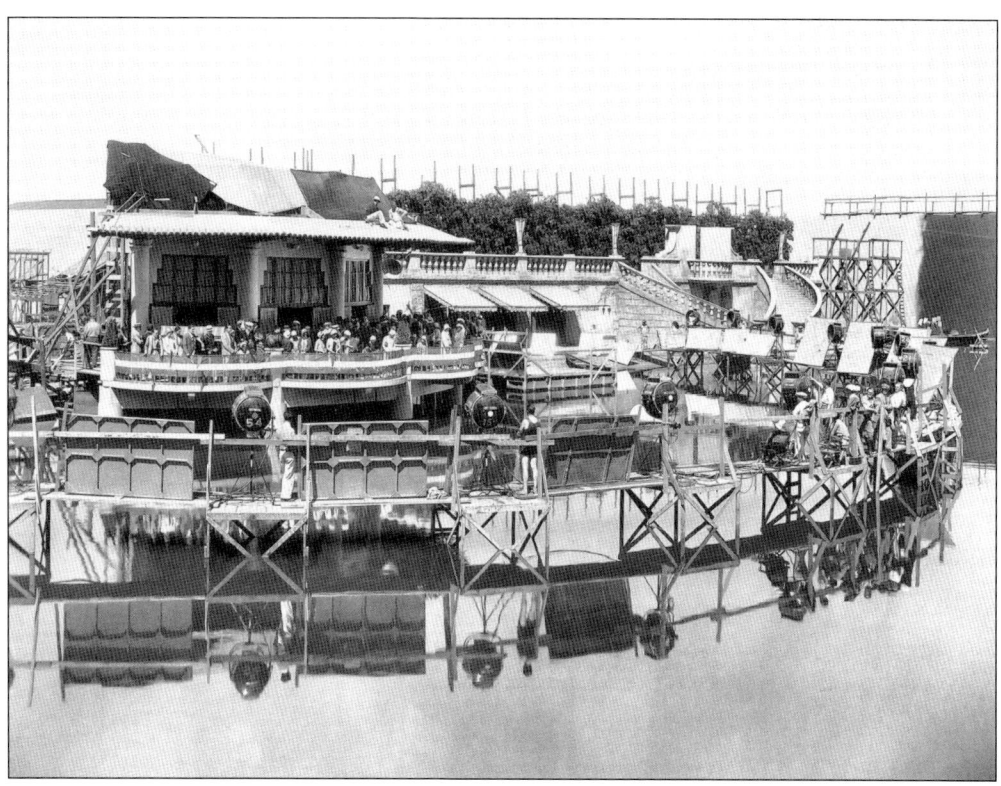

THE HOLLYWOOD NORCONIAN, 1930. Several movies were shot at or near the Norconian. Two films, *Top Speed* and *Love in the Rough*, used the resort as a prime story ingredient and went so far as to build sets replicating the Norconian in Hollywood. This set from *Love in the Rough*, overlooking "Lake First National," in Los Angeles replicates the Pavilion and tea room. (Courtesy of the Academy of Motion Picture Arts and Sciences.)

CORONA THEATRE, C. 1939. On the theatre's gala opening night, August 29, 1929, Harry Richmond was the master of ceremonies, Irving Berlin sang several of his own songs, and dozens of stars were in attendance: Clara Bow, D. W. Griffith, Laurel and Hardy, Delores Del Rio, John Barrymore, Charlie Chaplin, Al Jolson, Hoot Gibson, Buster Keaton, and dozens of others. They all bunked at the Norconian. (Corona Public Library.)

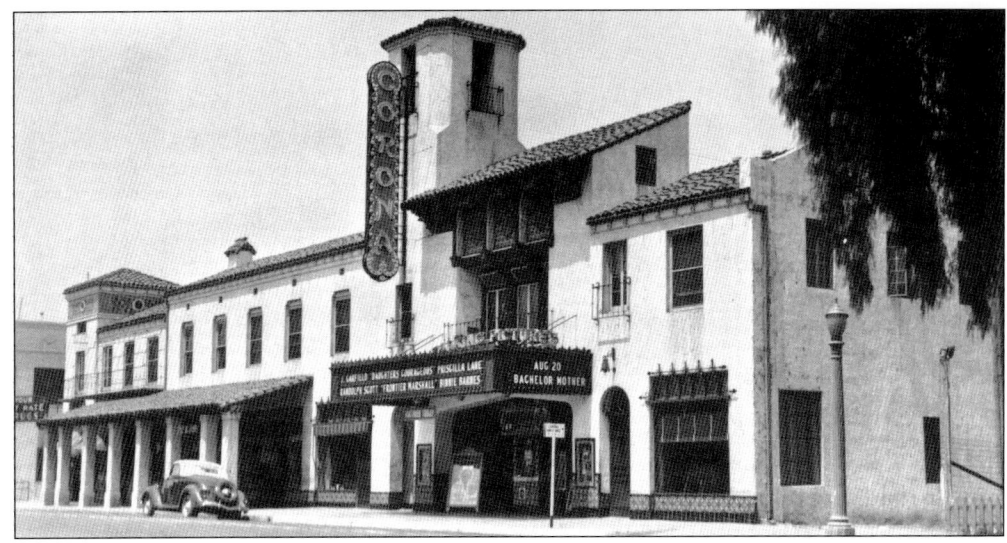

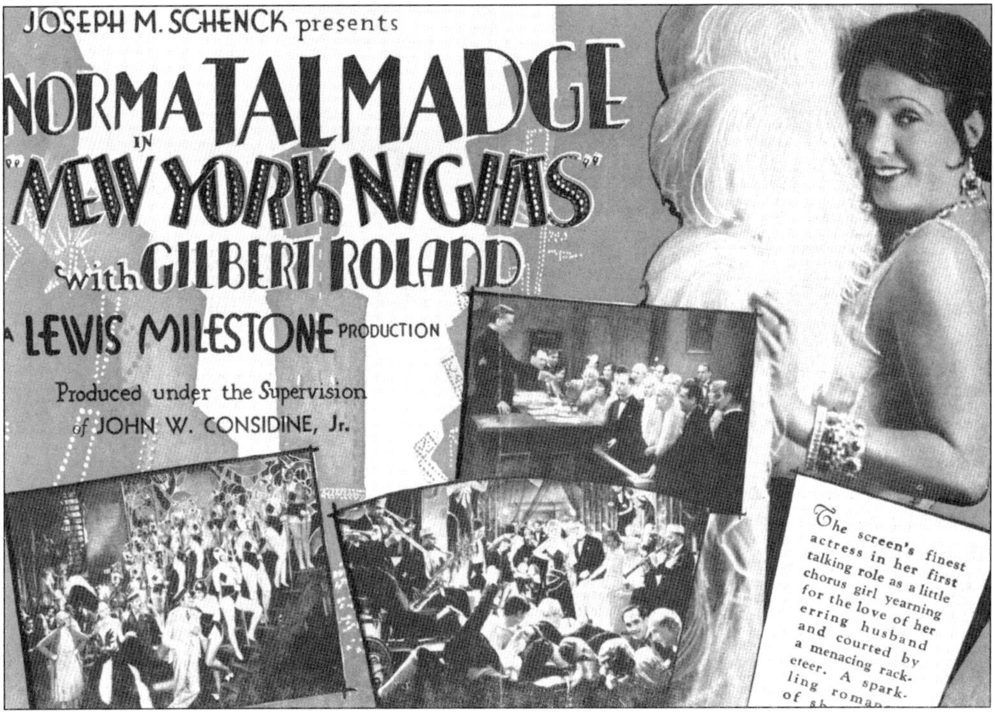

NEW YORK NIGHTS, 1929. Theater owner Glenn Harper, to kick-off the first film shown at his Corona Theatre, held a star-studded luncheon at the Norconian. That night, audiences heard silent screen star Norma Talmadge for the first time, and her picture career was soon over. Director Billy Wilder said silent films ended with her line to autograph hounds, "Get away, you little B******ds, I don't need you anymore!"

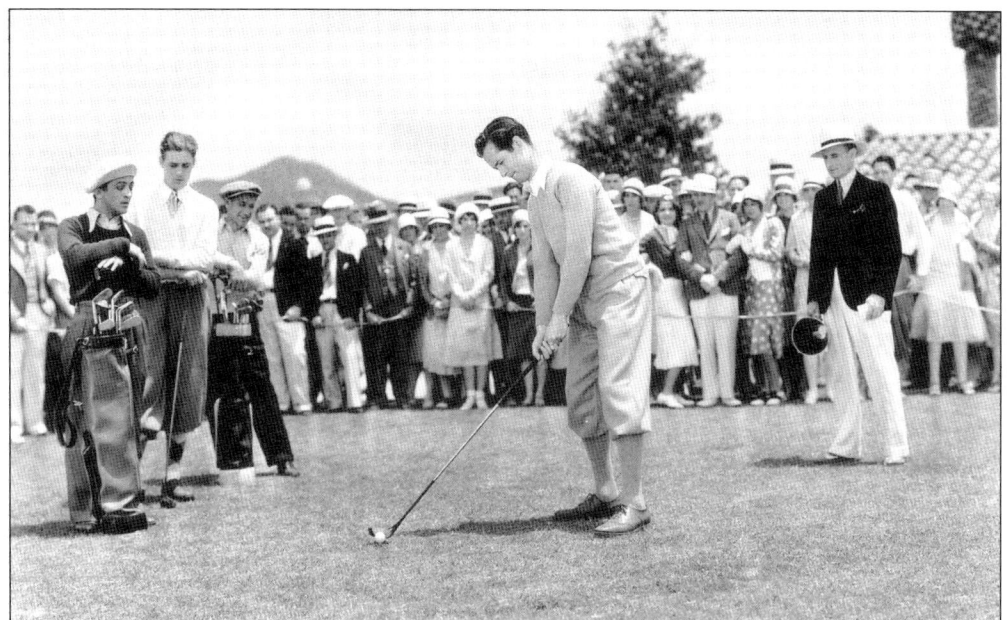

ROBERT MONTGOMERY, 1929. The frequent guest of the resort is shown filming a scene from *Love in the Rough* (note Beacon Hill in the background). The father of television's *Bewitched* star, nose-twitching Elizabeth Montgomery, made personal appearances onstage at the Corona Theatre to promote his films *Three Live Ghosts* and *Their Own Desire*. (Courtesy of the Academy of Motion Picture Arts and Sciences.)

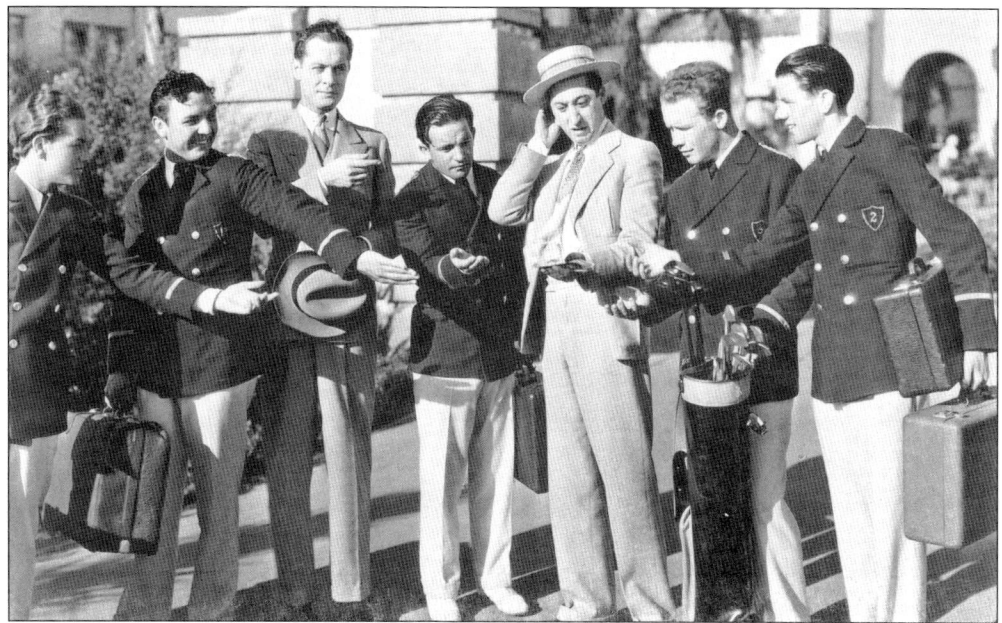

BENNY RUBIN, 1930. Standing in front of the Norconian Hotel, Robert Montgomery (third from left) and character comedian Benny Rubin (in the straw hat) clown with extras during filming of *Love in the Rough*. Ironically, if you were Jewish, it would be impossible to get a membership card at the resort; however, it appears there was no such restriction for movie people. (Courtesy of the Academy of Motion Picture Arts and Sciences.)

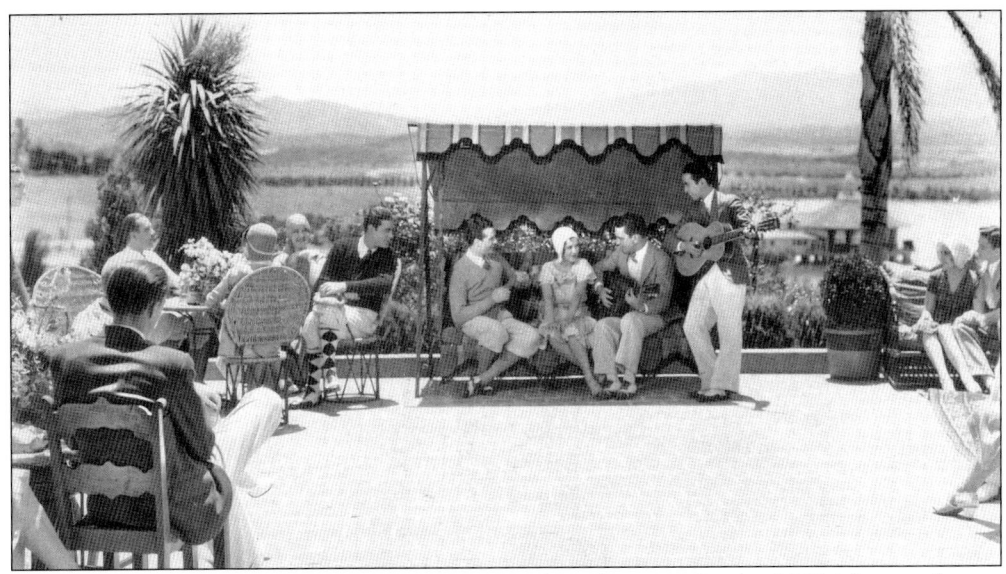

KELLY'S VACATION, 1930. The Norconian was used as a location for this MGM feature about a shipping clerk who gets and loses the girl, but gets her again because of a talent for golf. When the feature reached theaters, it had a new title, *Love in the Rough*. The film starred Robert Montgomery, Dorothy Jordan, and Benny Rubin. Extras were sought locally with the primary requirement being "well-groomed and sporting clothes of the latest lines." Above, with the Norconian Lake as a backdrop, Dorothy Jordan is serenaded by three young men with two guitars and a ukulele; known as the "The Biltmore Trio," they were the rage in 1929. Below, Jordan dances away on the tea room patio supported by a bevy of extras. In 1933, Dorothy Jordan was cast as Honey Hale in *Flying Down to Rio* opposite Fred Astaire, his first film. Jordan backed out at the last minute to honeymoon with new husband Merian Cooper, the producer of the original *King Kong*. The part went to an unknown blond named Ginger Rogers.

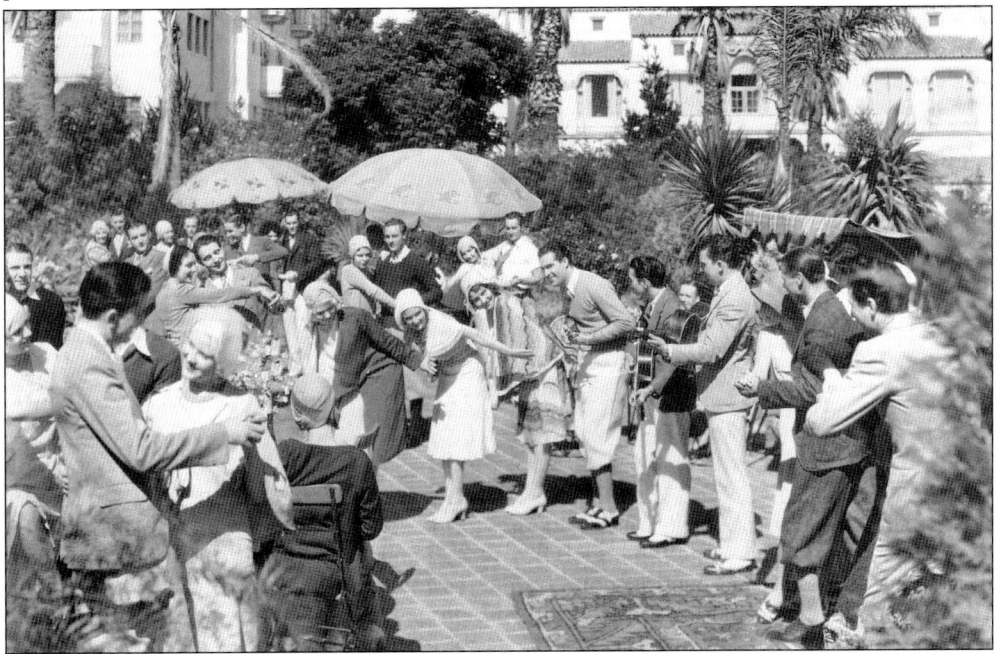

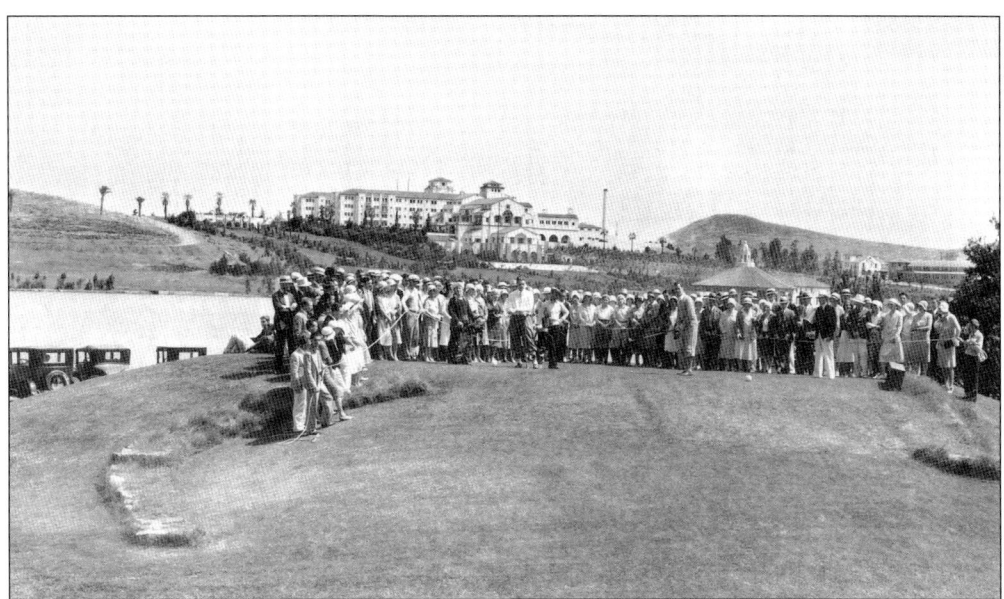

NORCONIAN 17TH TEE, 1929. Surrounded by well-dressed Corona and Norco residents as extras is the stirring climax where our hero is about to win Dorothy Jordan with a golf club. Montgomery being penniless and with a bleak future matters little to his future and very wealthy father-in-law because the kid can play golf well enough to beat the pants off dad's wealthy friends. Behind Montgomery are the hotel and Pavilion, and to the right, notice the small guest bungalow. It was reported that Clark built several of these, but little is known about them regarding size, shape, or locations; this is the only known photograph of one of these structures. Below, filming on the 15th green, note the familiar Norco ridgeline in the background. During production, Norco's famed Santa Ana winds kicked in and filming was delayed several days, driving the astronomical $9,000 a day budget even higher.

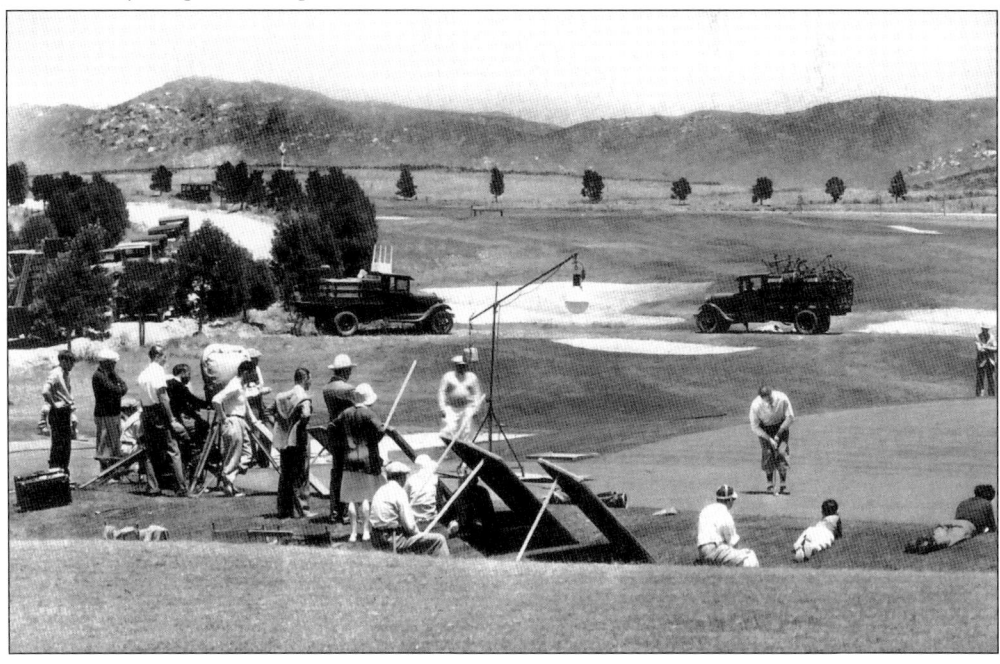

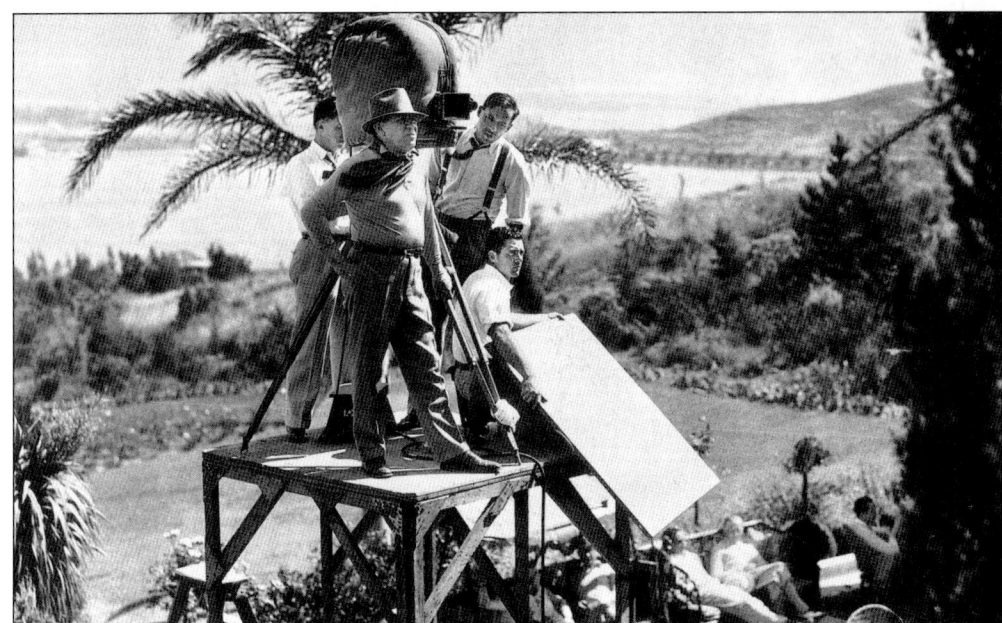

FILMING, 1930. With Lake Norconian as a backdrop, director Charles Reisner (in front of the platform) films a scene from *Love in the Rough*. Rex Clark saw to it that local residents were invited to watch as the movie crew went through their paces. Very likely, just out of view, hundreds of people with autograph books in hand are star-watching. (Courtesy of the Academy of Motion Picture Arts and Sciences.)

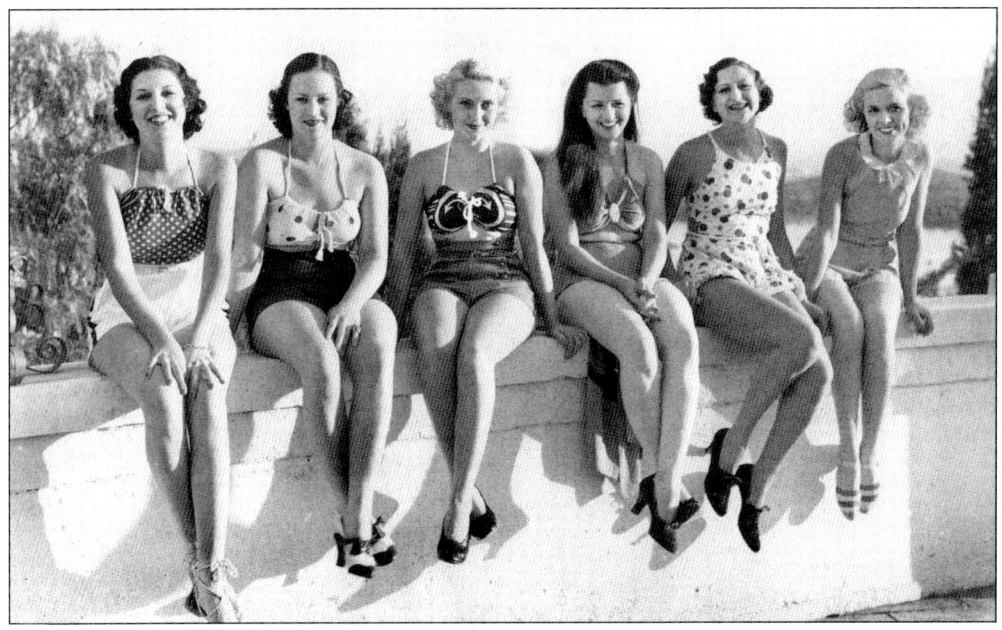

PRETTY GIRLS, 1935. Pictured are six models/actresses brought from Los Angeles to appear in publicity photographs for the Norconian resort. From left to right are Virginia Morrison, two unidentified, Marie Deauville, Marie Spizak, and Mellisa Miller. Deauville was an MGM contract player and the mother of Ronnie Deauville, a marvelous, sweet-voiced singer before he was stricken with polio.

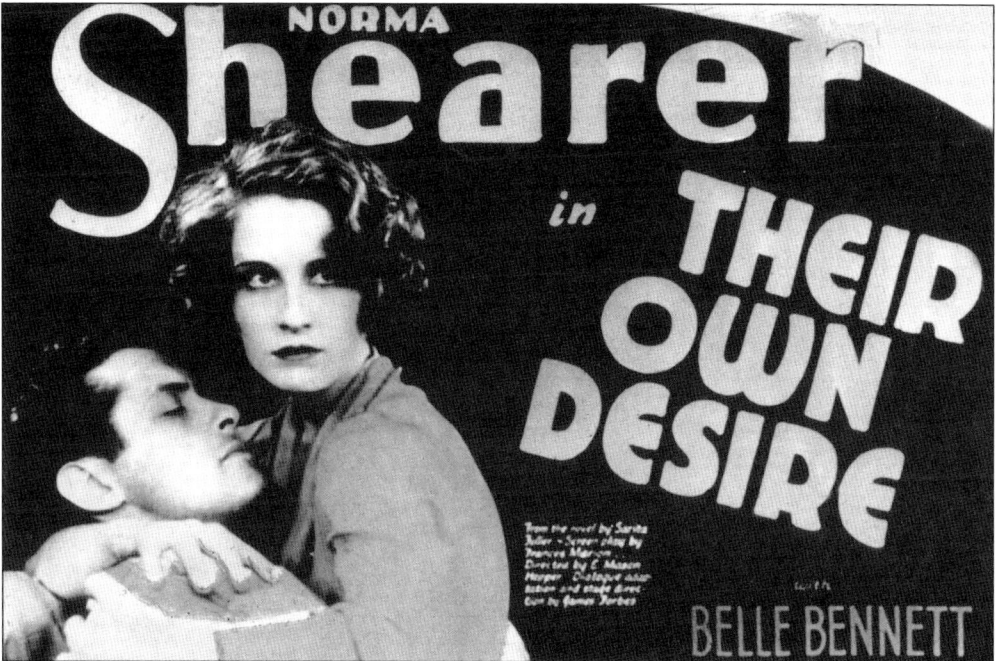

THEIR OWN DESIRE, 1929. Scenes for this Robert Montgomery/Norma Shearer tearjerker were filmed around the tea room, hotel, and particularly the pool. Shearer, one of the most popular stars in the world, was nominated for a best actress Oscar on this one. Horseback riding was a passion, and Shearer was often a guest and on horseback at the Norconian. (Courtesy of the Academy of Motion Picture Arts and Sciences.)

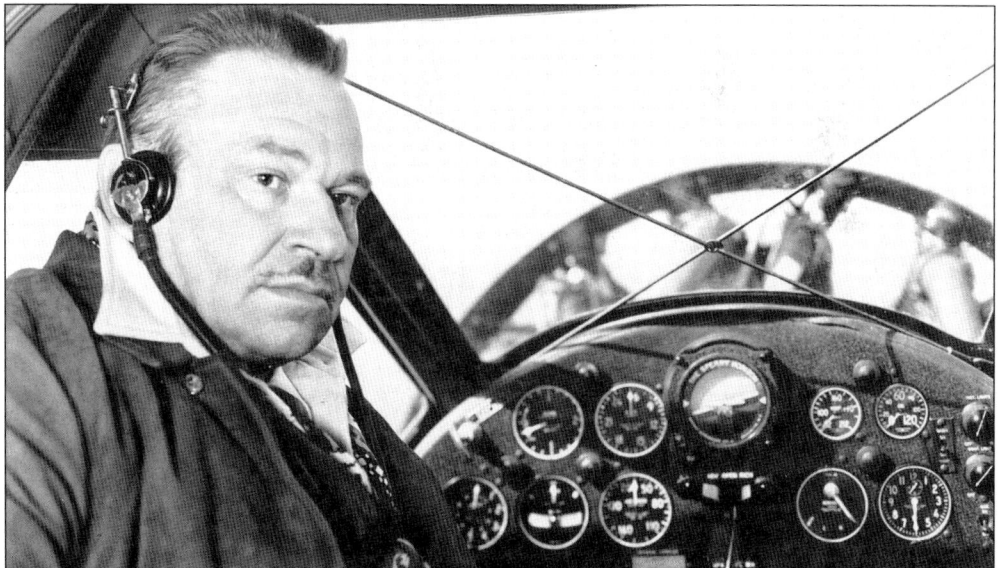

WALLACE BEERY, 1938. Film star Beery was squadron leader to a group of 60 planes, known as the "Air Country Club of Southern California," that visited the Norconian Airfield. One local resident remembered well the deafening noise and looking up to see "dozens of planes circling Norco, they just kept coming." Later residents flocked to the Norconian Airfield to look at the planes "all neat in rows." (Bison Archives.)

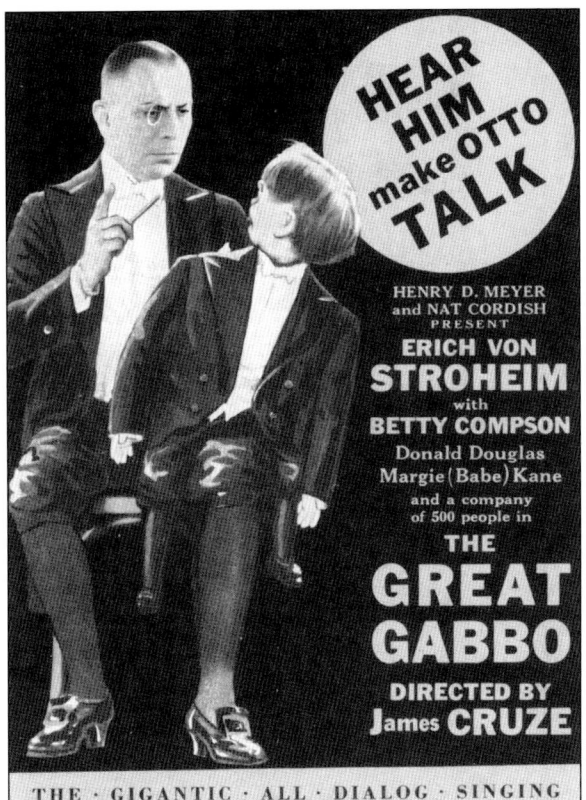

THE GREAT GABBO, 1929. This strange film, starring Eric von Stroheim in his first talkie, was about a brilliant ventriloquist who goes mad between lavish and mesmerizing musical numbers. Rex Clark produced a live version on the north shore of Lake Norconian. Stroheim directed stars Betty Compson, Babe Kane, Don Douglas, and 70 beautiful girls and young men in three elaborately staged musical numbers complete with stunning costumes and mammoth settings.

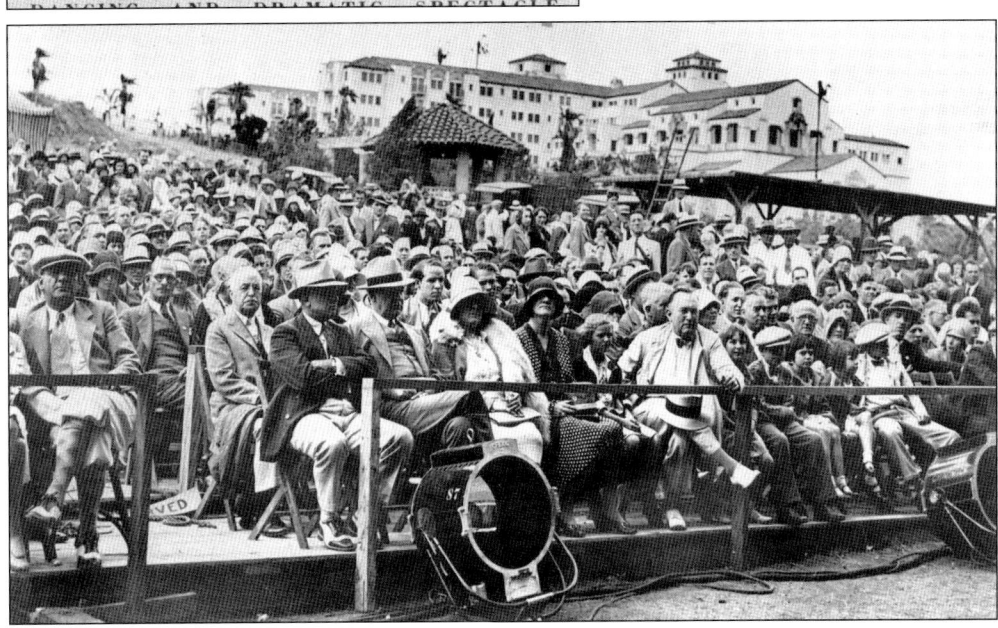

THE GREAT GABBO AUDIENCE, 1929. Before the 2:00 p.m. performance, the audience was treated to speedboat races and comic routines on the lake as well as diving and swimming exhibitions in the outdoor pools. A crowd of 50,000 was projected; unfortunately, rain kept the crowd to about 2,000; nevertheless, news accounts relate that the event was a dramatic success.

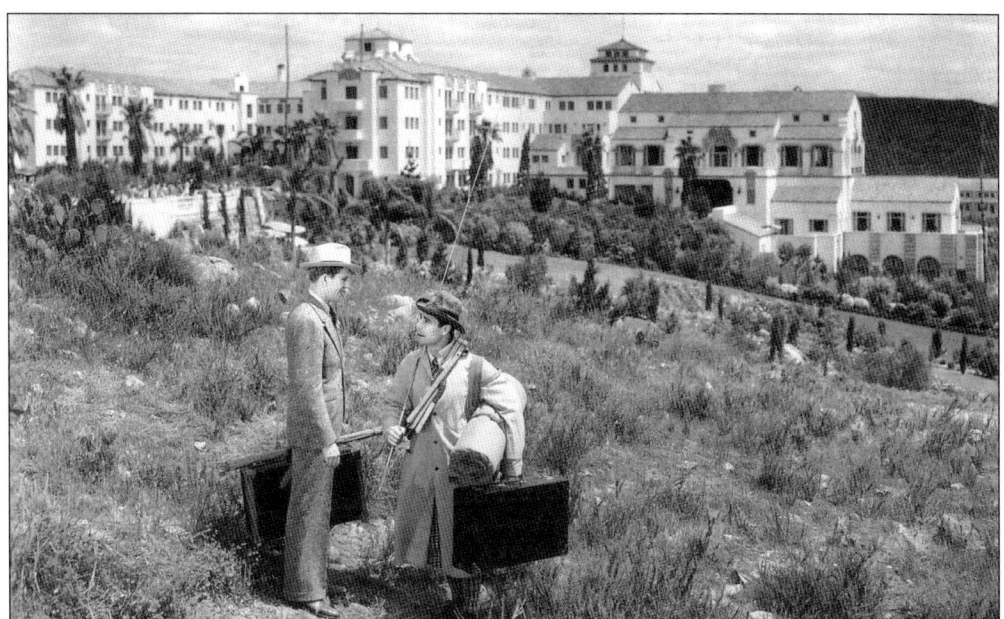

TOP SPEED, 1930. Joe E. Brown (right) starred in this comedy about two clerks posing as millionaires who save the day and get the girls because of a boat race. The film contains wonderful scenes of Lake Norconian, the Pavilion, boathouse, and hotel. Here Jack Whiting (left) and Brown film a scene with the east view of the hotel as a background. (Courtesy of the Academy of Motion Picture Arts and Sciences.)

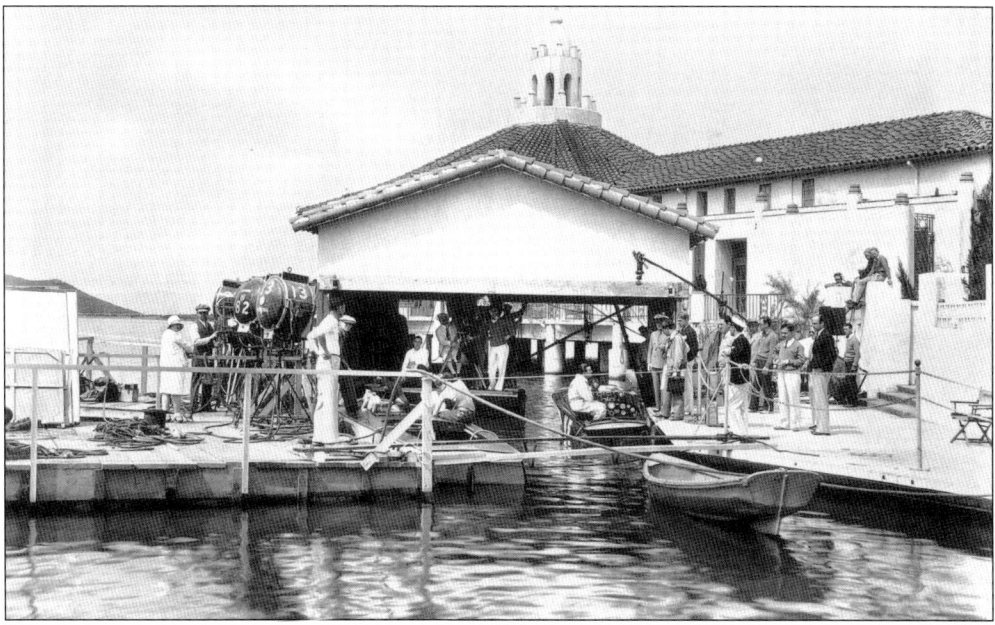

THE BOATHOUSE, TAKE TWO, 1930. Here a scene from the climactic boat race in *Top Speed* is filmed. Hundreds of local extras turned out to appear in the crowd scenes. Joe E. Brown starred in several films around the Riverside County area, including baseball pictures *Alibi Ike* and *Elmer the Great*, and he frequently stayed at the Norconian. (Courtesy of the Academy of Motion Picture Arts and Sciences.)

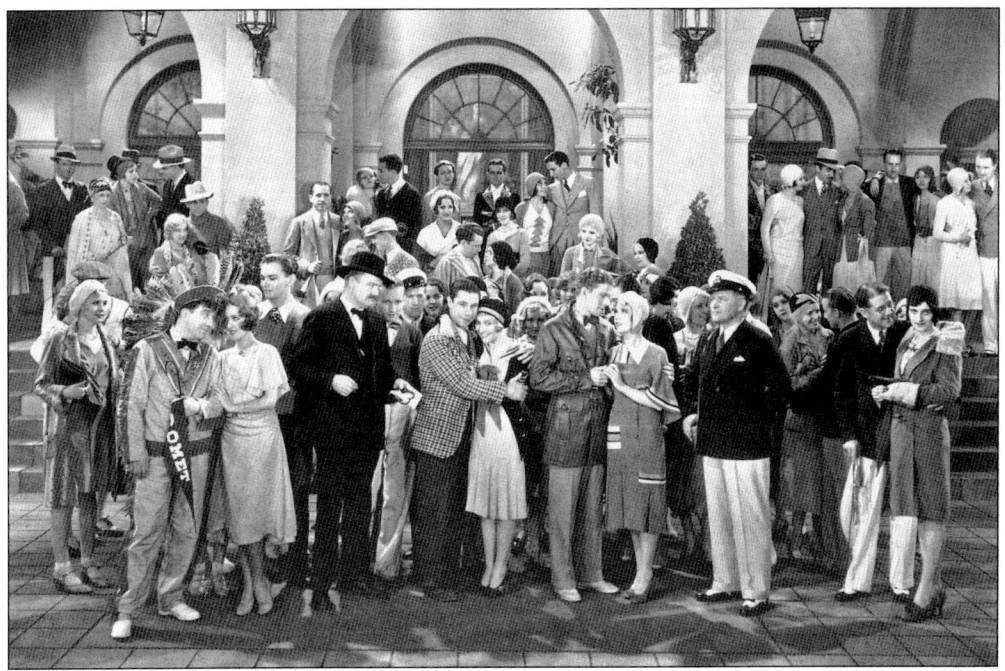

HOLLYWOOD MAGIC, 1930. The stars of *Top Speed* pose for a group shot in front of what appears to be the Norconian Hotel entrance; in fact, they are standing before a very good replica in Tinseltown. Pictured in the front are, from left to right, Frank McHugh, Rita Flynn, Wade Boteler, Joe E. Brown, Laura Lee, Jack Whiting, Bernice Claire, and Edwin Maxwell. (Courtesy of the Academy of Motion Picture Arts and Sciences.)

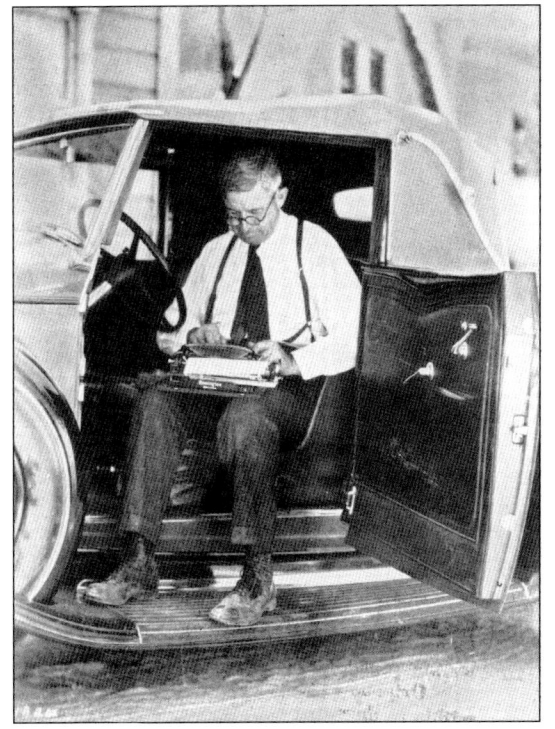

WILL ROGERS, 1932. Local Ray Harris recalls Will Rogers doing exactly what you see in this photograph—churning out the most widely read news column in the country. Rogers made several pictures in the area and was a frequent Norconian guest. Ben Cricket met the humorist and Wiley Post on the Norconian Airfield in 1935; the aviators actually gave a plane ride to Cricket's companion. (Los Angeles Public Library.)

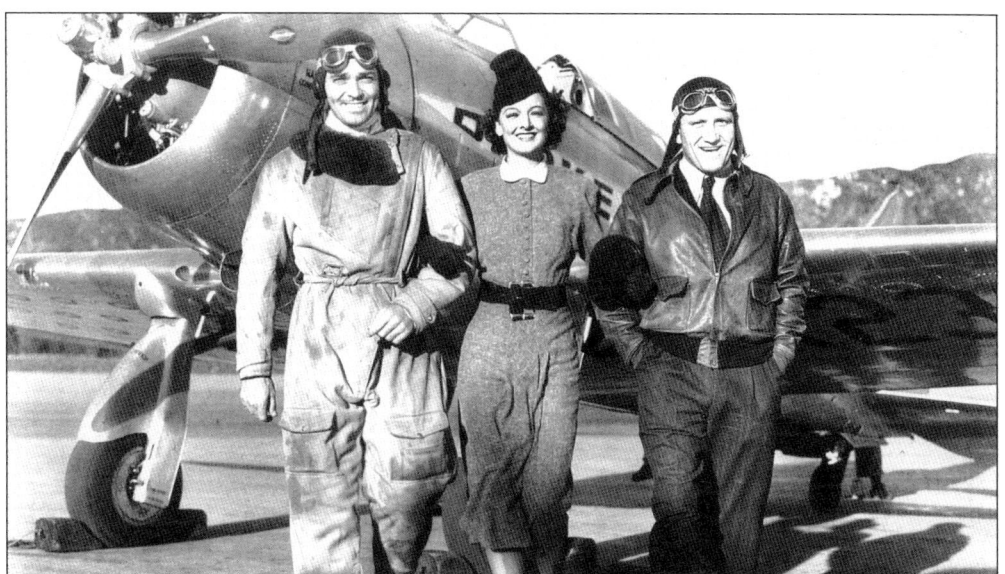

TEST PILOT, 1937. This MGM feature starred Clark Gable, Myrna Loy, and Spencer Tracy, with several scenes shot at the Norconian and nearby Chino Airfield. Norco residents Dale Crickett and Doris Gorrell, acting as reporters for Riverside City College, wangled interviews with Gable and Loy in the resort dining room. Later Crickett spent time at Loy's home as her guest. (Courtesy of the Academy of Motion Picture Arts and Sciences.)

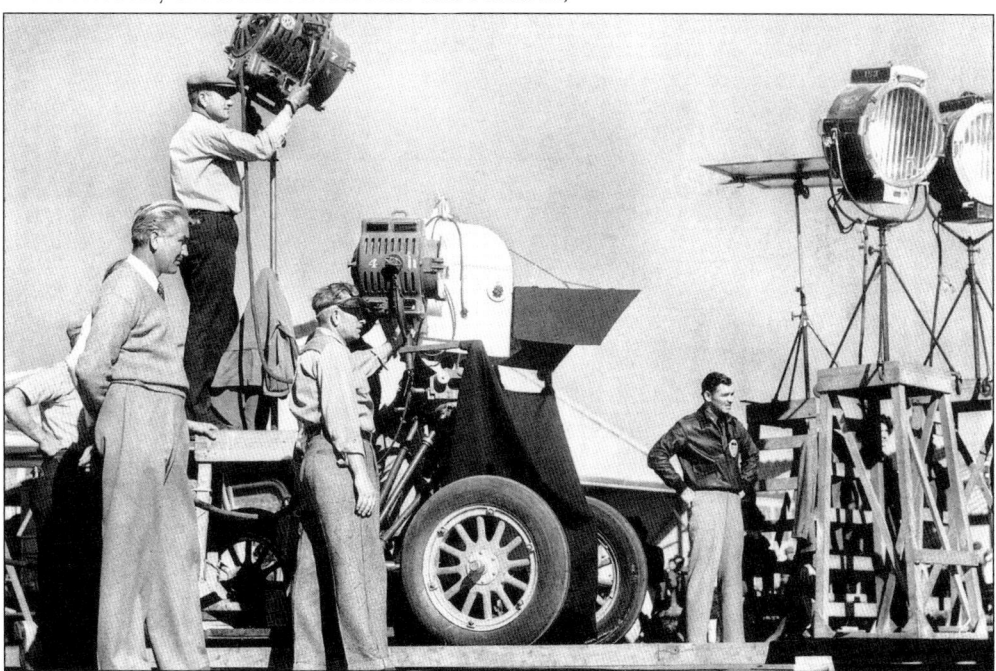

GONE WITH THE WIND, 1938. North of the Norconian, director Victor Fleming (left) and Clark Gable (right) watch a scene from *Test Pilot*. Fleming was a frequent resort guest and perhaps his most famous stay was in 1939, the evening *Gone with the Wind* (Fleming directed and Gable starred) was successfully previewed at nearby Riverside's Fox Theatre. (Courtesy of the Academy of Motion Picture Arts and Sciences.)

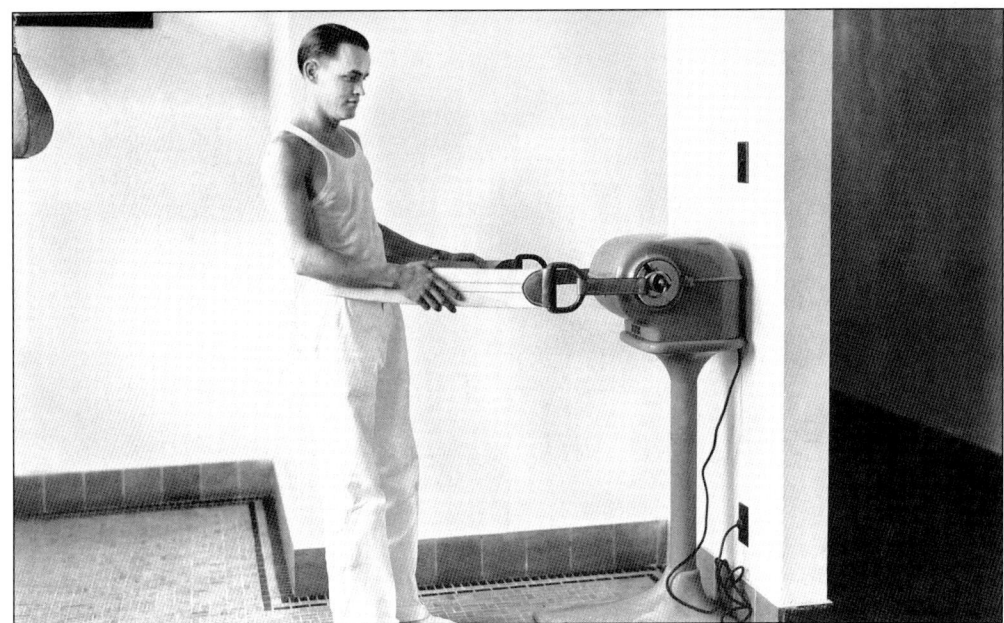

BOB HOPE, NORCONIAN GYMNASIUM. Hope was a frequent visitor at the Norconian (and later entertained at the Corona Naval Hospital). A very partial Norconian list of Hollywood guests would include Jeanette McDonald, Joan Crawford, Leslie Howard, Laurel and Hardy, Basil Rathbone, Gayle Sondergard, James Cagney, Bing Crosby, Robert Young, James Stewart, Cary Grant, Randolph Scott, Mae West, Harold Lloyd, Marion Davies, Buster Keaton, Charlie Chaplin, and Greta Garbo.

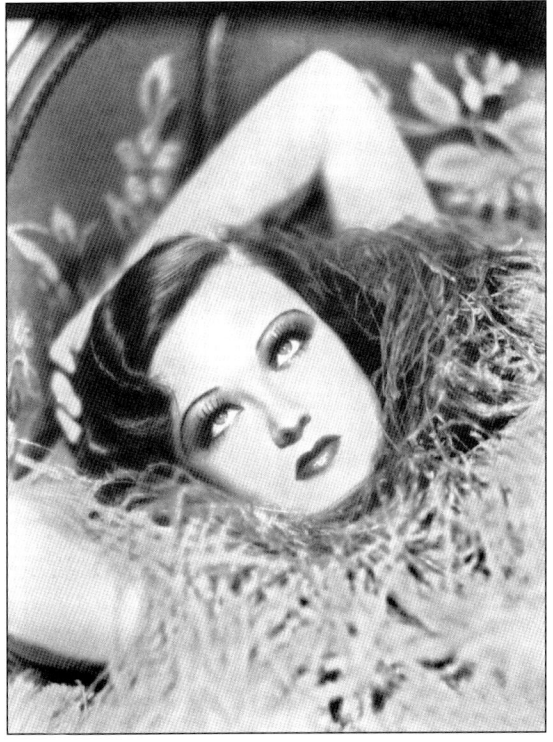

LONA ANDRE, 1938. This actress began with great promise but skidded into B movies such as *Slave in Bondage* and *What Price Passion*. However, on the Norconian golf course in 1938, 21-year-old Lona gained a moment of positive publicity by setting the world's golfing record for women, shooting 156 holes of golf in 11 hours and 55 minutes for a score of 875.

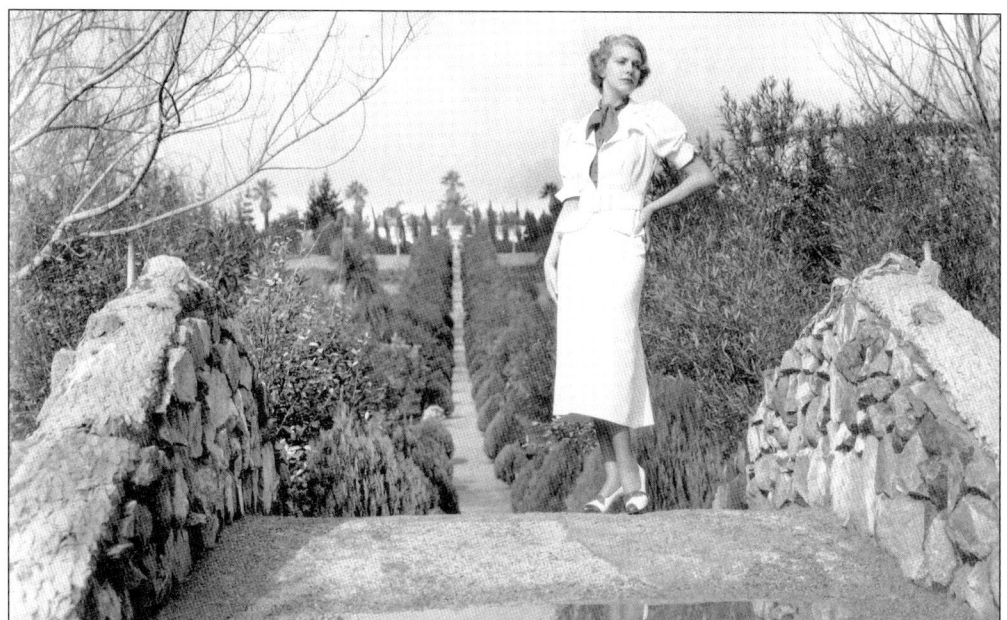

TEA ROOM WALKWAY, 1936. *Walking On Air* starred Ann Southern and Gene Raymond (husband of Jeanette McDonald, both frequent Norconian guests). Unfortunately, none of the footage shot at the resort made the final cut. Pictured is completely deleted Anita Colby. Also known as "The Face," she was the first $100-an-hour model and turned down marriage proposals from both Clark Gable and Jimmy Stewart.

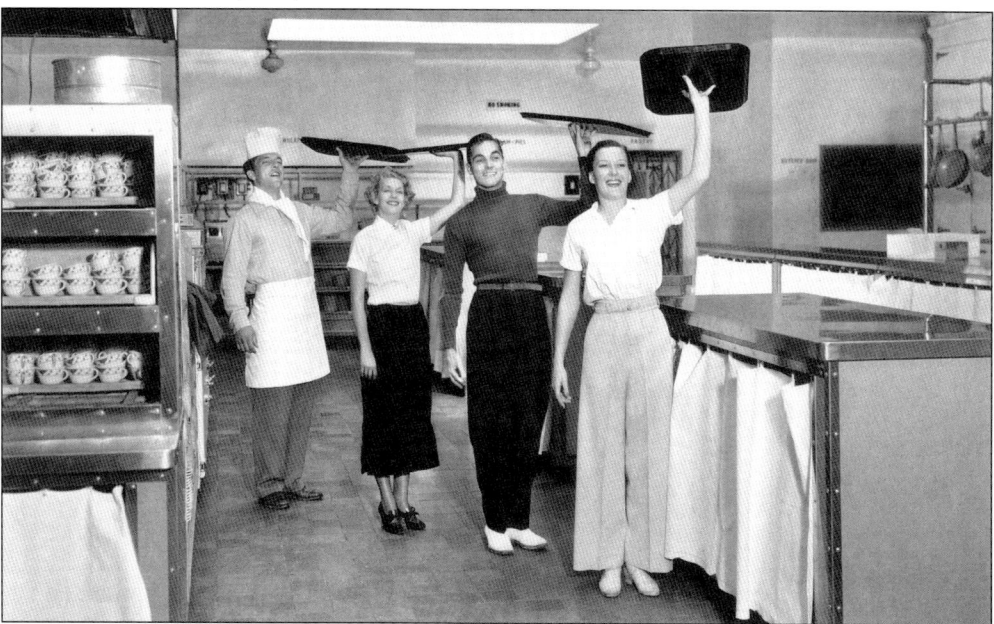

RKO'S *WALKING ON AIR*, 1936. This is one of several scenes shot at the Norconian that ended up on the cutting room floor. Marching through the resort kitchen are, from left to right, Gordon Jones (the Green Hornet in the 1940 serial and Mike the Cop from the *Abbot and Costello* show), Anita Colby (famed model), Alan Curtis (leading man of the 1940s), and comedienne Maxine Jennings (a longtime resident of Riverside, California).

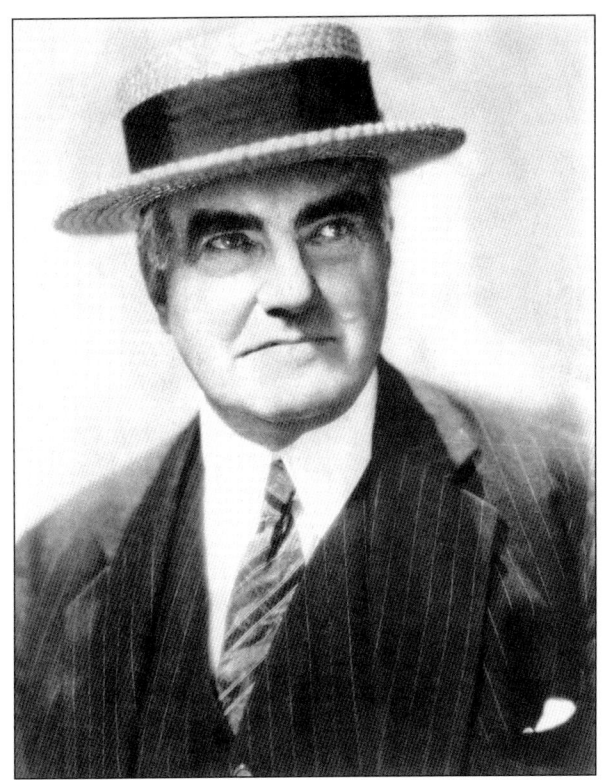

THE CHEERFUL PHILOSOPHER, C. 1932. Forgotten Burr McIntosh was a publisher/editor, actor, poet, public speaker, veteran of the Spanish-American War, and the resident "greeter" at the Norconian in the mid- to late 1930s. Living at the resort during summer months, he hosted several popular get-togethers where he would "say hello to his friends." (Courtesy of the Motion Picture Academy of Arts and Sciences.)

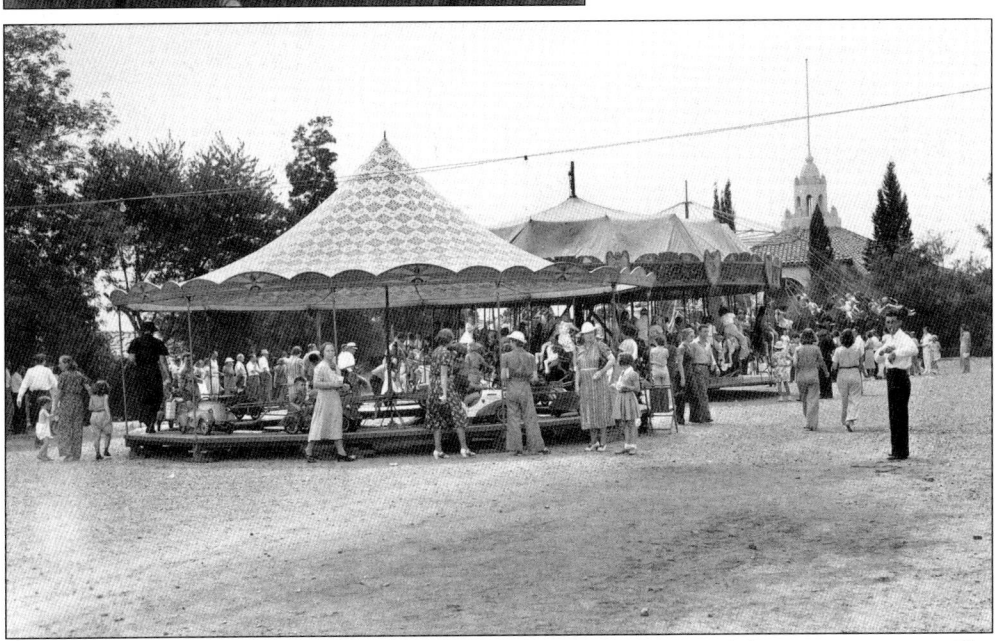

MGM PARTY, 1938. Fourteen thousand employees, including stars, of the most prestigious film studio in the world attended the 1938 company picnic. Merry-go-rounds, Ferris wheels, and other carnival rides awaited the employees, who began arriving Saturday night and filled every room. Sunday morning, thousands more began arriving by bus and private car. Spencer Tracy, Clark Gable, Greta Garbo, and Lionel Barrymore mixed in with the lowliest gofer.

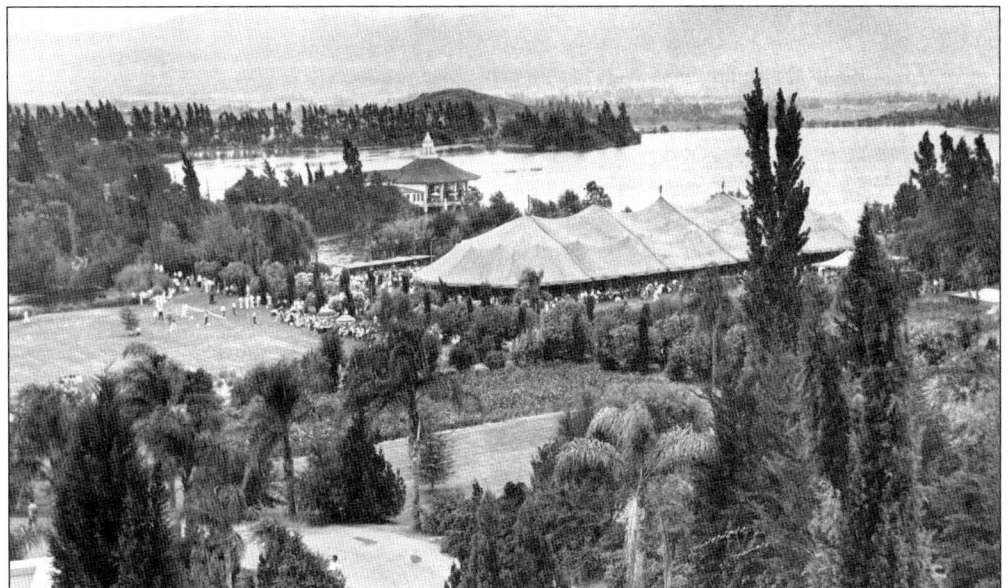

FOX STUDIOS PARTY, 1940. Employees (roughly 5,000), including the biggest stars, turned out for Fox's company picnic. Mammoth tents were erected to promote a circus atmosphere with guests enjoying boating races, fly casting, puppeteers, swimming and diving contests, tennis, golf, Ping Pong, badminton, and an Olympic diving and swimming exhibition featuring Marjorie Gestring. Nurses were brought in to specifically care for infants while the parents partied and played.

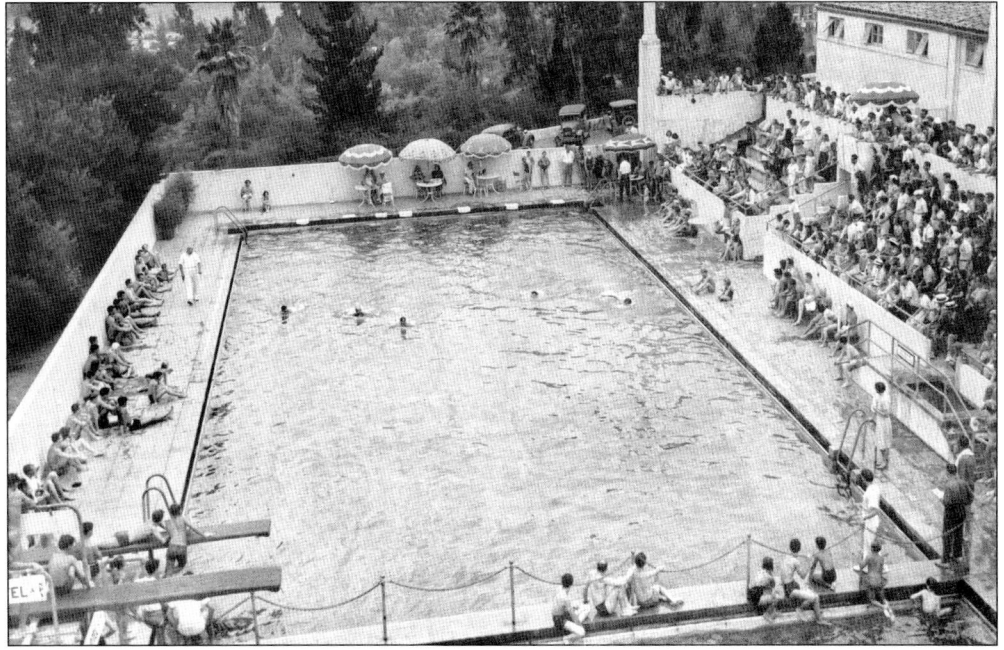

SWIMMING COMPETITIONS, C. 1940. It is unknown which studio party this photograph is from; however, all featured races in the pools with pretty extravagant trophies. Stan Yerkees, son of an MGM employee and young attendee to the company picnic, stated, "These competitions were a big deal especially if you could beat the pants off one of the star's kids or better yet beat Mickey Rooney; you could really tell a tale then."

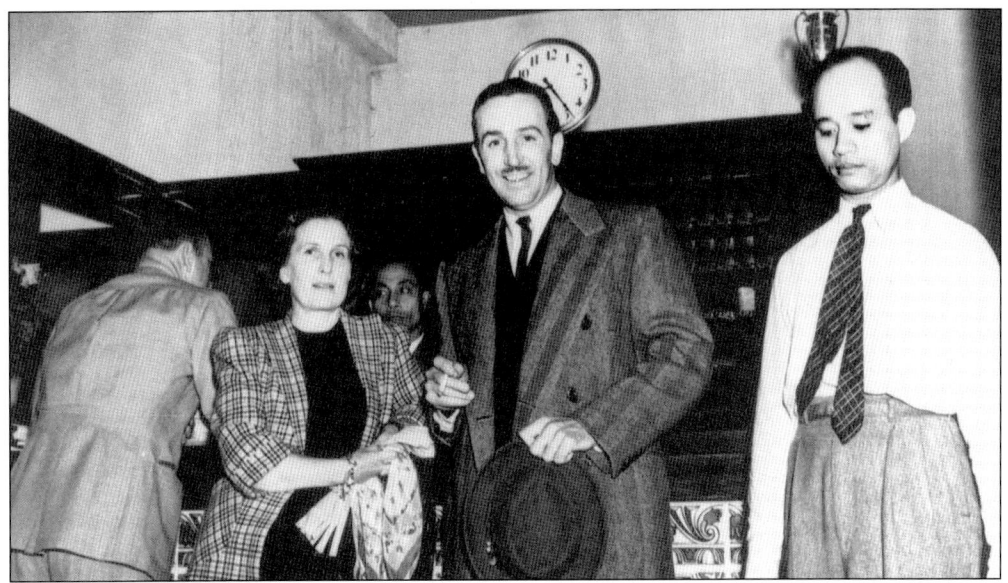

LILLIAN AND WALT DISNEY, 1938. The success of *Snow White* prompted Disney to throw a thank-you party, with all expenses paid, for everyone who worked for him and their families. That Norconian weekend has become the stuff of legend, and according to one attendee, Disney was so mortified at his employees' shenanigans that, for years after, if you dared mention the event in Walt's presence, you would be fired immediately.

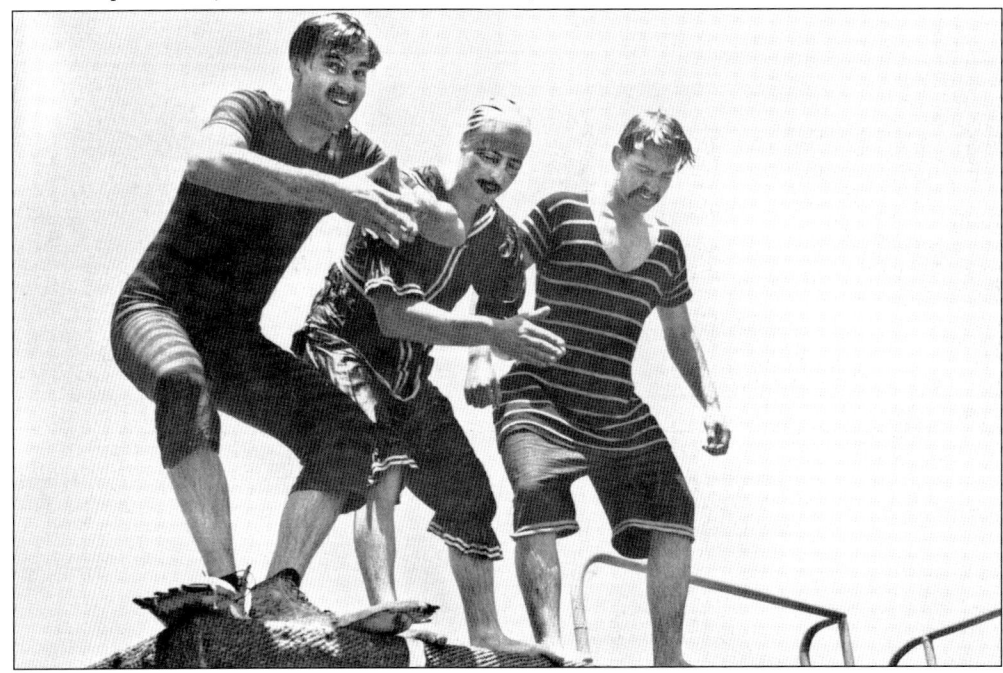

DISNEY ANIMATORS ANIMATING, 1938. Standing on the Norconian springboard, three Walt Disney employees—Jack Dunham (left), Joe Rinaldi (center), and Curt Perkins—wearing comic dress and false feet, prepare to demonstrate their unique versions of diving. Rinaldi wrote such classics as *Cinderella*, *Alice in Wonderland*, *Peter Pan*, and *Sleeping Beauty*. Perkins was a background artist on such projects as *Fantasia* and *Scooby-Doo, Where are You!* (Tom Sito.)

Seven
PATIENTS, PRISONERS, AND PH.D.s

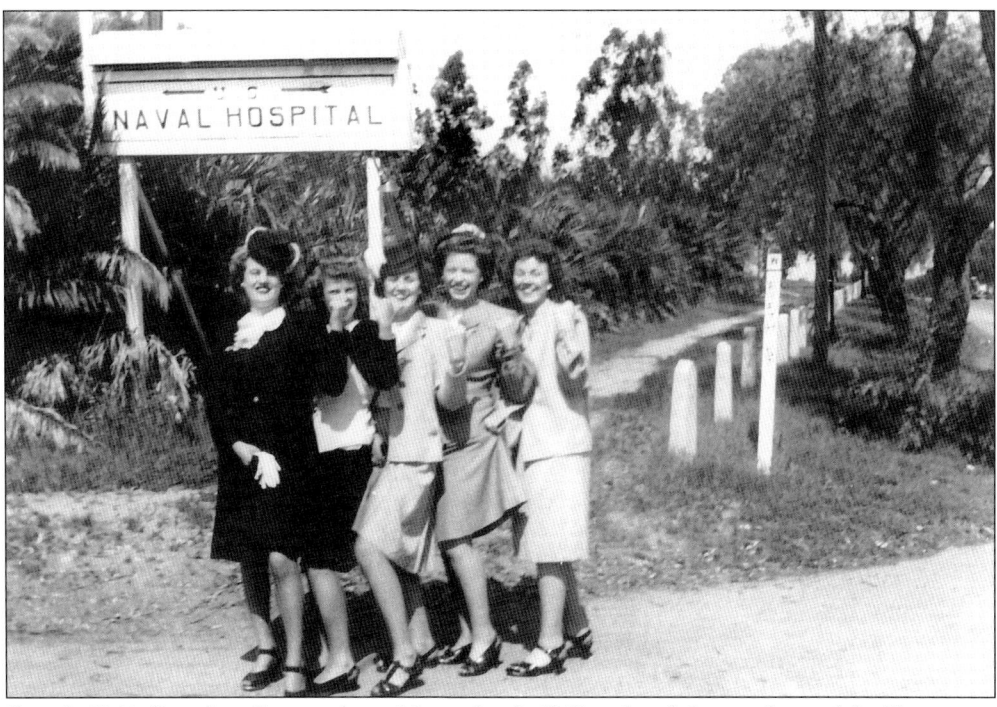

SOLD!, 1941. President Roosevelt, on November 8, 1941, ordered the purchase of the Norconian as the future site for the Corona Naval Hospital and set aside $2 million from his War Emergency Fund to pay for it. Unfortunately, amidst accusations of corruption and greed by both sides, payment was withheld, forcing Rex Clark into a vicious court battle. Though victorious, Clark's wife, Jimmie, later stated they received only $400,000.

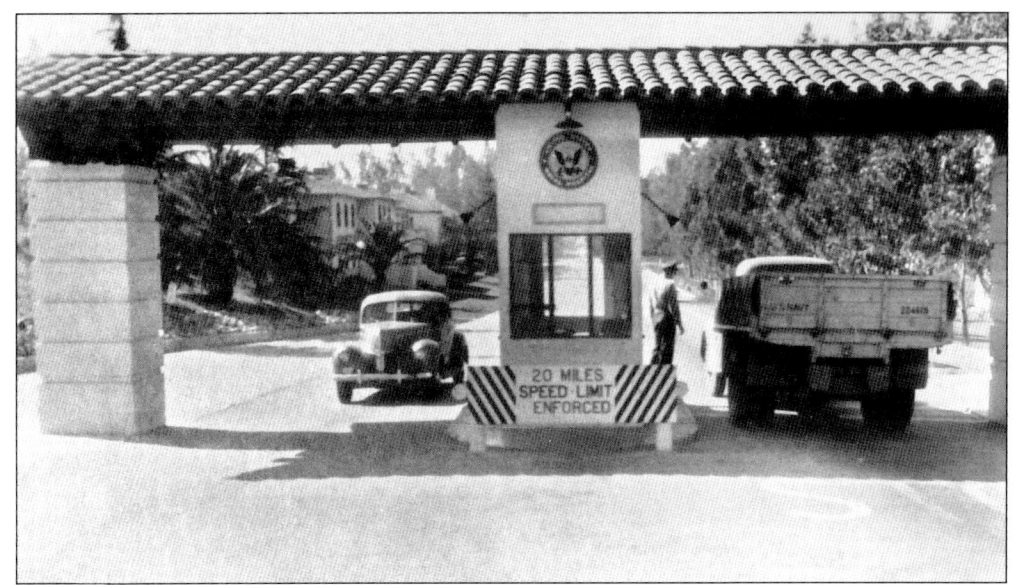

FIFTH STREET ENTRANCE, C. 1943. According to *The Navy in Corona*, initially the hospital capacity was 500 beds, utilizing all 250-resort bedrooms and the large public rooms. By February 1945, the number of patients had swelled to 4,050, with wounded pouring in from all over the Pacific theater. At the war's peak, there were 99 naval officers, 46 medical officers, 74 nurses, and 410 hospital workers.

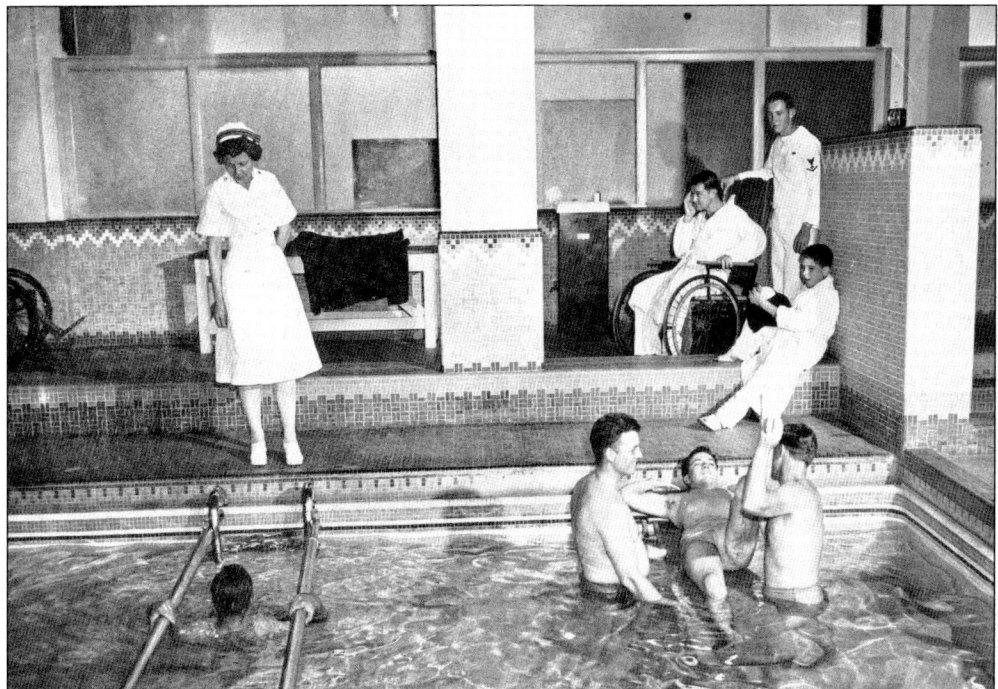

NOTHING BUT THE BEST, C. 1943. By May 1, 1942, there were roughly 100 patients at the naval hospital, two-thirds of whom were Pearl Harbor wounded. The navy utilized the luxurious indoor spas as a "hydrotherapy" treatment center. Rex Clark, in 1943, despite his bitterness toward the navy, stated, "I can think of no better use for the Norconian." (University of Southern California.)

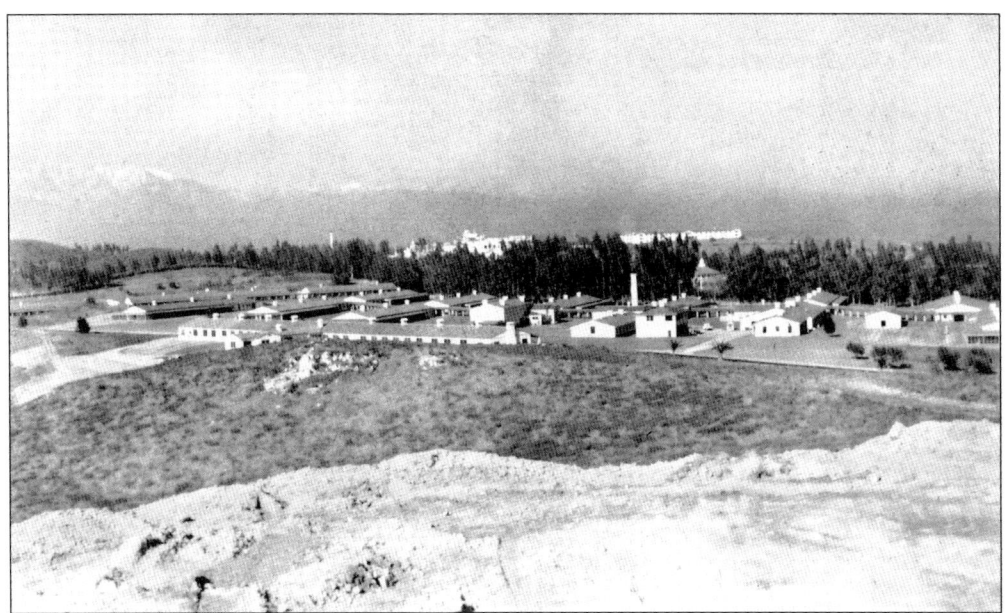

RESPIRATORY WARDS, C. 1947. Built on the northeastern portion of the Norconian golf course was the respiratory disease center, "a complex of 15 one-story interconnecting ward buildings" isolated and self-contained with facilities to treat marines and navy servicemen . . . suffering from rheumatic fever, tuberculosis, malaria and polio." The wards were designed with wide, open porches to provide "fresh air and sunshine." Today they house the Naval Surface Warfare Assessment Center.

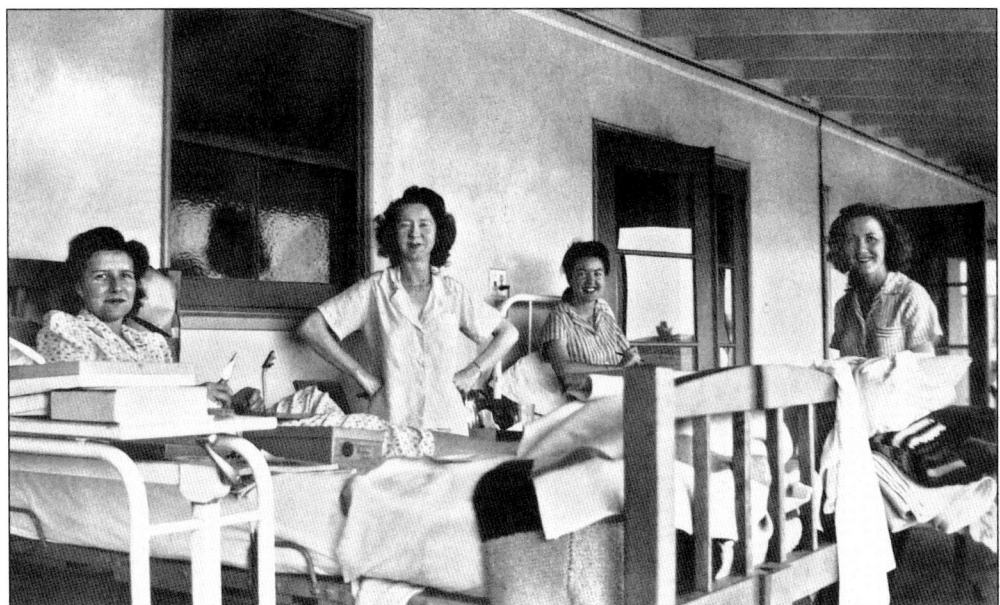

RESPIRATORY WARD PORCH, C. 1945. Standing center is Anna Rylaarsdam Lotterman, navy nurse, surrounded by women who contracted tuberculosis while treating patients. Lotterman, like many other nurses and corpsmen, later spoke of the difficulties of "night duty" as this was when most patients died. It was widely reported in 1944 that the first use of penicillin for tubercular patients occurred at this hospital site. (Ed Lotterman.)

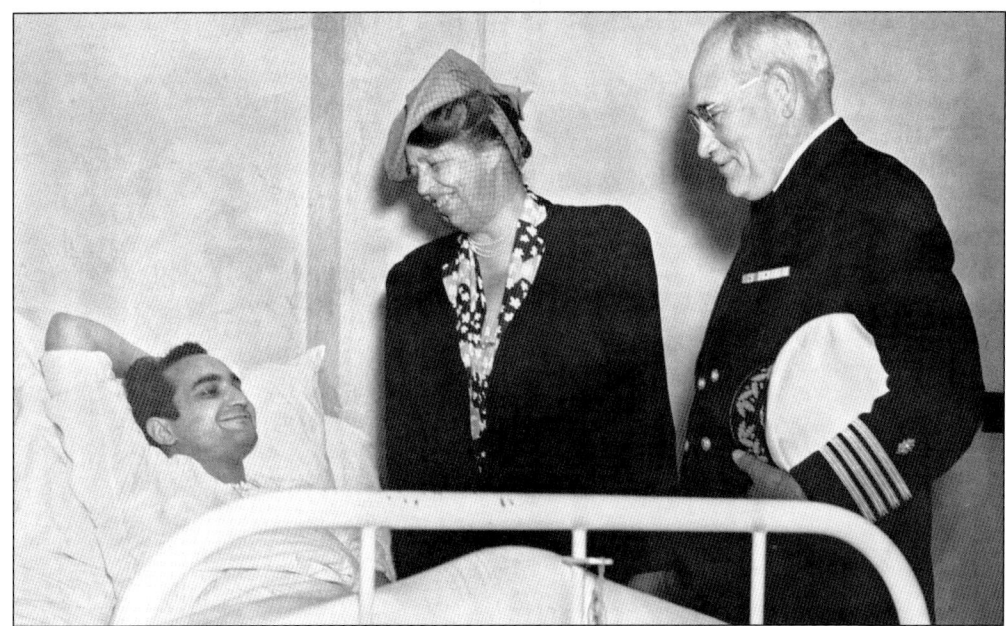

ELEANOR ROOSEVELT, APRIL 25, 1943. The president's wife spent the afternoon meeting with patients and considered the hospital an "admirable place for the navy to take care of its men." The patient is unidentified; however, the captain was the hospital's first commanding officer, H. L. Jensen. Intriguingly, two navy corpsmen independently claim that President Roosevelt secretly visited the hospital to make use of the soothing mineral waters. (Corona Library.)

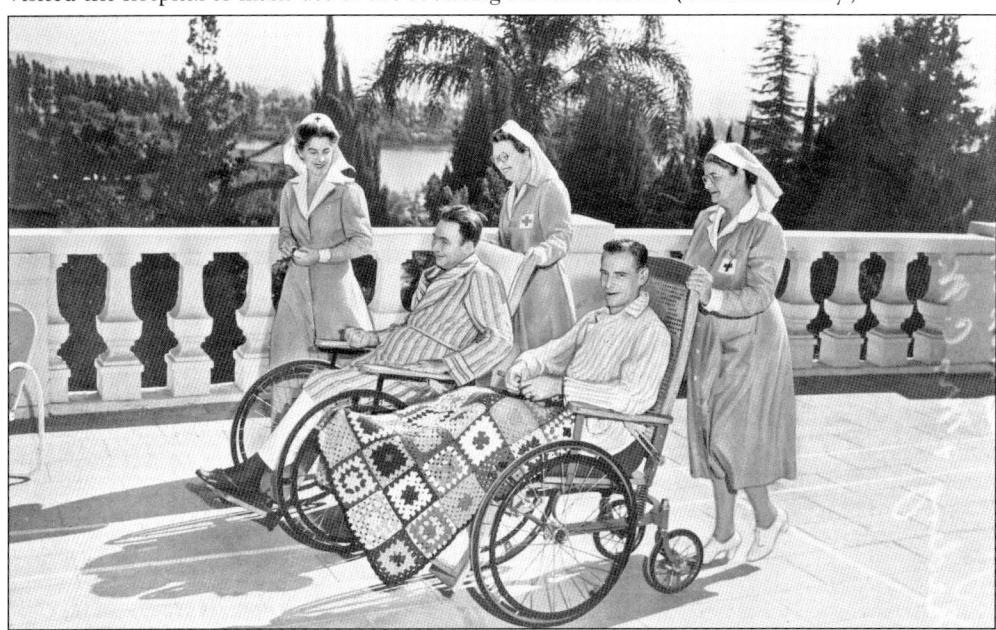

THE GRAY LADIES, 1942. Originally known as the Hostess and Hospital Service and Recreation Corps of the American Red Cross, this organization of women volunteers became known affectionately as "the gray ladies" because of their customary gray veils and dresses. The Corona-Norco branch was consistently praised for its efforts with patients. Note Lake Norconian in the background, as patients are wheeled along the tea room patio. (University of Southern California.)

HOLLYWOOD ANGEL, C. 1944. Kay Francis, left, with Constance Bennett, was an unsung hero during World War II. In charge of entertainment, Francis spent untold hours at the navy hospital. Every Thursday, she would arrive with a few of her friends to entertain the patients; her "friends" included Claudette Colbert, Red Skelton, Cary Grant, Errol Flynn, Humphrey Bogart, and James Cagney, among others. (Courtesy of the Motion Picture Academy of Arts and Sciences.)

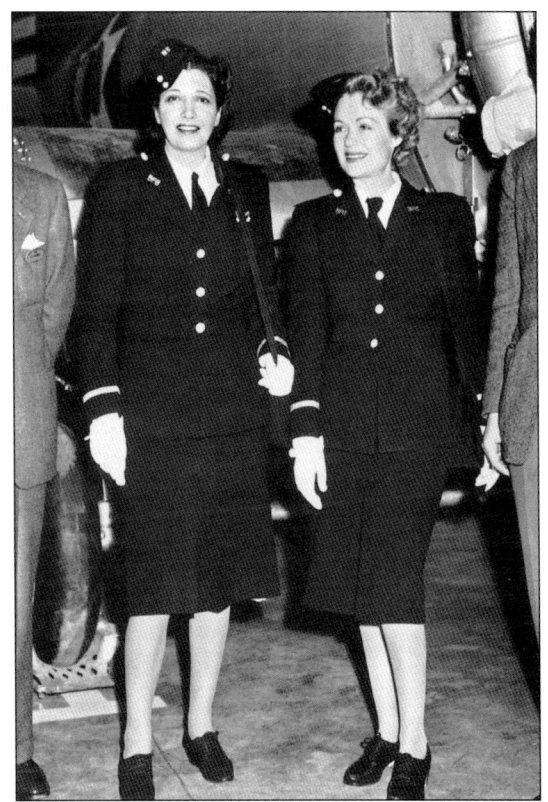

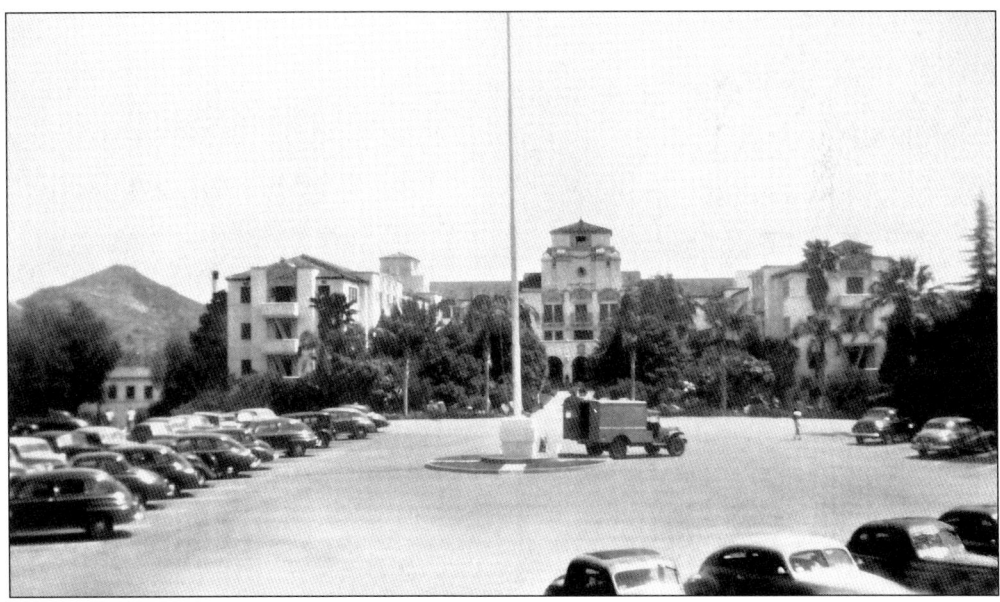

U.S. NAVAL HOSPITAL, C. 1945. In 1949, despite public outcry, negative impact on the surrounding communities, the genuine need for an area veterans hospital, and $15 million in recent improvements, the navy closed and stripped the facility, citing budget constraints and too few patients. Local citizens, dignitaries, veterans, and the American Legion conducted a "fill a hospital bed" drive to no avail.

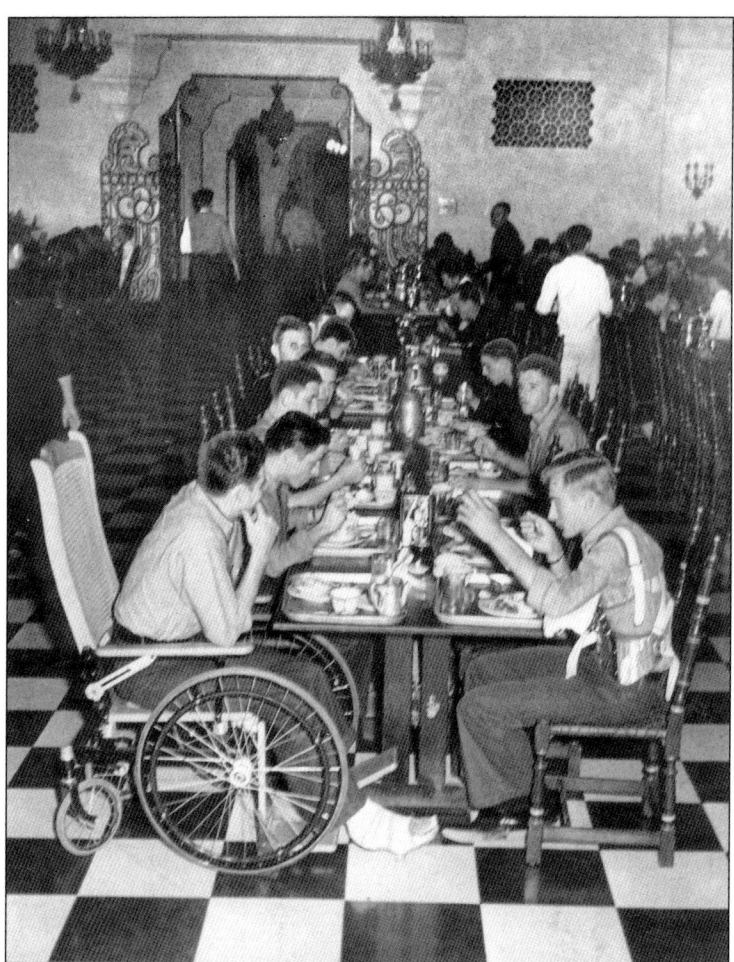

DINING IN LUXURY, 1942. Veterans with lost limbs chow down in the former Norconian grand dining room. Corpsman Bob Allen stated, "We didn't feel like we were in the service." Note the table is set with the original Norconian silver and china. The few resort artifacts that survive today are the result of patients taking home various items as souvenirs, which otherwise were simply tossed. (University of Southern California.)

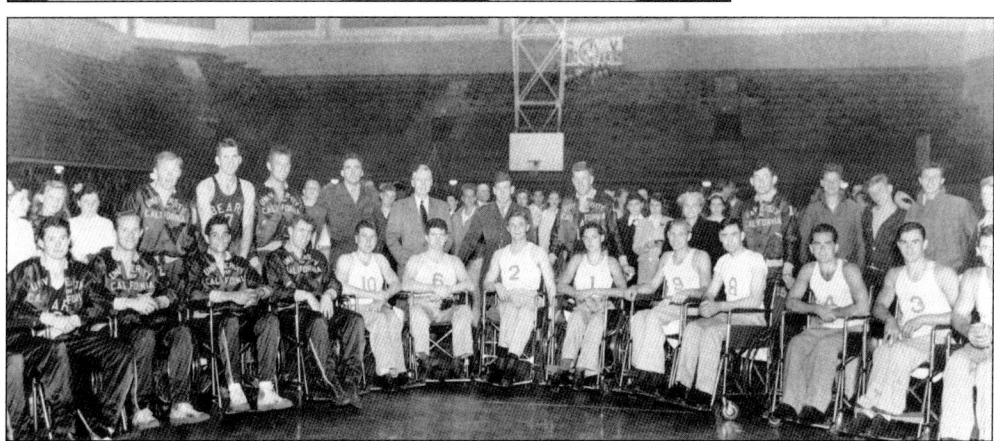

THE ROLLING DEVILS, 1942. Founded by Dr. Gerald Gray, the "Father of Wheelchair Basketball," the Rolling Devils were known as the "Globetrotters in Wheelchairs" and pretty much beat everybody. The program was begun as a way to get disabled soldiers "back into the world." The naval hospital pioneered prosthetic appliances and rehabilitation programs to get patients who had lost limbs "out of the shadows." (U.S. Navy Archives.)

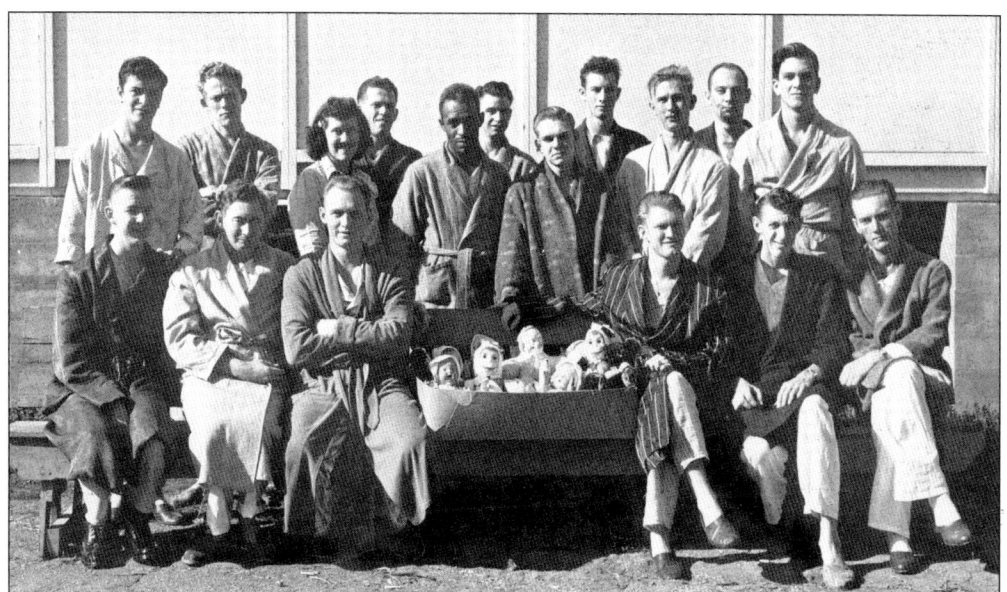

LEATHERNECK DOLLMAKERS, C. 1945. The hospital pioneered occupational therapy to better mainstream returning wounded. The facility boasted a carpenter shop, art studio, and toy factory. These marines gained back the use of fingers and limbs by making dolls for little girls. Famed artist Stanley Landsman once spoke of spending his recovery time at the hospital restoring wall murals the navy had covered over with "battleship gray." (University of Southern California.)

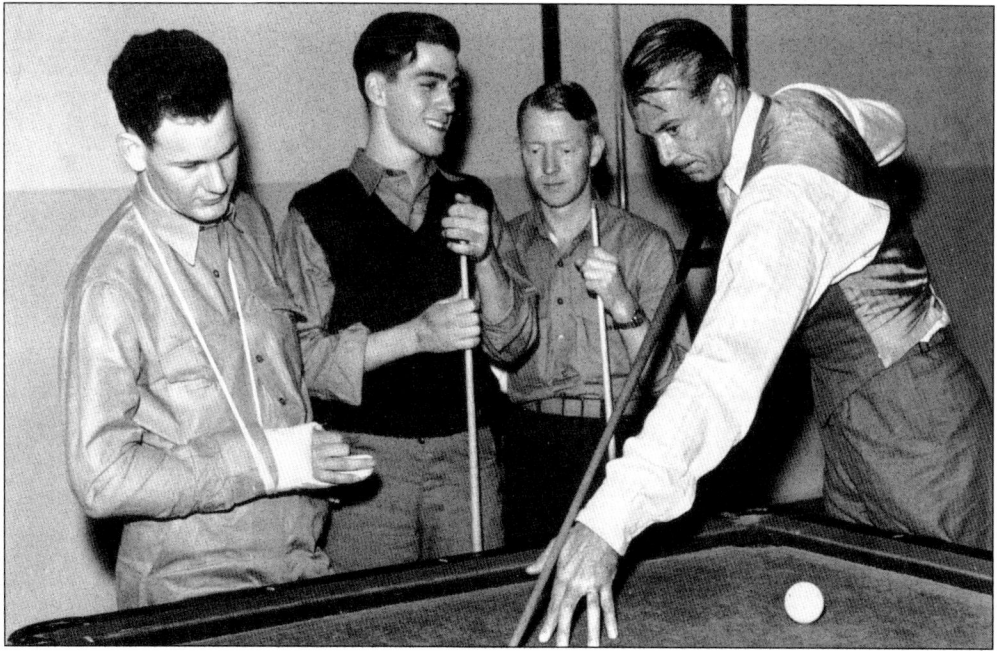

GARY COOPER AND THE BOYS, C. 1943. From left to right, marines James Tallant, John Virgopio, and Russell Twedt play pool with Gary Cooper. Cooper was a regular at both the Norconian and the naval hospital. He once introduced himself to a patient with, "Hi, I'm Gary Cooper," and the patient replied, "Sorry Gary, I know we know each other, just can't place you; was it Guadalcanal or Peleliu?" (U.S. Navy Archives.)

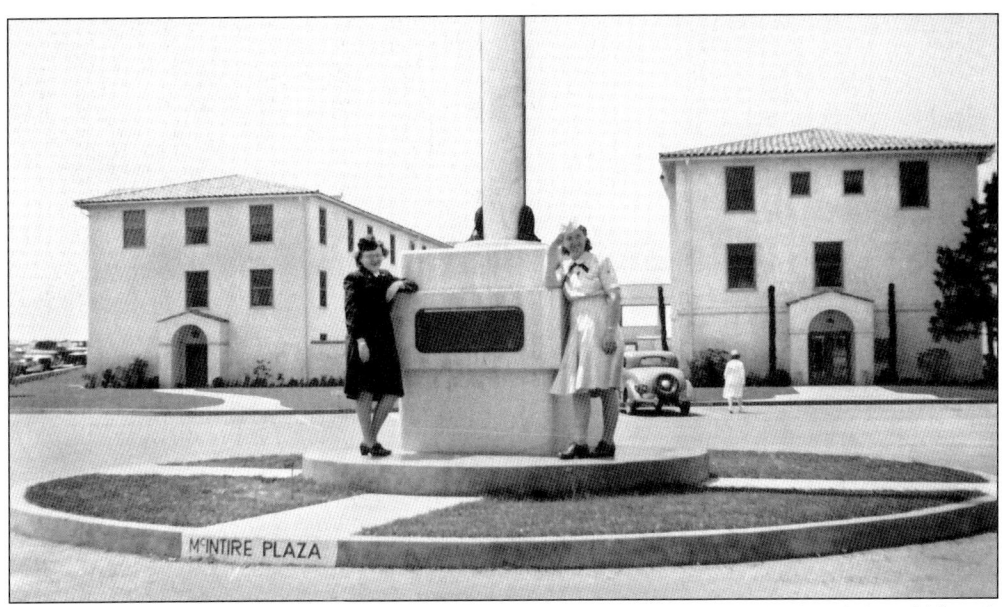

NURSES' QUARTERS, C. 1945. Built in 1944, the nurses' quarters directly faced the old hotel. Today the buildings house inmates and the flagpole was respectfully moved to a location several feet northeast. On this spot today are a cluster of portable prison administration buildings. The plaza was named after Vice Adm. Ross McIntire, former surgeon general of the navy and chief of medicine and surgery. (Ed Lotterman.)

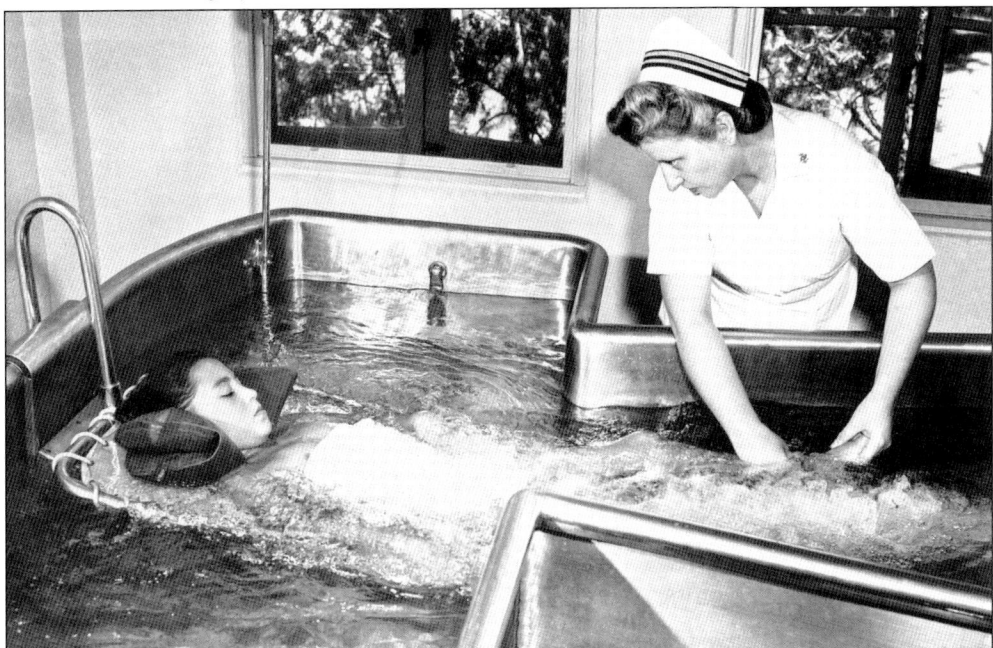

POLIO, C. 1947. In 1944, the hospital was designated the navy infantile paralysis facility on the West Coast and moved to the forefront of polio treatment in the United States. At the height of the epidemic, the hospital opened its doors to any and all afflicted with the dreaded disease. News accounts indicate this site was one of the first to be issued the new polio vaccine. (U.S. Navy Archives.)

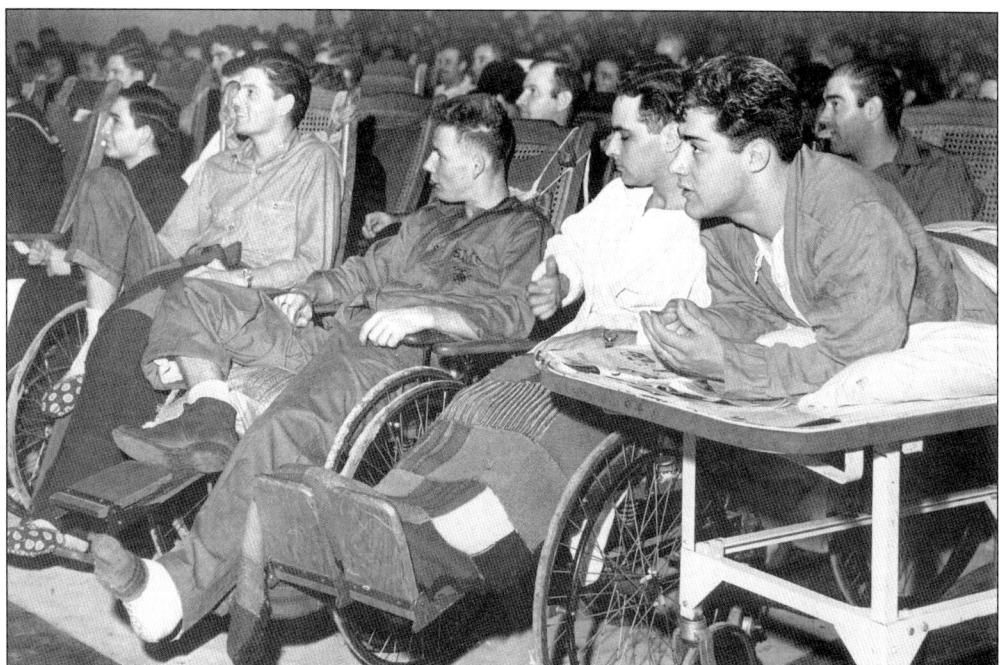

WORLD'S BEST AUDIENCE, C. 1945. Kay Francis saw to it that the biggest names and acts in show business entertained "the boys." The "Hollywood Victory Committee," Camel Caravan, and the USO Hospital Tour staged popular plays and musical reviews for the patients. Jack Benny, Harry James, Marlene Dietrich, and Tommy Dorsey, as well as navy-sponsored entertainment aired live radio broadcasts from this historic theater built in 1944. (University of Southern California.)

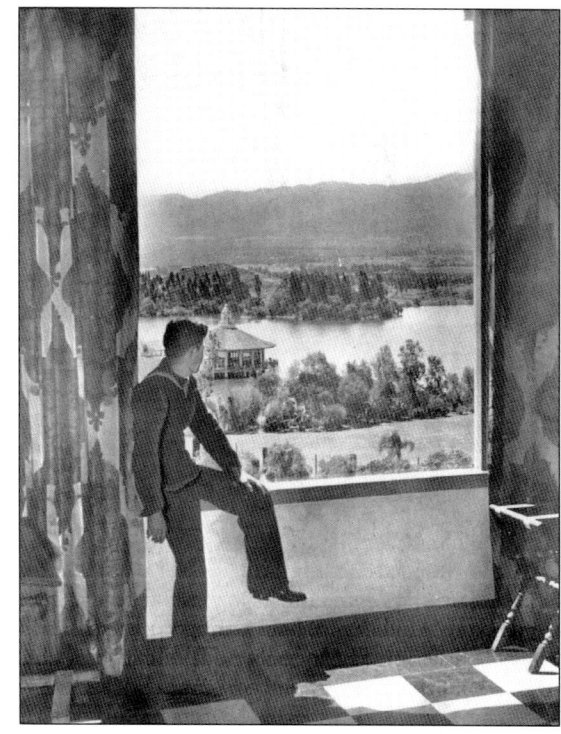

GOODBYE, C. 1944. In 1957, despite public outcry, the navy, again citing budget constraints and low patient load, closed the Corona Naval Hospital for good. Once again, the facility was quickly stripped for pennies on the investment dollar and abandoned. Like the Norconian before it, this preeminent hospital and its rich history has simply been forgotten—a shadow. (University of Southern California.)

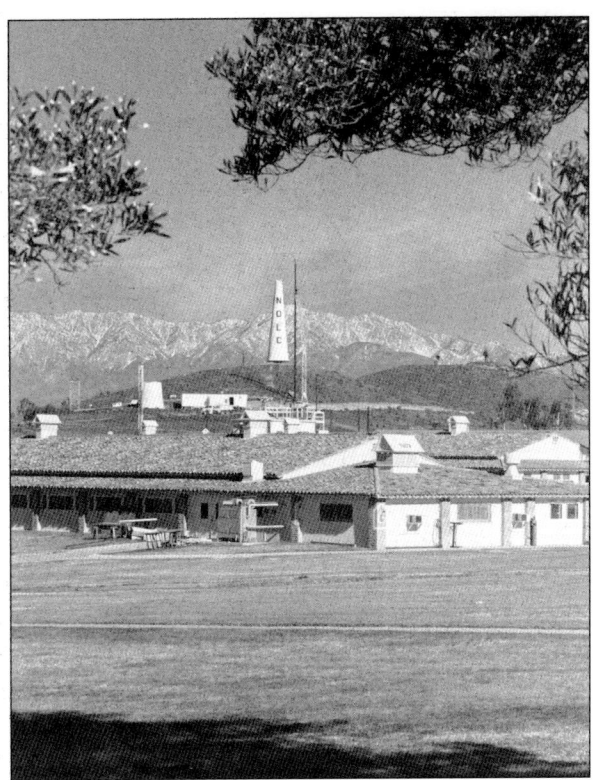

Top Secret, c. 1954. According to *The Navy in Corona*, the National Bureau of Standards (NBS) "assembled a distinguished corps of scientists" to develop "glider-type weapons and fin-controlled bombs." When the hospital closed in 1949, the NBS moved into the abandoned respiratory wards. Today this top-secret, 400-acre facility employs some of the best minds in the world and is known as the Naval Surface Warfare Assessment Center. (U.S. Navy Archives.)

California Rehabilitation Center, 1963. In 1962, ninety acres on the northern end of the old resort was declared government surplus and a bold experiment was born: the first drug treatment plan at a state level in the nation. In May, roughly 200 women and 760 men hoping to beat drug addiction were moved into the old resort/hospital. Heading the program was Roland W. Wood (left). (University of California, Los Angeles.)

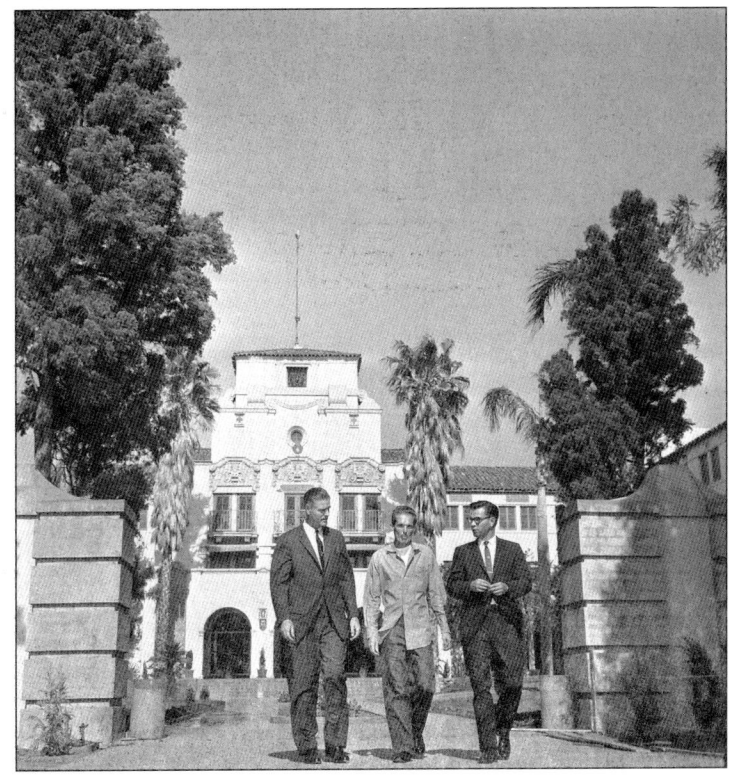

A NEW ERA, 1963. Roland Wood (right) stands in front of historic St. Luke's Chapel. The $75,000 chapel opened December 24, 1944, and was used by the navy for nondenominational services, weddings, counseling, and baptisms. On November 10, 1946, a stained-glass window was dedicated in honor of Col. Jane Murdoch, "who embodied the highest ideals of patriotic service"; it is still there. (University of California, Los Angeles.)

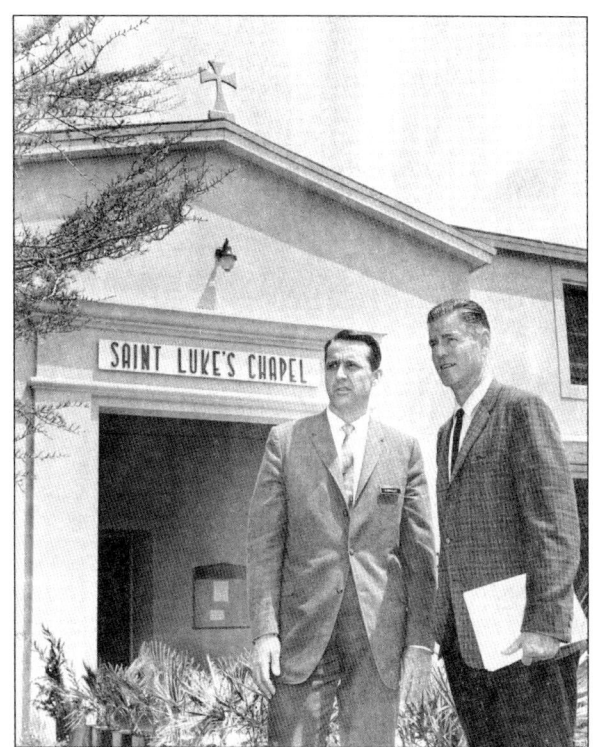

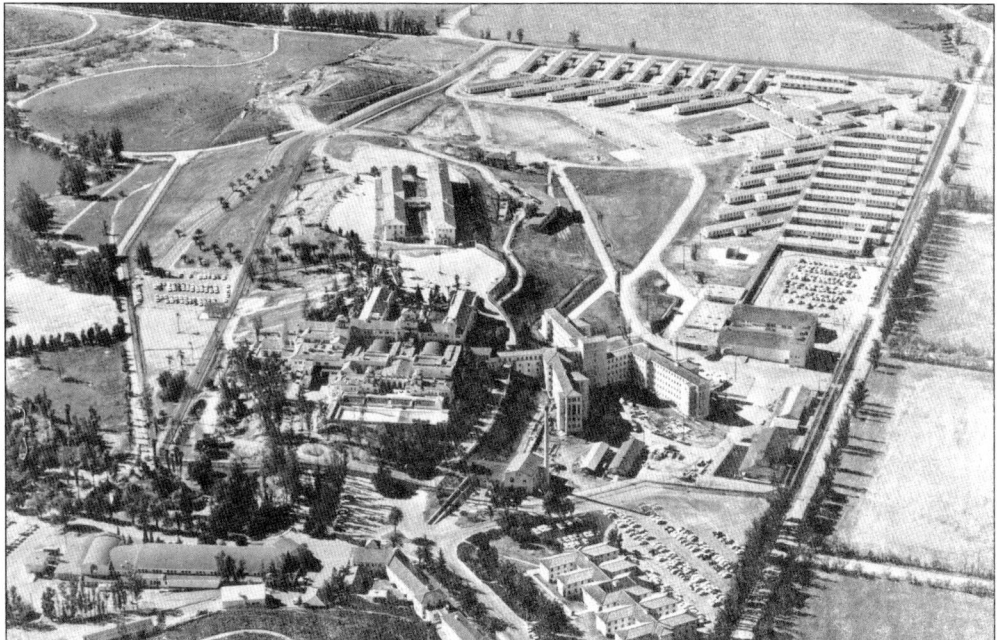

HOSPITAL/PRISON AERIAL, C. 1953. At center is the old Norconian hotel, above, the nurse's quarters and attached right, the navy hospital wing. In the upper right corner are the hospital wards known as "Splinterville," and down the right side are the gymnasium, theater, bowling alley, and chapel. Today, because of a population crisis in the California prison system, approximately 5,000 prisoners are housed in every nook and cranny on these 90-plus acres.

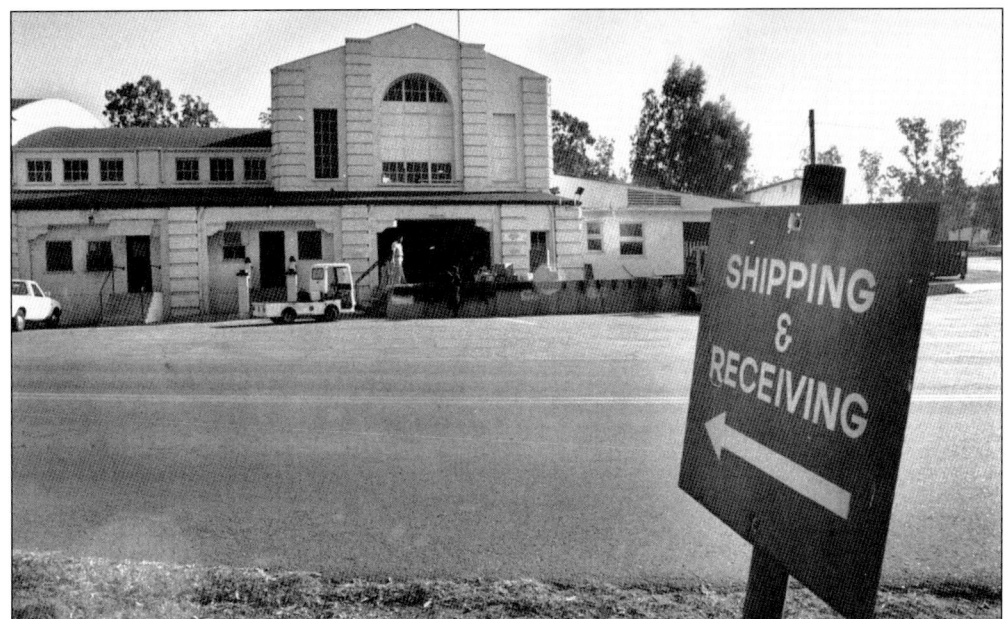

FORMER NORCONIAN LAUNDRY, C. 1991. Used as a shipping and receiving building until torn down in 1996, the laundry was one of only two structures from the original Norconian Resort not to survive; the other was the boathouse. Regardless of a building's condition and history, there seems to be a government policy that for every new building that goes up, another must come down; a concrete slab remains. (U.S. Navy Archives.)

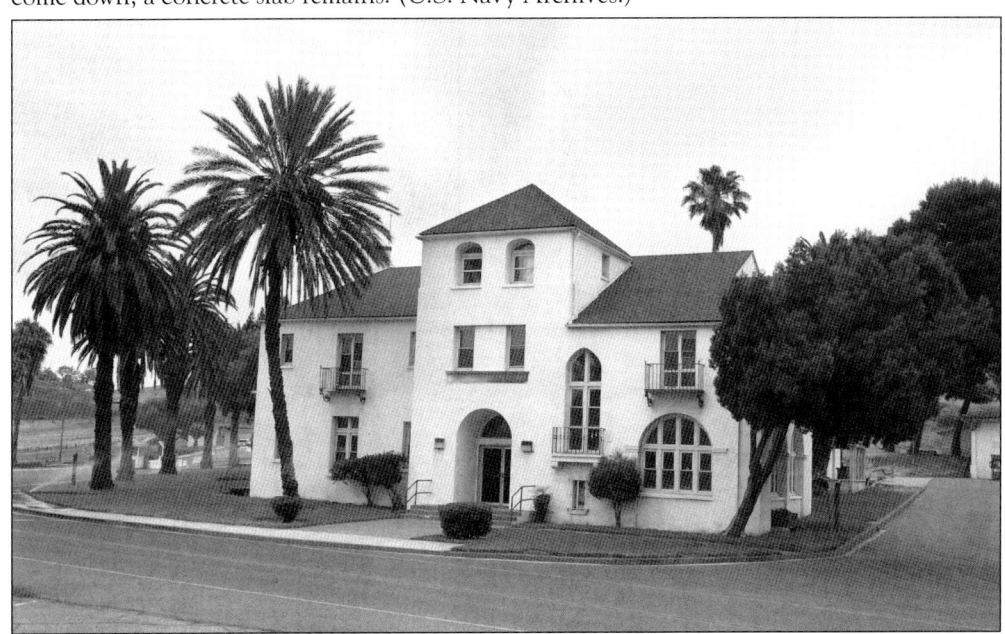

FORMER CHAUFFEURS' QUARTERS, 2006. Since the closing of the resort in 1941, this marvelous building has served as personnel quarters, offices, and even a school. Today it is abandoned and may well be demolished despite its placement on the National Register of Historic Places. Hopefully a future use will be determined for this national treasure, designed by Mission Inn architect G. Stanley Wilson. (Brigitte Jouxtel.)

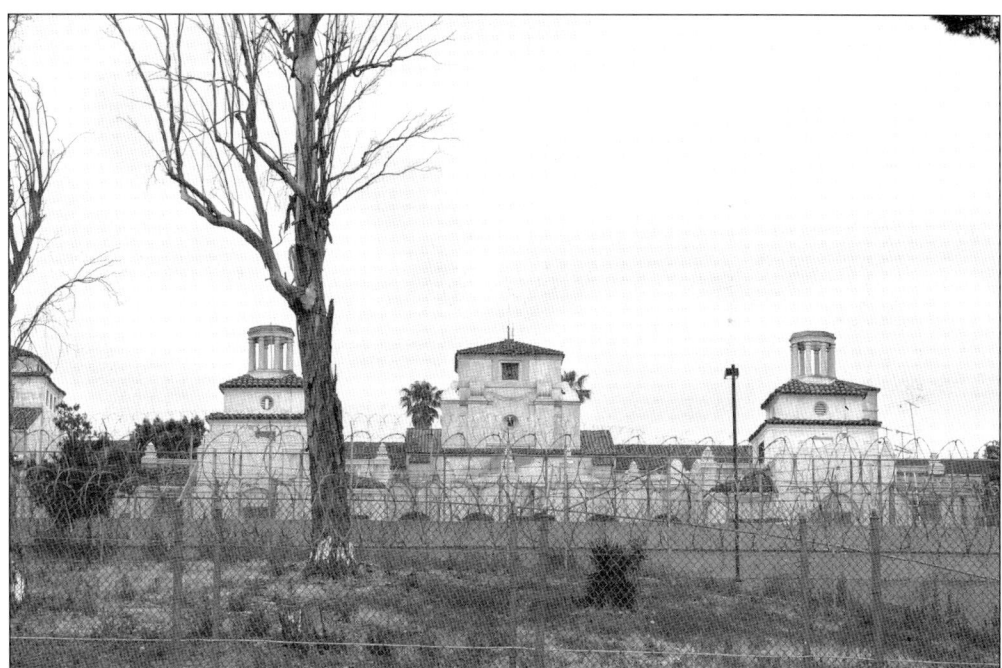

WEST VIEW, 2006. In the mid-1990s, a seismic retrofit was recommended for the former hotel that ultimately was deemed too expensive. In 2002, despite placement on the National Register and laws to the contrary, the old hotel was abandoned and officially declared a "black building," meaning cut off the power and water, seal it up, and let it die. (Brigitte Jouxtel.)

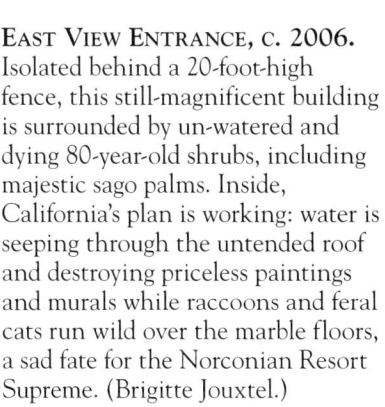

EAST VIEW ENTRANCE, C. 2006. Isolated behind a 20-foot-high fence, this still-magnificent building is surrounded by un-watered and dying 80-year-old shrubs, including majestic sago palms. Inside, California's plan is working: water is seeping through the untended roof and destroying priceless paintings and murals while raccoons and feral cats run wild over the marble floors, a sad fate for the Norconian Resort Supreme. (Brigitte Jouxtel.)

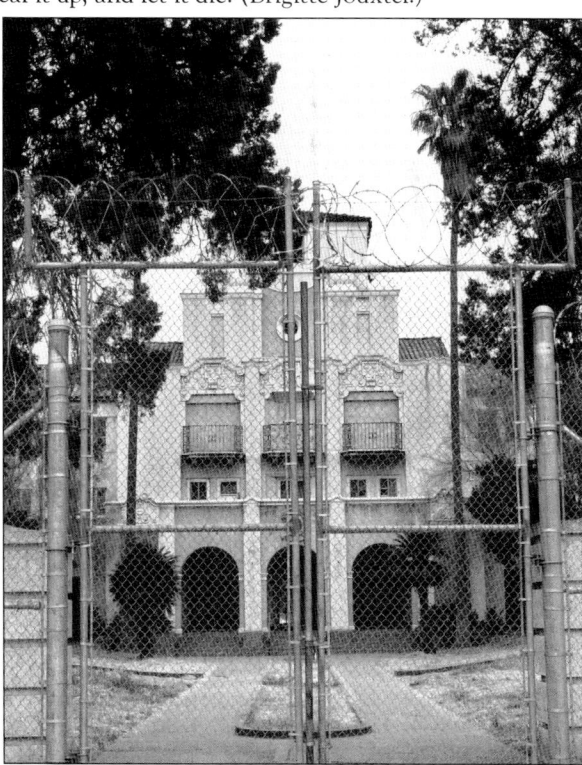

Across America, People are Discovering Something Wonderful. Their Heritage.

Arcadia Publishing is the leading local history publisher in the United States. With more than 3,000 titles in print and hundreds of new titles released every year, Arcadia has extensive specialized experience chronicling the history of communities and celebrating America's hidden stories, bringing to life the people, places, and events from the past. To discover the history of other communities across the nation, please visit:

www.arcadiapublishing.com

Customized search tools allow you to find regional history books about the town where you grew up, the cities where your friends and family live, the town where your parents met, or even that retirement spot you've been dreaming about.

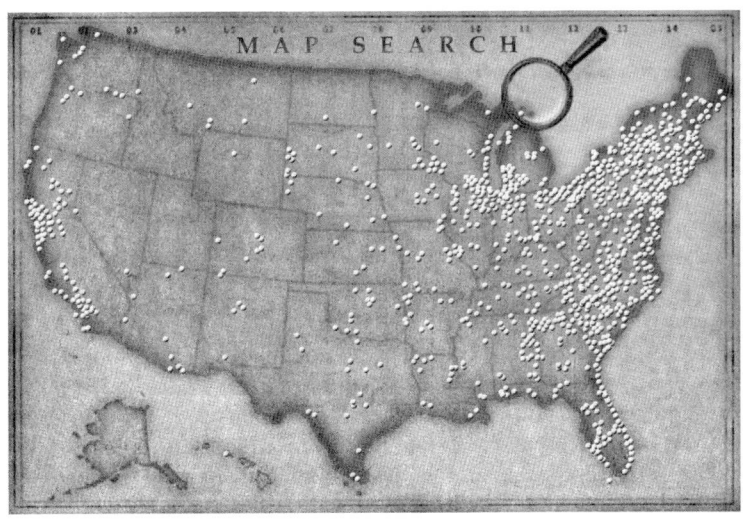